A Brief History *of the*
BODLEIAN
Library

Revised Edition

Mary Clapinson

Bodleian Library
UNIVERSITY OF OXFORD

First published in 2015, revised edition published in 2020 by the Bodleian Library
Broad Street, Oxford OX1 3BG
www.bodleianshop.co.uk

ISBN: 978 1 85124 544 4

Cover design by Dot Little at the Bodleian Library
Designed and typeset by Ocky Murray in Baskerville and Sabon
Printed and bound in China by C&C Offset Printing Co. Ltd
on 120gsm Chinese Baijin Texture paper

British Library Catalogue in Publishing Data
A CIP record of this publication is available from the British Library

Contents

Preface

Writing the history of an institution that has flourished for over four hundred years is a challenging project, but for the Bodleian Library the task is greatly facilitated by the seminal works of three earlier historians: William Dunn Macray, Sir Edmund Craster and Ian Philip. Macray's *Annals of the Bodleian Library Oxford* (2nd edn, 1890), Craster's *History of the Bodleian Library 1845–1945* (1952, repr. 1981) and Philip's Lyell lectures *The Bodleian Library in the Seventeenth and Eighteenth Centuries* (1983) are all invaluable sources and all supply much more factual detail than this brief account can provide for the period up to 1945. My debt to them all will be obvious to those who are familiar with their classic works. For the years since the end of the Second World War, I have relied on the library's well-preserved archives, on the record of developments regularly reported in the notes and news section of the *Bodleian Library Record*, on the recollections of colleagues and above all on the knowledge and advice of David Vaisey, Bodley's Librarian Emeritus.

Mary Clapinson
St Hugh's College, Oxford

Note to the revised edition

This revised and expanded edition of *A Brief History of the Bodleian Library* provides additional material on the university's medieval library and on the growth of Sir Thomas Bodley's foundation over the following centuries. It also brings the account up to date with details of recent developments, and is enhanced by the addition of a great many more illustrations of the Library's collections, buildings, staff and benefactors.

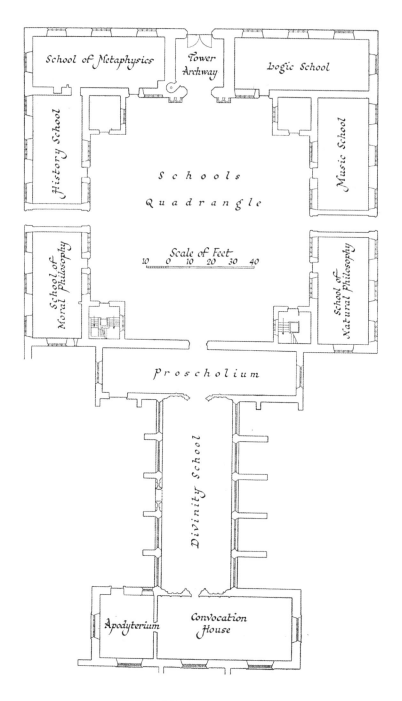

THE OLD BODLEIAN
GROUND FLOOR

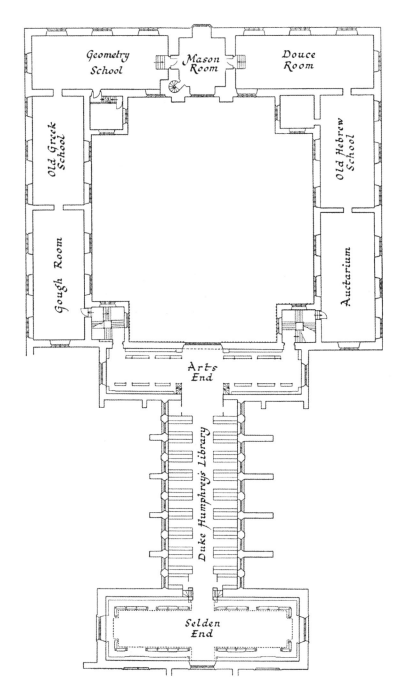

THE OLD BODLEIAN
FIRST FLOOR

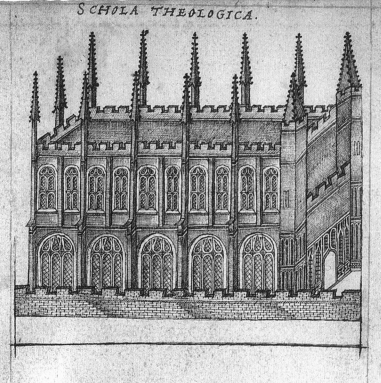

Cancell. E minet, & mediæ fastigia suspirit vrbis,
        Dux Humfrede, tuis sumptibus ista schola.
Surgit in immensum turritis vndiq; pinnis.
        Sectaq; perpulchro marmore, quadra domus.
Splendida luminibus crebris laquearia fulgent,
        Artificiumq; nitent pendula saxa manu.

Cæpit sub Henrico 6º per dominū Humfredum
Ducem Glocestriæ. Anno domini.   1441

CHAPTER I

The first university library

I N 1320 THE BISHOP of Worcester, Thomas Cobham, gave
money to Oxford University for the construction of a two-storey
building adjoining the University Church of St Mary's on the High
Street.[1] As a young man Cobham had studied arts in Paris, canon
law in Oxford and theology in Cambridge before entering the king's
service as a diplomat, where he developed an unrivalled expertise in
French affairs. He intended the new building to provide a centre for
the administration of the university, with a room on the ground floor
for meetings of its governing body (Congregation) and a library room
above (fig. 2). When Cobham died in 1327 the building was far from
finished, but he bequeathed to the university 400 marks to contribute to
the cost of finishing it. Unfortunately, his own library, which he also left
to the university, had to be pawned to pay for his funeral expenses, as
he died heavily in debt. Adam de Brome, rector of St Mary's, redeemed
the books, and gave them to the hall he had recently founded (which
later became Oriel College) to form a library for the students there.
Although the university took possession of the books in 1337, their
ownership was a matter of dispute with Oriel College for decades.
It was probably in 1367 that Cobham's books were, as decreed in a

Fig. 1 John Bereblock's drawing of the library building in 1566, with the
then empty Duke Humfrey's Library above the Divinity School.

Fig. 2 **The upper room in the fourteenth-century addition to the University Church of St Mary's which originally housed the first university library.**

university statute of that year, eventually housed in the library room over the Congregation House. They were to be arranged, chained and made available to scholars 'at convenient times'. Some were to be sold, to raise £40 in order to provide an income for a chaplain who would take care of the library.[2]

Another, more detailed, library statute followed in 1412, aiming to prevent the 'great evils' of 'careless management'.[3] It confirmed the arrangement by which one man was to be elected by Congregation to serve as both librarian and chaplain for the university, and fixed the librarian's salary at 100 shillings per annum (to be paid faithfully, in two instalments, 'lest the loss of his stipend should render him careless'), in addition to the payment of six shillings and eight pence for celebrating the university masses. 'That the librarian may not be overtaxed . . . by being all day in the library, nor the readers inconvenienced by his inattention', the library was to be open just five hours each day, from 9 to 11 in the morning and from 1 to 4 in the

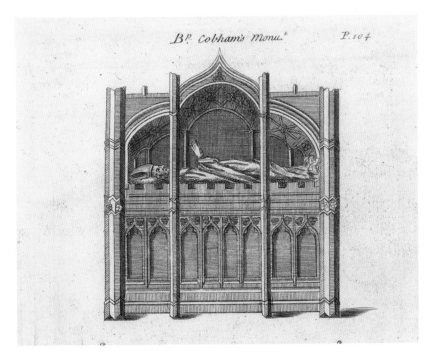

Fig. 3 Engraving of Thomas Cobham's tomb in William Thomas, *A Survey of the Cathedral Church of Worcester* (1737).

afternoon, except on Sundays and the days on which the university masses were celebrated, when it would be closed. Another exception was to be made if a distinguished visitor wished to use the library, when it should be open for him from sunrise to sunset, provided he was not accompanied by 'a disorderly crowd'. The statute also listed the principal benefactors of the library who were to be remembered at the university masses. They were the king (Henry IV), the Prince of Wales (later Henry V) and his brothers (Thomas, John and Humfrey); Thomas Arundel, archbishop of Canterbury; Philip Repington, bishop of Lincoln; Edmund Mortimer, earl of March; and Richard Courtenay, chancellor of the university from 1406 to 1408 and from 1411 to 1413. A large and conspicuous board was to be displayed in the library, listing 'in fair writing' all the books, with the names of their donors. To ensure that constant attendance to library duties did not damage the librarian's health, he was to have one month's leave of absence every year. The statute also restricted the right to study in the library to senior members

of the university 'in order that the books may not be injured by the
multitude of readers, nor students disturbed by throngs of visitors'.

Humfrey, duke of Gloucester (youngest brother of King Henry
V, with whom he had fought during the Hundred Years War and
at the Battle of Agincourt), was a great patron of Italian humanists
and collector of manuscripts, and had been noted as a benefactor of
the library in the statute of 1412 (fig. 4). He gave the university the
major part of his library in two main instalments, in 1439 and 1444,
the first comprising 129 volumes and the second 134. The collection
was a great storehouse of classical texts and of the writings of

contemporary humanists, many in beautifully illuminated manuscripts commissioned by the duke himself. Encouraged by the expectation of more manuscripts and an endowment from Duke Humfrey, and in order to provide appropriate accommodation for his splendid gifts, the university decided to add a new library room above the Divinity School – a lecture room for theological teaching and debate, which began to be constructed around 1424 (fig. 5). Progress on the building was slow because of shortage of funds, and in the event there was no legacy for the university when Duke Humfrey died in 1447. The delays continued until 1478, when the gift of 1,000 marks from the bishop of London, Thomas Kempe, enabled the university to complete both the Divinity School and the library room above it in 1488. All the university's books were then moved from the room by St Mary's Church into the new building, and Duke Humfrey was named the founder of this the second library of Oxford University.

A drawing of the building made almost eighty years later survives in a little volume that was presented to Queen Elizabeth I when she visited Oxford in 1566. It contains an account in Latin verse of the college and university buildings at that time, and was illustrated by John Bereblock, a fellow of Exeter College. His drawing of the 'Schola Theologica' shows the exterior of the free-standing, two-storeyed building from the south-west, with fine windows and pinnacles and the old city wall in the foreground. The manuscript was given to the Bodleian in 1630 by John More.[4] No illustration of the interior of the library exists, although the original walls and windows, with their carved corbels, survive more or less unaltered to this day. These and the evidence revealed during extensive restoration work in the 1960s enabled the architect Robert Potter to suggest what the library might have looked like in 1488 (fig. 6). It was furnished with lecterns about five foot six inches high, to which the manuscripts were chained, and at which the students stood to read. Light was provided by ten windows down each side of the long room, and by two magnificent large windows at the east and west ends. With a lofty ceiling of oak beams, it must have been an

Fig. 4 (opposite) **Sixteenth-century portrait of Humfrey, duke of Gloucester, from a collection of royal portraits in the municipal library at Arras.**

Fig. 5 (following spread) **The Divinity School was built in the fifteenth century as a lecture room for theological teaching and debate.**

Fig. 6 Duke Humfrey's Library during restoration work in the 1960s which revealed the outline of the fifteenth-century lecterns.

impressive place to study (fig. 7). Alas, it survived as a library for little more than sixty years. There is no record of the university spending any money after 1488 on the upkeep of its library or on the acquisition of new books. At a time when the wealthier and more active colleges were adding to their libraries the new, printed editions of classical and theological works that were the basis of most studies, the university library became increasingly irrelevant to the needs of its members. Meanwhile its manuscripts could be borrowed, and many of them were never returned. The university steered an uneasy course through the religious troubles of the last years of Henry VIII's reign; its colleges and members, all to an extent dependent on the king's favour, were divided between reformers and traditionalists. With the accession of the young King Edward VI, control of the government in London passed into the hands of the reformers, who were determined to ensure the university's loyalty to the new order. A formal visitation, with sweeping powers to alter statutes, confiscate endowments and enforce Protestant forms of

Fig. 7 **The architect Robert Potter's drawing of the library as it may have looked from 1488 until the mid-sixteenth century.**

worship, was instituted in 1547. It also encouraged the destruction of 'popish' books and manuscripts in the university and college libraries. The seventeenth-century antiquary Anthony Wood recorded that some of them were burned, some sold 'for Robin Hoods pennyworths, either to Booksellers, or to Glovers to press their gloves, or to Taylors to make measures, or to Bookbinders to cover books bound by them, and some also kept by the Reformers for their own use'.[5] In January 1556 the lecterns in Duke Humfrey's library were sold to Christ Church, and the once grand university library room was empty.

Thus it was that when, at the age of fourteen, Thomas Bodley came to study at Magdalen College, there was no central library in the university and, as for all his contemporaries, his college library was his only source of books. Thomas had been born in Exeter in 1545, the son of John Bodley, a publisher of strongly Protestant views, prominent in local politics, who was forced to take refuge abroad with his family when the Catholic Mary Tudor became queen. So from 1557 the young

Fig. 8 **Miniature of Sir Thomas Bodley by Nicholas Hilliard, 1598.**

Thomas received his early education in Geneva. There he lodged at the house of the French physician and schoolmaster Philibert Sarrasin, and attended courses at the newly founded Geneva Academy, studying Hebrew, Greek and theology under leading Protestant scholars of the day: Antoine Chevalier, Matthaeus Beroaldus, John Calvin and Theodore Beza. It was no doubt in Geneva that the foundations of Bodley's interest in modern European languages was laid.

Towards the end of 1559, with the Protestant Elizabeth I on the throne, the Bodley family returned to England and settled in London. Thomas graduated in 1563 and became a fellow of Merton College the following year. After ten years or so, he began to tire of Oxford. In 1576 Merton granted him leave of absence and he spent the next four years in France, Germany and Italy, becoming proficient in foreign languages while gradually being drawn into the complicated diplomacy of a Europe divided between Protestant and Catholic states. Although he returned to Merton, Bodley spent an increasing amount of time away from Oxford as he became more deeply involved in state business. In 1580 he was in Paris, assisting the English ambassador in complicated negotiations with a group of expatriate Italians. He was elected member of parliament for Portsmouth in 1584 and for St Germans in Cornwall in 1586, but he does not seem to have been an active parliamentarian. He was dispatched on his first major diplomatic mission – to Denmark and Brunswick – in April 1585, charged with what turned out to be the fruitless task of forming an alliance between the king of Denmark and a number of north German Protestant princes against Catholic Spain. In May 1588 he was sent with letters in the queen's own hand on a mission to Henri III of France, which may well have contributed to the toppling of the Catholic party of the duc de Guise the following September. Bodley's appointment to The Hague as ambassador to the Netherlands in December 1588 marked the summit of his diplomatic career. Support for the revolt of the Protestant Netherlands against Catholic Spain had been a principal part of Elizabeth I's foreign policy since 1585, when she had agreed to maintain troops in the Netherlands and had loaned them considerable sums of money. It was the ambassador's task to keep relations on an even keel, persuade the Netherlands that they should provide assistance in the military campaign against Spain, pay the expenses of the English forces and repay the queen's loan. Bodley found his duties frustrating and exhausting. His failure to achieve her objectives often incurred the queen's displeasure and he frequently asked to be recalled – describing his duties as like striving to keep water in a sieve. He finally returned to England in 1597, and seemed destined for higher public office, most likely as Secretary of State. But his hopes for preferment were thwarted by the rivalries between Lord Burghley and the earl of Essex at the court of the ageing Queen Elizabeth, and he decided to retire from public life. In 1598, 1601 and 1602 he was again proposed for embassies to France and the Netherlands, but rejected the offers, for in February 1598 he had written to the vice-chancellor of his old university, offering to assist with the renovation of its library.

CHAPTER 2

The early years, 1602–1652

I N 1 5 9 8, AT THE AGE OF FIFTY-THREE, Thomas Bodley was still ambitious to seek influence in another sphere in which to 'doe the true part of a profitable member of the State',[1] as he put it in his autobiography. He rightly reckoned that his scholarly and linguistic background and his diplomatic experience would be useful assets, and we know that he had sufficient means to finance the enterprise, for he had not only inherited a modest fortune from his father but had also married a rich widow. His wife Ann's first husband, John Ball, a wealthy merchant and mayor of Totnes in Devon, had died in March 1586, leaving her with seven children (the eldest of whom was only twelve) and a considerable fortune amassed through trade with northern France. Bodley married Ann Ball in July 1586, and it was to a large extent her fortune that enabled him to turn his attention to his old university and in particular to the restoration of its library 'which then in every part lay ruined and wast[e]'.[2] Later historians were to point out the irony of a library so closely associated in its early years with Protestant theology having been founded with money made by selling pilchards to Catholic France.

Writing to the vice-chancellor in February 1598, Bodley offered to rectify this sorry state of affairs, and 'to take the charge and cost'[3] of

Fig. 9 **The Divinity School from William Combe,** *A History of the University of Oxford* (1814).

renovating the library upon himself. He undertook to make the new library 'handsome with seates and shelfes and deskes and all that may be needful to stirre up other mens benevolence, to helpe to furnish it with bookes'.[4] He brought his considerable organizational skills as well as his money to the task, and at his request the university appointed a committee of six delegates to consider a design that Bodley had discussed with his old friend Henry Savile, now warden of Merton College, and to advise how best to fit out the library 'aswell for shewe, and statly forme, as for capacitie and strength and commoditie of Students'.[5] In order to make more room for an ever-increasing collection of books, Savile had in 1589–90 overseen the transformation of the west wing of the library at Merton, replacing the old lecterns with double-sided bookcases consisting of two shelves above sloping desks. Like the lecterns, the bookcases were at right angles to the walls, between the windows, but for the first time benches were provided for the students to sit on while they studied the books (which, as before, were chained to the cases). This was the design adopted for Bodley's library, though in the large room above the Divinity School the bookcases could be longer and taller, each providing three shelves for the storage of large books, and three desks for readers (fig. 11). The structure of the building also needed attention. The roof timbers were found to be badly decayed and had to be replaced. In April 1599 it was rumoured that the library was costing Bodley more than he had anticipated, and in the light of this it is interesting to see from the university's accounts that in the years 1597–99 it contributed over £54 to repairing the roof. Throughout the restoration work Bodley was very seldom in Oxford, relying on Henry Savile and the university delegates, who included three of his close friends, all of Gloucester Hall – Thomas Allen, William Gent and John Hawley, principal of the hall – to make decisions and supervise the work. There are no contemporary references to the decoration of the ceiling, but it is always assumed that Bodley was himself responsible for the design of what remains one of the finest features of his magnificent library room. The ceiling is divided into square panels on which are painted the arms of the university, with, at the intersections of the ribs, shields

Fig. 10 (opposite) **Portrait of Sir Thomas Bodley, late 1570s.**

Fig. 11 (following spread) **Duke Humfrey's Library with its original book presses and panelled ceiling displaying the university's and Bodley's arms.**

displaying Bodley's own arms. On 24 December 1599 Bodley wrote that he expected the 'carpenters, joiners, carvers, glasiers, and all that idle rabble' to have completed their work within a fortnight, and that the only 'mechanical workes' remaining were those concerned with bars, locks, chains for the books and other ironwork.[6] By June 1600 Bodley was able to report to the vice-chancellor that the restoration work was complete and that he would now be able to turn to the business of collecting books. To run his library, he had in 1599 appointed his first librarian, Thomas James, a fellow of New College, who like Bodley came from a staunchly Protestant background (fig. 12). He was working at this time on a catalogue of the manuscripts in Oxford and Cambridge colleges. James wrote to a friend in April 1600 reporting progress on his catalogue and expressing the expectation that he would soon be able to take his ease and pursue his research in his new post. How wrong he was! The task on which he was embarking was far from easy and his employer left him very little leisure over the next fourteen years.

On 8 November 1602 the library was officially opened, with more than 2,000 volumes on the shelves of its impressive three-decker book presses in the beautifully restored fifteenth-century room. On 10 November Bodley wrote to his librarian, thanking him for 'the best tidings, of any that yow sent, at any time unto me. For nowe me thinkes my long designe is come to some perfection: sith the place is frequented, and yow established in your charge.'[7] Bodley proved a very skilful fund-raiser, securing benefactions of both books and money from all the great and the good. He had a large Benefactors' Register, handsomely bound and beautifully illuminated with the donors' coats of arms, put on display at the entrance to the library, as a way both of recording in perpetuity every benefactor and of encouraging more donors (fig. 13). As early as 1598, one contemporary remarked in a letter to a friend that 'every man bethinks himself how, by some good book or other he may be written in the scroll of benefactors',[8] and within two or three years the library managed to accumulate an impressive number of volumes. Many of the donors of these books and manuscripts had,

Fig. 12 (opposite) **Portrait of Thomas James, Bodley's first Librarian, 1620, attributed to Gilbert Jackson.**

Fig. 13 (following spread) **The first ninety pages of the Benefactors' Register, begun by Bodley in 1604, were printed; thereafter entries were added by hand.**

Ioſ. Langij Polyanthea. fo. Lugd. 1604.

A. Veſalius de vſu radicis Chynæ. fo. Baſ. 1546.

Rodericus à Caſtro de vniuerſa mulierum medicina. fo. Hamb. 1602.

And. de Iſernia in vſus Feudorum Comment. fo. 1597.

Iac. Gretſeri exercitationes Theologicæ. 4. Ing. 1604.

Collegium Conimbricenſe in Ariſt Logicam. 4. 1604.

Luc. Oſiandri Epitome Hiſtoriæ Eccleſiaſt. Centuriæ reliquæ ix. x. &c. 4. Tub. 1604.

Rob. Marantæ Conſilia. 4. Col. 1599.

C. Sigonius de reb. Bononienſib. fo. Franc. 1604.

La Bibliotheque du Sieur de la Croix-du-maine. fo. Par. 1584.

Caniſij Antiquæ lectionis to. 5. 4. Ing. 1604.

Io. Philippus Ingraſſias in Galenum de Oſſib. fo.

GEORGIVS SAYNTPOLL Miles, donauit xx. libras, quibus empti ſunt hi libri.

Ouum Teſtamentum cum Annot. & editione Galt. Delœni Biblioſcopi regis Angliæ. 4. Lond. 1540.

Euangelia & Epiſt. lingua Slauonica. 4.

Les Annales de Poloigne per B. de Vigenere. 4. Par. 1573.

Ant. Fabri Rationalia in Pandectas. fo. S. Ger. 1604.

La Conference des Couſtumes de France par Pierre Guenoys 2. vol. fo. Par. 1596.

Guil. Gilbertus de Magnete. fo. Lond. 1600.

Er. Oſwaldus Schreckenfuchſius in Sphæram Io. de Sacrobuſto. fo. Baſ. 1569.

Seb. Munſteri Rudimenta Mathematica. fo. Baſ. 1551.

Io. Bapt. Coſta de Facti ſcientia & ignorantia. fo. Pap. 1603.

Linſchotten his Diſcourſes of Voyages into the Eaſt and Weſt Indies. fo. Lond.

Io. à Wower de Polymathia. 4. Baſ. 1602.

Diſcorſo armonico di Herc. Bottrigaro. 1602.

Stromateus Prouerbiorum Græcorum p Scaligerum. 4. Leid. 1600.

C. Dibuadij in Geometriam Euclidis D. ſtratio linealis. 4. Arn. 1603.

Eiuſdem in eundem Demonſtratio numera

Aſtrolabij Canones quo primi mobilis motu prebenduntur. 4. Ven. 1502.

Rich. Knolles Generall Hiſtorie of the T fo. Lond. 1603.

Statuta Agriculturæ vrbis per Serlupium & os. 4. Rom. 1595.

Fr. à Chriſto in 3. lib. Sententiarum. fo. 1586.

Il Ripoſo de Rafaello Borghini. 8. Fior. 1

Pet. Sacratus in 33. Pſalm. cum quibuſdam milijs. 8. Bon. 1588.

Gr. Corteſij Epiſtolæ & Tract. contra nega Petrum Apoſt. fuiſſe Romæ. 4. Ven. 1

Fr. Paniçarollæ Diſceptationes Caluinic Med. 1594.

An. Monteterentij Scholia ad Statuta tam uilia quam Criminalia Ciuit. Bononia Bon. 1582.

Impreſe illuſtri di ca. Camilli. 4. Ven. 1585

Balthaſaris Etzelij Florilegia Chryſoſtom Mog. 1603.

Alf. Salmeronis tomus 6. 7. 8. fo. Col. 160

Porphyrius de Abſtinentia ab eſu anima Lat. 4. 1547.

Statuta Iadertina. 4. Ven. 1564.

Lettere di Annibal Caro. 4. Ven. 1597.

Il Conſolato del Mare, col Portolano del M 4. Ven. 1599.

Lettere di Luigi Groto. 4. Ven. 1601.

Tempio al Card. Cinth. Aldobrandini. 4. 1600.

Io. Bacho Anglicus ſuper ſententias 2. vo Med. 1510.

Venantij Honorij Clementiani &c. Carm Mog. 1603.

Polycarpi Lyſeri Adamus. 4. Lipſ. 1604.

Chriſt. Pelargus in Exodum. 4. Lipſ. 1604

Sermones B. Umberti. 4. Ven. 1603.

Asia Bapt. Grimaye. 4. Ant. 1604.

Jo. Hier. Puluerinus de curandis singulis huma-
ni corporis morbis. fo. Ven. 1600.

Maur. Cordæus in 1. lib. Hip. de Morbis Mulierum. fo. Par. 1585.

Doctissimorum virorum Comment. in Catullum
Tibul. & Propert. fo. Lut. 1604.

Philippi Scherbij Theses Philosophiæ. 4. 1603.

Gio. Marinello delle copie delle parole 2. vol.
Ven. 1602.

Remigius Altissiodorensis & Varlenius in
Psal. fo.

Ant. Butrius in 6. Decret. fo. Ven. 1575.

Q. Horatius cum Comment. Adr. Turnebi. fo.
Par. 1605.

Di Bart. Dionigi parte 5. delle Historie di Tar-
cagnota. 4. Ven. 1603.

Meditationes in Theriacam & Methridicam
Antidotum. 4. Ven. 1576.

Donum ROBERTI BARKER Regiæ
Maiestatis Typographi.

Rigenis Homiliæ super vet.
Testamentum. fo. MS.
The new Testament, with
some parts of the olde in
ancient English. fo.
The Mirrour of the world
written by a Friar at the instance of King
Philip of France. An. 1289. fo. MS.
Foure books of Honour Militarie & Ciuill. fo.
Lond. 1602.

Fr. Gonzaga de Origine Seraphicæ Re-
ligionis Franciscanæ. fo. Rom. 1587.

Donū GVIL. BALLOW Academiæ
Procuratoris.

Augustinꝰ de non iurando. fo. MS. De
trib. hostibus hoīem impugnātibꝰ. De
verbis Domini & Apostoli. Ad fratres
in Eremo. Epistola ad Iulianū Co-
mitem. De igne purgatorij.

De 10. plagis et de 10. præceptis. De gau-
dio & supplicio damnatorū. Stimulus
conscientiæ. Sermo Aug. de tremendo
Iudicio. De ebrietate. De fuga
mulierum. Sermo ad parochianos.
Epistolæ variæ Hieronymi ad diuersos.
Notabilia excerpta de epistolis Hieronymi. Aug. de perfectione iustitiæ.
De vita christiana. Eiusdem meditationes de dilectione Dei. De decimis
reddendis. Expositio S. Bernardi super Magnificat. Stourton de laude
B. Mariæ. Distinctiones bonæ per
Alphabetum.
Aug. sup Gen. ad literam. fo. Ms.
Boetius de hebdomadibꝰ. Aug. de Tri-
nitate. De vera religione. De
libero arbitrio. De natura boni.
De natura et gratia. Liber retracta-
tionū. De præsentia Dei ad Darda-
num. De fide ad Petrum. De
prædestinatione. De gratia & libero
arbitrio. Ad inquisitiones Ianuarij.
De fide & symbolo. Sermo ad iuuenes. De cura gerenda pro mortuis.
De moribus ecclesiæ et Manichæorum.
Hypognost. Contra Epistola Mani-
chei. De mendacio. Contra men-
dacium. De duabus animabꝰ. De
videndo Deū. Ad Macedonium.
Soliloq. De assumptione B. virginis.
Ep. ad Volusian. De virginit.
Sermo Ambrosij de assumptione. Sermones in monte. De adulterinis con-
iugijs. De utilitate credendi.

De

בְּרֵאשִׁית בָּרָא אֱלֹהִים אֵת הַשָּׁמַיִם

וְאֵת הָאָרֶץ ׃ וְהָאָרֶץ הָיְתָה תֹהוּ וָבֹהוּ

וְחֹשֶׁךְ עַל פְּנֵי תְהוֹם וְרוּחַ אֱלֹהִים

מְרַחֶפֶת עַל פְּנֵי הַמַּיִם ׃ וַיֹּאמֶר אֱלֹהִים

יְהִי אוֹר וַיְהִי אוֹר ׃ וַיַּרְא אֱלֹהִים אֶת

הָאוֹר כִּי טוֹב וַיַּבְדֵּל אֱלֹהִים בֵּין הָאוֹר

וּבֵין הַחֹשֶׁךְ ׃ וַיִּקְרָא אֱלֹהִים לָאוֹר יוֹם

וְלַחֹשֶׁךְ קָרָא לַיְלָה וַיְהִי עֶרֶב וַיְהִי בֹקֶר

יוֹם אֶחָד ׃

וַיֹּאמֶר אֱלֹהִים יְהִי רָקִיעַ בְּתוֹךְ הַמַּיִם

וִיהִי מַבְדִּיל בֵּין מַיִם לָמָיִם ׃ וַיַּעַשׂ אֱלֹהִים

אֶת הָרָקִיעַ וַיַּבְדֵּל בֵּין הַמַּיִם אֲשֶׁר

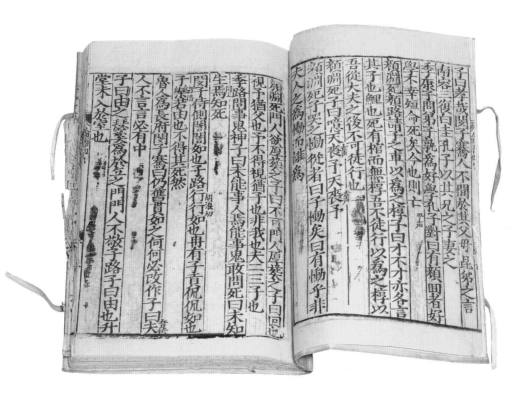

Fig. 14 (opposite) **The first oriental manuscript in the Bodleian was a copy of the Book of Genesis in Sephardic script, given by Sir John Fortescue in 1601.**

Fig. 15 (above) **The first Chinese book in the Bodleian was bought by Thomas Bodley in 1604 with money given by the earl of Northumberland.**

like the founder of the library and his first librarian, lived through the upheavals of the Reformation, when the monastic libraries (and the university's fifteenth-century library) had been destroyed and their fine collections dispersed. They regarded Bodley's foundation as a safe haven should such troubles recur, and many of the manuscripts presented to the Bodleian in its early years had belonged to English monasteries before their suppression. For example, in 1602 Sir Walter Cope gave the library forty-seven manuscripts, including many early English ones from monastic houses, among them a volume of homilies in Anglo-Saxon which on its last leaf has a sentence (added probably in the late eleventh century) that is reckoned to be the oldest specimen of the Dutch language. In 1603 Sir George More's gift of twenty-seven volumes included a group of manuscripts from Newark Priory, while the thirty-four manuscripts given by William Burdet in 1608 had for the most part originated at Reading Abbey.

Francis Bacon memorably described the Bodleian in 1605 as 'an ark to save learning from deluge',[9] and such it proved to be. In 1600 the earl of Essex gave 252 books that he had brought back from the bishop's palace in Faro, Portugal, after defeating the Spaniards in a naval battle off Cadiz in 1596. In 1601 the Oxford mathematician Thomas Allen, a close friend of Bodley, gave the library a volume that included three ninth-century booklets on subjects such as Latin grammar and Ovid's *Art of Love*, which are annotated by St Dunstan, probably when he was abbot of Glastonbury in the middle of the tenth century. The same year Sir John Fortescue, Chancellor of the Exchequer, gave several manuscripts and books, among them a manuscript of the Book of Genesis, written in Sephardic script with a Latin word-for-word translation – the first oriental manuscript in the Bodleian collections (fig. 14). In 1603 Sir Walter Ralegh joined the ranks of library benefactors, with a gift of £50. The following year the diplomat and poet Sir Henry Wotton presented a late sixteenth-century manuscript of the Qur'ān. Many of the library's early benefactors were men who had known Bodley when they served as soldiers or diplomats in the Netherlands; among these were Robert Sidney, earl of Leicester; Charles Blount, Lord Mountjoy; Thomas Sackville, Lord Buckhurst; Henry Percy, earl of Northumberland (fig. 15) and Sir William Knollys, later earl of Banbury. Each of them contributed substantial sums of money (£50 or £100) to the new library. Institutions as well as individuals added to the store. Merton College, at the warden's instigation, gave about forty books in 1600. The dean and chapter of Exeter Cathedral, no doubt through the influence of Bodley's brother Laurence who was a canon there (and had himself presented thirty-seven 'very fayre and new-bought bookes in folio' in 1600[10]), gave over eighty of their manuscripts to the library in 1602, including treasures such as the missal given to their predecessors by the first bishop of Exeter, Leofric, in the reign of Edward the Confessor (fig. 16) and a copy of Boethius's *De consolatione philosophiae*, written in the late tenth century at Canterbury. Ten years later the dean and canons of Windsor followed suit, presenting over one hundred books and manuscripts.

Fig. 16 **The Anglo-Saxon missal given to Exeter Cathedral by its first bishop, Leofric, was one of eighty manuscripts given by the dean and chapter to the Bodleian in 1602.**

ERE

DIGNV

& iustum est æquum

BEATI PACIFICI

REGNANTE D. IACOBO REGVM DOCTISSIMO
MVNIFICENTISSIMO OPTIMO HÆ MVSIS
EXTRVCTÆ MOLES. CONGESTA BIBLIOTHECA
ET QVÆCVNQVE ADHVC DEERANT AD SPLEN
DOREM ACADEMIÆ FELICITER TENTATA
COEPTA ABSOLVTA. SOLI DEO GLORIA.

Bodley was knighted in 1604 and his library was formally named the Bodleian Library, though many (including the founder himself) continued to refer to it as the 'public' library of the university – that is, a library open to all members of the university, in contrast to college libraries, which were only for the use of members of the foundation.[11] In August of the next year King James I visited the Bodleian and spent a long time examining a selection of books and manuscripts on its shelves. He was so moved by the magnificence of the collections that, on the spur of the moment, he offered to add to them any manuscripts that Bodley might choose from the libraries of the royal palaces. Nothing came of this extraordinary offer. On leaving the library, the king, who had from his youth developed a love of learning, declared that if he were not king, he would like to be a member of the university and that, were it ever his misfortune to be a captive, he would, given a choice, want to be imprisoned in the library where, bound up with chains as the books were, he could spend his days in study. Fifteen years later, King James gave a copy of his *Works* to the library, which was received with great ceremony by the university. The presentation is commemorated on the west side of the Tower of the Five Orders in the Schools Quadrangle, which shows the king with Fame blowing a trumpet on his left and the university meekly kneeling on his right (fig. 17).

Between 1600 and 1605 Bodley raised about £1,700, which enabled him to employ two enterprising London booksellers, John Norton and John Bill, to buy books for his library in Continental Europe.[12] Norton bought and sold books at the Frankfurt book fair and Bill regularly travelled to France, Germany, Spain and Italy. In 1597 Norton had published John Gerard's *Herball*, a copy of which he presented to Bodley's new library in 1601 (fig. 18). One of the books Bill bought for Bodley in Spain in 1604 was the first edition of *Don Quixote*. The first catalogue of the library's contents, compiled by Thomas James and published in 1605, reveals the wide range of material Norton and Bill were able to purchase: dictionaries, grammars and other works in Hebrew, Persian, Arabic, Hungarian and Chinese, as well as in the standard Latin and Greek, with literature by modern European authors, among them Boccaccio, Dante, Petrarch, Ronsard and Montaigne.

Fig. 17 **The west face of the Tower of the Five Orders in the Schools Quadrangle commemorates King James I's gift of a copy of his *Works* to the university.**

Bodley's purchasing of Chinese books was remarkable, for serious Chinese studies began in England only much later, and it is doubtful whether in the first decade of the seventeenth century anyone in Oxford was able to read the language. Indeed, in June 1607, sending a consignment of books from London, Bodley explained to James, 'Of the China Bookes, because I cannot give their titles, I have written on every volume the name of the giver.'[13] The 1605 catalogue includes very few works in English, a reflection both of the prevailing use of classical languages for scholarly works and of Bodley's own view that works in English, whether literature or pamphlets, were too frivolous to be preserved in an academic library. As early as 1602, he instructed his librarian 'to take no riffe raffe bookes' from the collection offered by Sir Richard Fermor (of Somerton in Oxfordshire) 'for suche will but prove a discredit to our Librarie'.[14] On 1 January 1612 he wrote to James complaining that the librarian had included in his catalogue 'idle bookes and riffe raffes' which 'will raise a scandal upon it [the library], when it shall be given out, by suche as would disgrace it, that I have made up a number, with Almanackes, plaies, and proclamations'.[15] Only a fortnight later, on 15 January, Bodley again wrote to James: 'I can see no good reason to alter my opinion, for including suche bookes, as almanakes, plaies, & an infinit number, that are daily printed, of very unworthy maters', which, he was confident, 'the keeper & underkeeper should disdaine to seeke out, to deliver unto any man'. He did concede that some plays might be worth preserving, but 'hardly one in fortie', and those mainly in foreign languages.[16]

The catalogue of 1605 was dedicated to the king's eldest son, the 11-year-old Prince Henry Frederick, whom Bodley thought likely to prove a more generous benefactor than his father. But any hopes of royal munificence were dashed by the prince's early death from typhoid fever in 1612. In his preface to the 1605 catalogue, Thomas James, surveying the rapidly filling bookshelves, had written that there seemed more need of a library for the books than of books for the library, but that did not prevent him from suggesting that Bodley should ask the Stationers' Company of London to donate copies of all the books they printed. The result was an agreement between the university and the

Fig. 18 **The London bookseller John Norton presented a beautifully coloured edition of John Gerard's** *Herball* **to the library in 1601.**

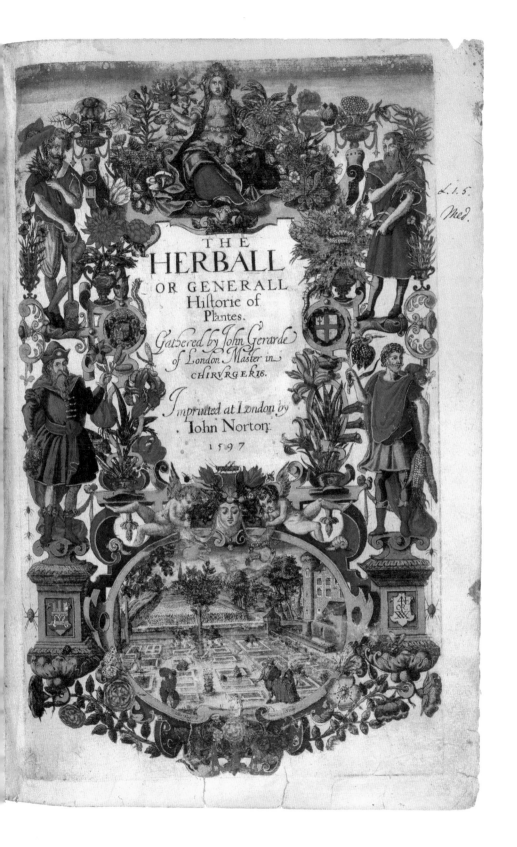

THE
HERBALL
OR GENERALL
Historie of
Plantes.

Gathered by John Gerarde
of London Master in
CHIRVRGERIE.

Imprinted at London by
Iohn Norton.
1597

company in 1610 that provided for one copy of every item printed by company members to be added to the Bodleian's collections free of charge (fig. 19). Not only did this guarantee a regular supply of newly published books for a while, but it also formed the basis in England of the concept of copyright or legal deposit, and ensured that the Bodleian was among the nine libraries listed in the 1709 Copyright Act as entitled to receive a copy of every book registered at Stationers' Hall. It remains a 'copyright library' to this day, having to all intents and purposes fulfilled the role of the national library until the British Museum, with its library, opened in 1759.

Thomas Bodley's munificence was greeted with enthusiasm in Oxford, and later generations described him as the ideal benefactor – a man blessed with plenty of money, energy and contacts in high places, who used these assets tirelessly in pursuit of his great venture. But Thomas James must have found him a hard taskmaster. The librarian was expected to provide weekly reports on progress, and in return received a constant stream of letters which reveal Bodley's at times obsessive interest in the minutiae of library management. For example, in September 1602 he complained about James's handwriting, especially in the lists that were designed to guide readers to the position of the books on the library shelves: 'I shall request yow ... would with your penne express your letters as full as yow can. For it chaunceth many times that your writing is both ill to be read and understood, by reason of sundrie letters but half drawen, when your paper taketh not the inke, which causeth obscuritie.'[17] He went on to give his librarian precise instructions on how to paste the sheets of paper together without the join showing. For good measure, he sent James some better-quality ink. Several of his letters rebuke his librarian for not keeping the library open for the hours set out in the statutes (six hours each day, from 8 to 11 throughout the year, and from 2 to 5 on spring and summer afternoons, or from 1 to 4 during the winter months). Bodley had provided a bell in 1604, which he replaced in 1611, with instructions that it should be rung to give notice when the library was about to be opened and again when it was about to close. It is clear from the first library statutes that it was no easy matter to keep regular hours in the days before accurate clocks were common, and the provision of a bell does not seem to have solved the problem, despite hopes that it would ensure that 'no one will come too early nor stay there too late,

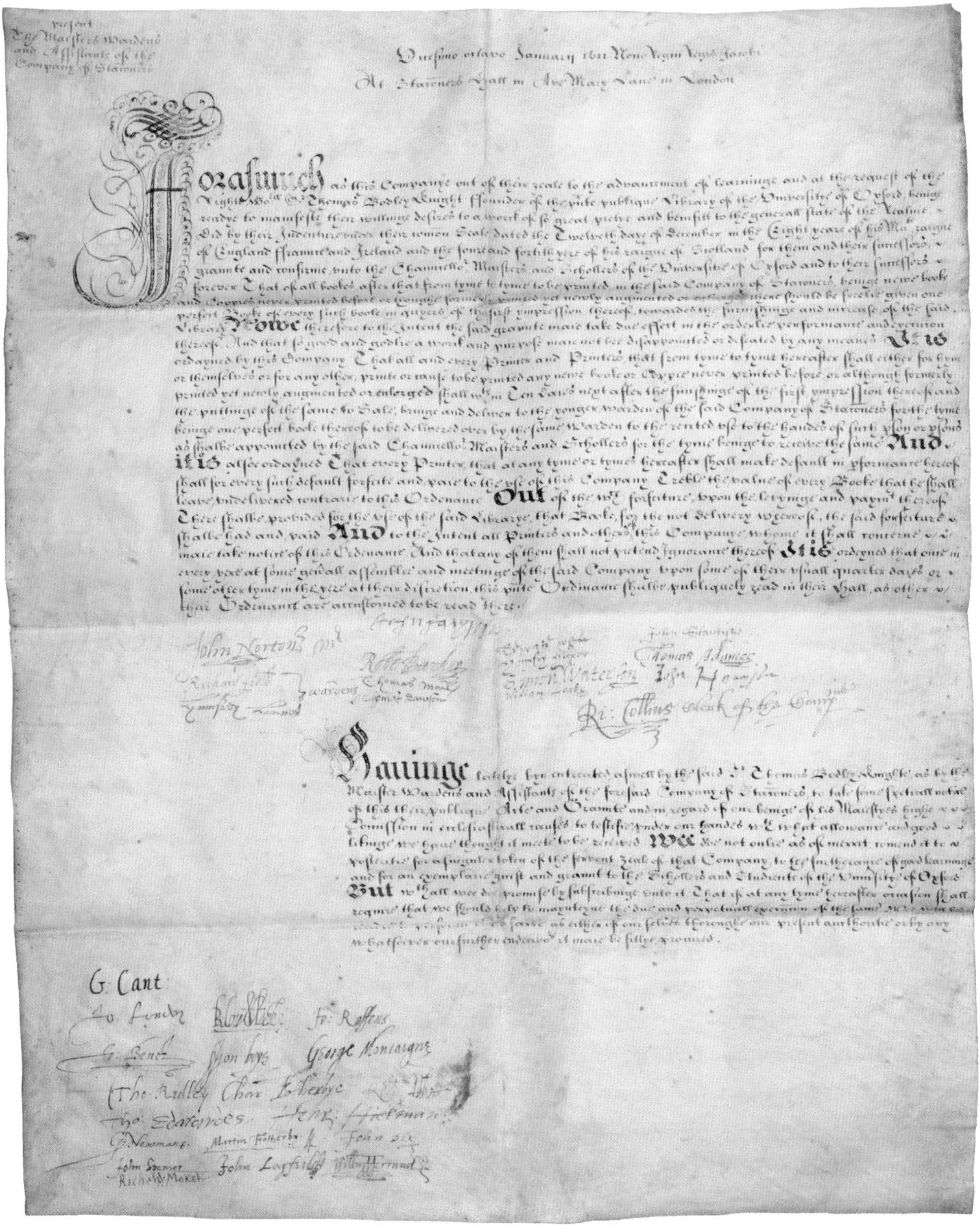

Fig. 19 The Stationers' Company's agreement with the university in 1610 provided for the gift to the library of one copy of every book published by its members.

Fig. 20 **The first book received under the agreement with the Stationers'
Company was Thomas Cartwright's** *Christian Religion* **(1614).**

which the disagreement of clocks may often cause, to the grievous
inconvenience of the librarian and the students'.[18] Twenty-six years
later, in 1636, the university statutes refer to the same difficulty:

> As the time fixed by the Bodleian Statutes for keeping the library
> open is mostly shorter than it ought to be through the unequal
> going of the clock, and so works no inconsiderable prejudice to the
> students, it is enacted, that a three hour sand-glass shall be set up in
> some conspicuous spot in the library, which immediately after the
> ringing of the library-bell is to be set on end, and be the standard
> time allowed to be spent in the library.[19]

Bodley's concern about the regulation of the time his library was open
continued to preoccupy him; his last letter to his librarian – written on
3 January 1613, the day after he had dictated his will and just twenty-
five days before he died – was wholly concerned with a report he had

received from a friend in Oxford that the library had been closed for a fortnight. Bodley made it clear that this was totally unacceptable – a state of affairs

> which is highly disliked of all that understand it, but of no man more then of my self ... I cannot choose but request yow for heerafter, to alter your course (which nowe I hear is too common) in taking that libertie [of closing the Library]. For my meaning was ever ... that still there should be that access for students ... as was formerly allowed by the ancient statutes, which never permitted so large vacations.[20]

In fact, Bodley was conveniently forgetting that the regulations for the earlier university library had allowed the librarian a month's leave each year – a precedent he failed to follow. From the beginning he had been very reluctant to allow the librarian to take any holiday, despite the fact that no formal provision was made for assistance until 1610 – although there was probably, from 1601, a servant who cleaned the library[21] and, from 1602, an assistant or underkeeper.[22]

It was only in June 1610, with the promulgation of library statutes in the university's governing body of Convocation, that the staffing of the Bodleian was established as consisting of three men: a librarian, a sub-librarian and a porter. The librarian's duties were principally concerned with assistance to students, cataloguing of books as they came into the library and maintenance of the Benefactors' Register. He was to be 'a man of eminent celebrity and of a good reputation ... for truth, probity and prudence', a graduate, with knowledge of both classical and modern languages,

> free from the conjugal tie, and not an incumbent of any benefice with cure of souls, unless in the immediate neighbourhood. For it cannot harmonize with piety to undertake so great a charge in combination with public employments; and wedlock is mostly so rife with domestic engagements as to be unable to afford leisure for a man's free disposal of himself day by day.[23]

Thomas James had, despite Bodley's disapproval, married in September 1602. Most of the later librarians were married and many were also parish priests, contrary to statute until the prohibition was eventually removed with the revision of the library statutes in 1847. The sub-librarian was to be in attendance in the library 'to share in his [the librarian's] toils', principally the cataloguing, and to 'have some acquaintance with the tongues'. A porter – 'some needy and honest man' – was also to be appointed by the librarian 'to clean the books, and sweep the library, and to brush the tables, closets, seats, screens, windows, and in short, all the places which are sullied by dust or through disuse'.[24]

Bodley diverged from earlier library regulations in prohibiting the lending of books. He was convinced that one of the main reasons for the demise of the university's fifteenth-century library was that readers had been allowed to borrow books and manuscripts without there being any mechanism for enforcing the return of the items they had borrowed. Several times in his letters to Thomas James, Bodley stressed that this was not a matter that was open for negotiation. In July 1605 he wrote firmly: 'The lending of any booke out of the Librarie may be assented to by no means; neither is it a mater that the Universitie or Vicechancelour are to deale in.'[25] Again in March 1610 he refused to contemplate a loan that his librarian requested on behalf of a reader: 'For still the like may be alleaged [a precedent] in other cases hereafter, to the abuse of all good order, & totall ruine of the Librarie.'[26] When the provost of Oriel College asked to borrow a book, Bodley again turned down the request, but he followed up his refusal by sending from London a book on the same subject, instructing Thomas James to give it to the provost and to ask him to donate the volume to the library when he had finished with it – a neat way of satisfying the provost's needs without breaking the library's rules.

Despite the strict enforcement of the no-borrowing rule and the fact that all the larger volumes were securely chained to the shelves, there is evidence that books did occasionally go astray. A Mr Yates of New College was accused in November 1613 of not returning to the sub-librarian a book that had been fetched for him from the gallery in Arts End. He admitted the offence, was ordered to provide a replacement copy and 'promised so to do'.[27] Bodley was convinced that the greatest risk of what he called 'embezzlement' of the books was in the interval between their arrival in the library and their being placed on the shelves. He more than once urged Thomas James to choose only trustworthy scholars to help with the task of carrying up to the library the new books that were sent from London, especially when the consignment included small volumes in fine bindings. As for the larger (folio) books, James was instructed to have the smith on hand to chain them immediately on arrival, and to close the library to readers until the job was completed. From the outset, the folios were arranged alphabetically by author within each of the four faculties of Arts, Law, Medicine and Theology, and chained to the book presses. As early as 1605, Bodley was having some smaller (quarto) books that were expected to be heavily used bound in leather to facilitate chaining them among the folios, thus making them more readily accessible to readers than those bound in vellum that were kept in the cupboards and later in the galleries and had to be fetched by the librarian.

Thomas Bodley wanted his library to be a resource not only for his own university, but also for the scholarly world at large. In early discussions with the university about who should be entitled to use it, he agreed that there would have to be some restrictions on access, to ensure 'the ease of the Keeper [i.e. the librarian], the quietnesse of the students, the securitie of the books and the Honor and dignitie of the University'; otherwise the 'popular sort' would daily pester the room 'with their gazing, and babbling, and trampling up and down' and 'disturb out of all measure the endeavours of those that are studious'.[28] But he insisted that bona fide scholars from outside Oxford should be allowed to study in the library, once they had gone through the formalities of requesting permission and had taken the library oath, 'in order that study in any science may be the more happily advanced', as the first library statutes, drafted by Bodley, expressed it in 1610.[29] Many students from Cambridge, the Scottish universities and the London Inns of Court registered as readers in the early years. Bodley dissuaded the university from requiring caution money from visiting scholars as savouring 'of discourtesie'.[30] As for members of Oxford University, the university itself was not inclined to allow its more junior members to use the library – and the privilege was originally restricted to men who were already Masters of Arts, or Doctors or Bachelors of Divinity, Medicine or Law. In December 1602 Bodley wrote to James that he had been asked by a very good friend to help get a young Bachelor of Arts admitted as a reader, 'which I would willingly doe at the instance of his frindes … but sith it is thought fitte by the Universitie, that Bachelers of art shall be excluded, I may not my self give the first occasion of breache of their order'.[31]

We know who used the library during the first year, because Thomas James kept a record of the 248 scholars who came between 8 November 1602 and 7 November 1603. Fifteen of them were from Continental Europe – among them three from France, two each from Denmark, Silesia and Prussia, and one each from Switzerland and Saxony. Most of those studying in the Bodleian were resident members of the university who had recently graduated as Masters of Arts; only one was a more junior Bachelor of Arts, and he had had to obtain special permission. Thomas Bodley had been inclined to give Bachelors of Arts access to the library, but had deferred to the university's wish to restrict the privilege to its senior members. At first very few BAs registered as readers – just two in 1604, but twenty-two in 1605 and a similar number in the following years, until the number peaked at 113 in 1611, before dropping back to sixty-four the following year and stabilizing at around thirty or forty for each of the next five years. It is clear that by then the admission of BAs to read in the library had become a matter of routine, though their presence seems to have caused some problems. In 1610 they were required to wear the academic dress appropriate to their junior status. In 1613 they were exhorted to 'abstain from reading books ill adapted to their studies' and to 'show due observance and deference to the seniors by giving place to them the moment they see them approaching the bench or book-case where they are, or else by passing to them, if the case require it, the book which they were previously using'. And in 1615 they were ordered 'not to roam about from place to place but ... diligently to ply their studies in that part of the Library wherein the books of the faculty of arts (and those alone) are contained'.[32] It was not only the younger members of the university whose use of the Bodleian was governed by library regulations. All had to be formally admitted as readers, in the presence of the vice-chancellor and librarian, and to swear an 'oath of fidelity' to the library, undertaking that they would 'study in modesty and silence', and use the books 'in such manner that they may last as long as possible'.[33]

Down the centuries, all readers, when admitted to use the Bodleian, have been required to take an oath, or more recently to read aloud a declaration, which since around 1970 has been in the form:

I hereby undertake not to remove from the Library, or to mark, deface, or injure in any way, any volume, document, or other object belonging to it, or in its custody; not to bring into the Library or kindle therein any fire or flame, and not to smoke in the Library; and I promise to obey all rules of the Library.

Thomas Bodley's 'oath of fidelity' was considerably longer:

You shall promise and sweare in the presence of almightie God, that whensoever you shall repaire to the publique Librarie of this Universitie, you will conforme your self to studie with modestie and silence, and use both the bookes and every thing els appertaining to their furniture, with a carefull respect to their longest conservation; and that neither your self in person, nor any other whosoever, by your procurement or privitie, shall either openly or underhand, by way of embezeling, changing, razing, defacing, tearing, cutting, noting, interlining, or by voluntarie corrupting, blotting, slurring or any other maner of mangling, or misusing, any one or more of the saied bookes, either wholly or in part, make any alteration: but shall hinder and impeache, as much as lieth in yow, all and every such offendour or offendours, by detecting their demeanour unto the Vice-chancellour, or to his Deputie then in place, within the next three daies after it shall com to your knowledge, so helpe you God by Christes merites, according to the doctrine of his holy Evangelistes.[34]

By 1608 Bodley had decided to build an extension at right angles to the original library, at its east end, to house the ever-increasing collections. Yorkshire masons who had been working at Merton College moved across to the Bodleian and began work in July 1610. Timber was supplied without charge from the king's woods at Stow in Buckinghamshire and at Shotover immediately to the east of Oxford, and Francis, Lord Norris, gave twenty oak trees from his estate at Rycote, near Thame. Others, among them George Abbot, who had graduated from Balliol College in the 1580s and was in 1609 vice-chancellor of the university, contributed generously to the cost of construction. (He was to become bishop of London in 1610 and archbishop of Canterbury the following year.) The extension, known as Arts End, was completed, way behind schedule and over budget, in

the autumn of 1612 (fig. 21). It was the first example in England of a new type of library design – the walls shelved from floor to ceiling, with a gallery giving access to the upper half – and was in marked contrast to the traditional fittings in the original library room, with its book presses and desks at right angles to the walls between the windows, making best use of the available natural light for reading. The shelving in Arts End is evidence of the need to provide storage for the ever-increasing number of books that were rolling off the printing presses of the western world, and that the Bodleian was acquiring both from benefactors and from the Stationers' Company of London.

On the ground floor below Arts End the Proscholium provided an elegant entrance hall to the Divinity School (fig. 22). Bodley then directed his energies to persuading the university to raise money for the addition of three more ranges of buildings to form a quadrangle. He planned that these would, on the ground and first floors, provide rooms for teaching in the university faculties or 'schools', replacing the dilapidated houses adjoining the Divinity School, and on the second floor house his expanding library. The names of these schools were painted above the doorways, recording in Latin the range of subjects taught in the seventeenth-century university – jurisprudence, anatomy, metaphysics, moral philosophy, natural philosophy, languages, grammar, rhetoric, logic, arithmetic, geometry, music and astronomy – in addition to theology, which continued to be taught in the fifteenth-century Divinity School. But Sir Thomas did not live to see his plan materialize: the foundation stone of what came to be known as the 'Schools Quadrangle' was laid on 30 March 1613, the day after his funeral (fig. 23). By then his library contained some 15,000 separate works, bound into about 7,000 volumes. The collection included several hundred manuscripts, the most important of them medieval ones that had passed into private hands at the dissolution of the monasteries in the 1530s and then been transferred as gifts to the safer haven of the Bodleian.

Fig. 21 (previous spread) **Arts End, completed in 1612, was fitted with shelves from floor to ceiling to house the library's ever-increasing collections.**

Fig. 22 (opposite) **Engraving of the Proscholium, completed in 1612, which served as an elegant entrance hall to the Divinity School. From James Ingram, *Memorials of Oxford*, vol. 2 (1836).**

Bodley had at the outset made clear his view that one of the main reasons the university's earlier library had failed was because it was seen as only 'a store of bookes of diverse benefactors', which, without 'any lasting allowance for augmentation of the number ... came to ruine'.[35] Therefore, in 1609 he made provision for a regular income for the library by endowing it with land in Berkshire and houses in Distaff Lane, London. The indenture, preserved in the University Archives, affirms his opinion both that the 'principall occasion of the utter subversion and ruine of some of the famousest Libraryes in Christendome hath ben the wante of due provision of some certainety in revenwe, for their continewall preservation' and that his library was well on the way to being 'the most absolute and sufficient for the furtheringe of students of all kyndes of knowledge of good literature, that was ever yett in beinge, in any publique place of studie'.[36] Thanks to his forethought and his liberality, Bodley's library had a secure income of £157 per annum, while its regular outgoings amounted to about £68, leaving it an ample surplus with which to buy more books of relevance to Oxford scholars. A fine bust of Bodley, presented by a former chancellor of the university, Thomas Sackville, earl of Dorset, and admired by King James I when he visited the library in 1605, still presides over the entrance to Duke Humfrey's Library.

On the death of Sir Thomas Bodley, Thomas James became responsible to a governing body of university men – the curators of the Bodleian, whose number and role had been set out in the first library statutes of 1610. While careful to express every confidence in his first librarian, Sir Thomas thought it necessary to establish a committee of eight high-ranking members of the university (the vice-chancellor, both proctors and five professors) both to avoid the risk of problems with future holders of the post and to oversee the running of the Bodleian. Their duties were prescribed as visiting the library at least once a year (on the anniversary of its opening on 8 November) and 'to enquire with particularity into its state and condition'. It is clear that the curators soon realized that they would need to be better informed if they were to fulfil their statutory responsibilities. In 1615 ordinances decreed that they were each to be given a copy of the library statutes, to be supplied with copies of the handlists of the books on the shelves to facilitate their

Fig. 23 (previous spread) **The Schools Quadrangle, completed in 1618.**

stock check each November and to be convened by the vice-chancellor twice each year to look through the catalogues of new books available at Frankfurt.

Thomas James continued in post for seven years after Bodley's death. During this time, he produced another catalogue of the entire contents of the library. Its publication in 1620, financed by a judicious balance in the accounts accumulated for this purpose by the curators since 1613, marked the first library catalogue to list the books alphabetically by author – an arrangement that we now take for granted, as it eventually became standard practice in the western world. He also worked on more detailed subject guides to the books on theology, medicine and law. A fourth guide, to the wide range of books in the 'Arts' classification, was designed specifically for the younger members of the university, who, having graduated as Bachelor of Arts, were studying for the degree of Master of Arts and using the Bodleian in increasing numbers. The librarian's interest in and commitment to this task is demonstrated by his continuing to add to the guide for four years after his retirement. It was never printed, but we can tell how useful it was, for by 1645 the manuscript copy was 'all torne and worne out' and the library paid £3 to have it recopied for continuing use.[37]

Thomas James's published catalogues alerted scholars all over Europe to the great number of books available for study in Oxford, and Bodley's enlightened policy made the collections accessible to them. The advantages of studying in the Bodleian were publicized in a French treatise of 1627 on how to set up a library; written by Gabriel Naudé, it cited the Bodleian's catalogues as an example of good, indeed essential, practice. Naudé also praised the Bodleian as a library 'where one may freely enter and without difficulty'.[38] It is interesting to see that 520 foreign students signed on as readers in the Bodleian between 1602 and 1642, when the outbreak of civil war in England interrupted the flow. No new readers from abroad were registered between January 1642 and July 1647. Thereafter their numbers slowly increased and foreign scholars returned to Oxford throughout the second half of the century, many of them to study the Bodleian's famous manuscript collections – over three hundred foreigners registered as readers between 1647 and 1682, when the record briefly breaks off.

Very few early readers have left any account of their experience of using the Bodleian. The first was Jean Basire, a French student of civil law, who had already been in Oxford for three years when he became the first foreigner to be admitted to use the library, just three months after it opened. He wrote of his satisfaction in finding that he was allowed to study in the Bodleian for six hours each day, if, he added, he could survive working for so long. Lucas Holsten of Hamburg, admitted as a reader in 1622, wrote enthusiastically about being able to study the Greek and Latin manuscripts, which he thought were woefully neglected by Oxford scholars. He divided the two years he spent as a young scholar in England in the early 1620s between London and Oxford, researching manuscript collections for his *Geographi minores*. Almost a decade earlier, in 1613, the librarian had asserted that only two people consulted the manuscripts – Brian Twyne, fellow of Corpus Christi College, and Thomas Allen of Gloucester Hall. Twyne had been a pupil of Allen's who became particularly interested in the study of astronomy and navigation, staunchly defending the controversial views of astronomers like Copernicus, Kepler and Galileo. His only significant publication, *Antiquitatis academiae Oxoniensis apologia*, which appeared in 1608, was the first printed history of the university. In 1634 he became the first Keeper of the University Archives. Allen, a mathematician and astrologer, who had matriculated at Trinity College in 1561 and been a fellow there from 1565, resigned his fellowship in 1571, moving to Gloucester Hall to avoid having to take the oath of supremacy and thus acknowledge Elizabeth I as supreme governor of the Church of England. (Although formally a member of the established church, Allen inclined to Roman Catholicism, and in the first quarter of the seventeenth century Gloucester Hall contained a substantial number of Catholics.)

In 1613 Thomas James removed the manuscripts from the shelves of printed books in Duke Humfrey's Library and housed them more securely in a gallery accessible only to staff, who would fetch any volumes that readers wished to consult. Twyne complained to the curators about this 'locking away' of the manuscripts and – in a very early, if not the earliest, instance of the exercise of reader influence on library policy – the librarian was forced to relent. In 1639 we find another scholar from Hamburg, Johann Friedrich Gronovius, much less enthusiastic than Lucas Holsten. He too had come to work on the famous manuscript collections in the Bodleian, but his studies were hampered by a new regulation stipulating that non-members of the university had to be accompanied by an Oxford graduate of senior status whenever they consulted a manuscript. 'Where am I', Gronovius wrote, 'to find men willing to waste time to sit with me three or four hours studying my finger-nails?' He found people in Oxford in general more than a little xenophobic, apt to call all foreigners, regardless of their nationality, 'French dogs'.[39] Oxford students seem to have had fewer obstacles placed in the way of their studies. In the late 1620s Richard Napier, a young fellow of All Souls, wrote to his uncle about an interesting astrological manuscript he was transcribing in the Bodleian. He was frustrated at not being allowed to take it back to his rooms in college, but was delighted when the sub-librarian lent him a key so that he could 'go into the Library privately when I please, and there to sit from six of the clock in the morning to five at night'.[40]

While Thomas James compiled catalogues to make the library collections more accessible, and a steady stream of foreign scholars came to study in the library, work on the building of the quadrangle continued intermittently – to provide teaching rooms for the university faculties and, on the second floor, space for the expansion of the Bodleian. The basic structure, complete with essential fittings like doors and locks, was finished by 1618, thanks to almost £2,500 paid from Bodley's estate. In 1622 a new gate was inserted at the entrance to the Proscholium with an inscription above it commemorating Bodley's foundation of the library for Oxford University and the republic of the learned. But there were problems with both the funding and the design of the new quadrangle, and the work of masons, glaziers, painters and smiths dragged on for another ten years. To many members of the university it must have seemed interminable. In the vice-chancellor's accounts for May to July 1624 it is noted that Jeremy Lawes, a London plumber, had been paid £38 for all 'plummery done by him at the schooles from the beginning of the world to this day'.[41] The badly designed and poorly constructed floors were a problem from the start. As early as 1625, additional arches had to be erected in the School of Natural Philosophy to support the floor of the Anatomy School above, and clamps and bolts were supplied to truss up the sagging floors of the other rooms on the first storey of the quadrangle. In 1630 it was thought that the structure of the Schools was so poor that there was some danger of it collapsing. Fortunately this forecast proved unduly pessimistic, but to keep the Schools standing the university had to levy fees on its members to pay for maintenance and repairs throughout the seventeenth century and beyond.

The librarian himself contributed to the library building the design of the magnificent frieze which survives just below ceiling level around the second floor of the quadrangle (now the Upper Reading Room). It depicts eminent authors from classical times to 1619, and mirrors the arrangement of their works on the shelves of Duke Humfrey's Library. It also reflects Thomas James's reverence for the writers of ancient Greece and Rome, the Church Fathers, foreign Protestant reformers and English churchmen of his own time. James was renowned for his strong anti-Catholic views and envisaged the library as a powerhouse of Protestant learning. He is reputed to have recommended the papal *Index of Prohibited Books* as a useful guide for the selection of books to purchase. James resigned in 1620, and was succeeded by John Rouse, a fellow of Oriel College, who – like Thomas Bodley before him – had spent several years travelling around Europe, visiting libraries and improving his knowledge of foreign languages (fig. 24). Rouse shared his predecessor's strong Puritan views but, unlike James, was neither a theologian nor an ordained clergyman. He was a friend of the poet John Milton, who presented copies of his published works to the Bodleian, one with a complimentary inscription to the librarian as 'a most learned man and a good judge of books'.[42] Rouse had a reputation as a sound scholar and his own statement, written in the autograph album of a visiting scholar – 'I cannot tell a lie, or commend a book if it is a bad one'[43] – reinforces the impression of a man for whom books were all-important. It was largely due to Rouse that the library began to collect works of English literature, which, as we have seen, Bodley had not considered suitable material for his scholarly library. The founder's policy was set aside in 1649, when Robert Burton, student and from 1624 librarian of Christ Church, author of *The Anatomy of Melancholy*, died leaving instructions that the Bodleian should choose whatever it wanted from his large library. (It is intriguing to note that a 'Robert Burton' consulted Simon Forman in 1597 and was diagnosed as suffering from melancholy.[44]) Rouse was able to fill many gaps in the Bodleian's collections from Burton's library, especially in works of English literature, including Shakespeare's *Venus and Adonis* (today

Fig. 24 **Portrait of John Rouse, Bodley's Librarian from 1620 to 1652.**

An Active Swain to make a Leap was seen,
Which shan'd his Fellow Shepherds on the Green,
And growing Vain, he would Essay once more,
But lost the Fame, which he had gain'd before;
Oft' did he try, at length was forc'd to yeild
He Stove in Vain, — he had himself Excell'd:
So Nature once in her Essays of Wit,
In Shakespear took the Shepherd's Lucky Leap
But over-straining in the great Effort,
In Dryden, and the rest, has since fell Short.

Under Shakespear's Picture by B: Johnson

This Figure w.ᶜ.ᵏ thou here seſt put,
It was for gentle Shakespear cut,
Wherein y.ᵉ Graver was at Strife
With Nature to out-do y.ᵉ Life;
Oh.' could he but have drawn his Wit
As well in Brals, as he has hitt
His Face — The print would y.ᵉ surp
All y.ᵗ was ever Writ in Brals;
But since he cannot, Reader look
Not on his Picture, but his Book

Mr. WILLIAM

SHAKESPEARES

COMEDIES,
HISTORIES, &
TRAGEDIES.

Published according to the True Originall Copies.

the only surviving first quarto of this poem) and *The Rape of Lucrece*, and plays by Beaumont and Fletcher and Ben Jonson. Among the books that came into the library when Rouse was librarian was the collected edition of Shakespeare's *Plays*, published in 1623, long known as the First Folio (fig. 25). It is recorded in the 1635 supplement to the Bodleian catalogue, but was probably sold in a batch of 'duplicates' to an Oxford bookseller once the third edition was acquired, as it is not in the catalogue of 1674. Fortunately, another copy came in Edmond Malone's bequest in the early nineteenth century.

In the previous decade Rouse had overseen an enormous expansion of the library's collection of manuscripts, largely through the good offices of William Laud, who combined influence in Oxford (first as president of St John's College and then, from 1630, as chancellor of the university) with considerable power in church and state (as privy councillor, and successively bishop of London and archbishop of Canterbury). It was Laud who, early in 1629, persuaded the earl of Pembroke to buy an important collection of Greek manuscripts for the university. They had belonged to a wealthy Venetian, Jacopo Barozzi da Vignola, and their purchase by a London bookseller caused considerable interest in the scholarly world. Pembroke thought they 'would be of more use to the church in being kept united in some public library, than scattered in particular hands'.[45] Greek manuscripts were rare in England and their arrival greatly enhanced the Bodleian's reputation. They were accompanied by the gift of a further twenty-nine Greek manuscripts from Sir Thomas Roe, friend of John Donne and Ben Jonson, formerly ambassador to Mughal India, and from 1621 to 1629 ambassador to Constantinople. He later served as member of parliament for Oxford in the Long Parliament. In 1634 Sir Kenelm Digby, who had studied in Oxford and had inherited a fine collection of manuscripts from his old tutor, Thomas Allen, followed Laud's advice and gave them to the Bodleian. Allen was a mathematician, and many of his manuscripts are important works of medieval science. Laud himself began to

Fig. 25 (previous spread) **The original Bodleian copy of the First Folio of Shakespeare's *Plays* (1623), discarded in the mid-seventeenth century, was purchased by the library when it came on the market in 1906.**

Fig. 26 (opposite) **The 'Laudian Mahzor', a lavishly illustrated Hebrew community prayer book, *c.*1275.**

מִתְנַשֵּׂא לְכֹל לְרֹאשׁ׳ בַּחֲרֵבֹּאוּ
כְּאוֹם הַדֵּלֶת רֹאשׁ׳ כִּכְבֹוּדֵּךָ הַבְּתַאֲנַה
בְּרֹאשׁ בִּיטֶה׳ וְאֲתַה הַדְּרֹושׁ׳ מִכֹּל
אוֹם לְפְרֹושׁ׳ לְנַשֵׂאַה עַל כֹל לְרֹאשׁ׳
גַעֲלֹה תֵּשִׁית לְמֵצֹּד רֹאשׁ׳ וְהָיִיֵת
תֹרֵים רֹאשׁ׳ כִּכְבָא כְבֹד מֵרֹאשׁ׳

Fig. 27 **Bust of King Charles I by Hubert Le Sueur, *c.*1631.**

collect manuscripts, buying many that came on the market as monastic libraries on the Continent were despoiled in the campaigns of the Thirty Years War. Between 1635 and 1640 he gave 1,300 manuscripts to the library, almost doubling its manuscript holdings, and making it a renowned centre for oriental studies, especially Arabic, Persian and Turkish. His donations include many treasures such as the 'Laudian Mahzor', one of the finest examples of an early, lavishly illustrated Hebrew community prayer book, produced in southern Germany around 1270–80, and an album of Indian miniature paintings, dating from the early seventeenth century, which contains eighteen pictures from a set of *ragamala* icons, illustrations of musical modes. As chancellor of the university, Laud sought to encourage the development of a learned press in Oxford to publish editions of the writings of the early Fathers of the Church, in order to disseminate the truth embodied in them and to correct what he considered the erroneous views of many contemporary theologians. His gifts of manuscripts were all subject to the condition that they should never leave the library except to go to the university press for printing. He also presented, in 1636, a bust of his patron, King Charles I, which was placed on the right-hand side of the entrance to Duke Humfrey's Library, facing the bust of Sir Thomas Bodley. Five years later the university paid a local mason £6 for the carved surround in which it still stands (fig. 27).

With so many large donations, the library shelves were full to overflowing, and there was no space in the main library for the newly acquired manuscripts. In his will, Bodley had specified that part of the library's endowment was to be spent on building 'some bewtifull enlargment at the west end' of the fifteenth-century Duke Humfrey's Library,[46] but discussions about how best to achieve this dragged on for years. Eventually, in May 1634, the foundation stone of the university's Convocation House (fig. 28) was laid to the west of the Divinity School. By 1640 the elegant room above it was ready for use as the final seventeenth-century extension to the Bodleian, and Rouse was at last able to move the great manuscript collections to a secure home in its galleries.

Meanwhile, Rouse, like Thomas James before him, methodically catalogued the new books as they came in, and in 1635 published a supplement to the 1620 catalogue. But, unlike his predecessor or any of his successors, Rouse had to cope with civil war. Oxford became a garrison city, briefly (from August to October 1642) for the Parliamentarian army, then for the king's army. Neither was popular with the city or the university, particularly as the war dragged on. For four years after the Battle of Edgehill in October 1642, Oxford became the Royalist headquarters. The demands of the royal court and the army disrupted the work of the university, and soon brought it to a halt. The Court of Chancery took over the new Convocation House, and the Court of Requests sat in the School of Natural Philosophy. Other rooms around the Schools Quadrangle were used for the storage of army supplies and munitions – powder and muskets in the tower, many of the arms forcibly collected from city and university residents; victuals in the Law and Logic Schools; uniforms and cloth in the Astronomy and Music Schools; – with the result that Rouse had to run a library in the centre of what was in effect a military depot, in a city that became increasingly overcrowded, unhealthy and lawless. The king's headquarters were in Christ Church, where many courtiers, government officials and high-ranking army officers took up residence. Queen Henrietta Maria and her entourage lodged at Merton College. New College became the base of the ordnance office and a store for small arms and powder. Many members of the university left Oxford for safer and more salubrious places. The city was ravaged by epidemics in 1643 and 1644, and in the autumn of 1644 suffered a disastrous fire, which started uncomfortably close to the Bodleian near the North Gate and spread southwards, destroying many homes and businesses.

In 1642 £500 from the library's coffers was loaned to the king's cause. (This forced loan was never repaid but, together with £450 owed by one of Thomas Bodley's executors, continued to be recorded in the library's accounts for another 140 years, until both were finally written off as bad debts in 1782.) With Oxford cut off from London by the war, no rents could be collected from the houses the library owned in Distaff Lane, and there was no money to buy books or to pay the librarian's salary. To add to his problems, on 30 December 1645 Rouse received an order to take to Christ Church a book that the king wanted to read – a history of the world by Théodore Agrippa d'Aubigné. The slip of paper, firmly endorsed by the vice-chancellor 'His Majestyes use is in commaund to us',[47] survives to this day (fig. 29). Rouse had to hurry to Christ Church, taking with him a copy of the statutes which forbade the removal of any book from the library. He explained to the king ' that on taking up office he had sworn to observe the statutes, and so was unable to meet his request. No doubt much to the librarian's relief, Charles I 'would not have the booke, nor permit it to be taken out of the Library, saying it was fit that the will and statutes of the pious founder be religiously observed'.[48]

Academic activity all but ground to a halt during the war and the number of students coming to the university and admitted to read in the Bodleian dropped markedly. For example, between 1633 and 1635 over five hundred had signed on as readers, but during the years 1643–45 only about one hundred new readers registered. At the same time, some eminent scholars, brought to Oxford by business at the king's court, took the opportunity to consult the library's holdings. Among them were the herald and antiquary Sir William Dugdale and the

Fig. 28 **Convocation House was built in 1634–37 at the west end of the Divinity School. Its fan-vault ceiling was added in 1758–59.**

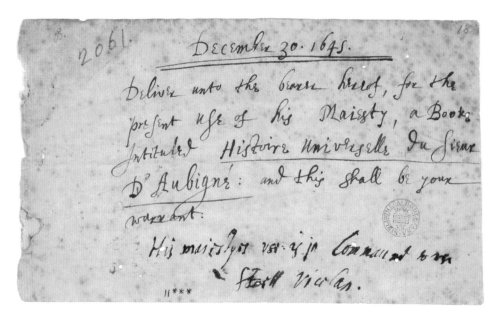

Fig. 29 **When Oxford was the Royalist headquarters during the Civil War, the king asked for a book to be sent from the Bodleian to Christ Church in 1645.**

archbishop of Armagh, James Ussher. In 1646 Oxford surrendered to the Parliamentarian army, and its enlightened general, Thomas Fairfax, is reputed to have immediately put a guard on the door of the Bodleian to prevent looting. He had certainly, in the negotiations that led to the city's surrender, informed the royal governor, Sir Thomas Glemham, that he was keen to preserve Oxford as a place famous for learning, and to that end he urged a speedy agreement to the terms on offer.

A little notebook surviving in the Bodleian's archives[49] gives us a rare glimpse of activity in the seventeenth-century library. It records the names of those readers for whom, in 1648 and 1649, the sub-librarian fetched books and manuscripts from the galleries and cupboards, and gives the shelfmarks of the volumes fetched. From this we learn that 218 of the readers were university men of MA or higher status, ninety-nine were BAs, two were students of civil law from London and three were foreign visitors. Many of them were men who had played a prominent role in university affairs. They included John Prideaux, former rector of Exeter College; John Greaves, professor of astronomy; Gerard Langbaine, Keeper of the University Archives and provost of

Queen's College; Richard Zouche, an eminent lawyer, who had drafted the articles of surrender to the Parliamentarian army in 1646; and Gilbert Sheldon, warden of All Souls College and future archbishop of Canterbury. The careers of others studying in the Bodleian during these two years still lay ahead – among them John Fell, the future dean of Christ Church and bishop of Oxford, and Ralph Bathurst, fellow of Trinity College, who went on to become physician to the Navy and one of the originators of the Royal Society. A striking feature of the picture provided by this record of Bodleian readers in the years after the end of the Civil War is how men of very different political persuasions studied together in the university library: staunch Royalists such as Gilbert Sheldon, John Prideaux and Richard Zouche and enthusiastic Parliamentarians such as Thankful Owen, president of St John's, and a group of Cambridge graduates, including the lawyer Peter Pett, who came to Oxford to fill vacancies in college fellowships caused by the removal of men loyal to the king.

Rouse continued in office until his death in 1652, aged seventy-eight, having not only enormously enhanced the library's collections but also preserved it intact through what can now be seen as the most turbulent years in its long history. At the end of its first half-century, the Bodleian, thanks to Thomas Bodley's foresight in providing it with an ample endowment and comprehensive regulations, enforceable within the structures of Oxford University, had been established on a firm footing. Its collections of books and manuscripts were already substantial and set fair to continue to grow. They were proving useful to hundreds of scholars from outside Oxford as well as to members of the university. The scholarship, acumen and devotion to duty of his first two librarians, Thomas James and John Rouse, had been essential to the success of the enterprise. Throughout the following centuries, the abilities and personalities of the librarians strongly influenced the development of the Bodleian, and for this reason the individuals in charge of the library provide the basis of this chronological account of its history.

PARS 2

CHAPTER 3

Consolidation, 1652–1700

JOHN ROUSE WAS SUCCEEDED by Thomas Barlow, who had been a fellow of Queen's College since 1633, and university reader in metaphysics since 1635 (fig. 31). He had gained the reputation of being a good teacher, an encyclopaedic scholar, a cautious theologian – though decidedly Calvinist in his own beliefs – and an expert on the controversies between Protestants and Catholics. Like Rouse, he had managed to survive the recent changes of regime within the university without losing his post. Barlow was assiduous in attending to his duties in the library, welcoming visitors and assisting scholars in their researches. But he seems to have been a traditionalist, content to continue in the old ways established by his predecessors. He was certainly not in sympathy with those in the university who, in keeping with their enthusiasm for the practical uses of academic studies, were keen to apply the techniques of the developing sciences to the Bodleian in order to make it more useful to the younger generation of scholars. A group of twenty-four eminent men, recruited by Gerard Langbaine, provost of Queen's College (including John Wilkins, warden of Wadham College; Seth Ward, professor of astronomy and future bishop of Salisbury; and Ralph Bathurst, physician and future president of Trinity College – all members of the Oxford Experimental Philosophy Club)

Fig. 30 **Selden End.**

embarked on an ambitious project, planning to look at every book in the library in order to compile a subject guide to the entire collection. Their aim was specifically to facilitate further research in experimental science, and some of them would have been aware that they were following in the footsteps of Bodley's first librarian, Thomas James, who had produced subject guides to the collections, the one for the books in the 'Arts' classification having been recopied in 1645. Each member of the group was allocated responsibility for a section of the library, and Seth Ward reported on their progress in a letter to Sir Justinian Isham in February 1652, optimistically predicting that they would complete their task by Lent. The only documentary evidence clearly relating to this undertaking is a catalogue in Langbaine's hand of the books classified as 'Jur', with a number of the books in the 8° Th. section. The catalogue was among the manuscripts found by the antiquary Anthony Wood 'among the waste papers' of Thomas Barlow at Queen's College in 1672. Wood noted on its flyleaf: 'Written in order to the making of a universal catalogue in all kinds of Learning – but he died before he could go half through with it.'[1] It seems likely that no substantial progress was made, though a slim volume in the Bodleian archives giving brief catalogue entries for books in the classification 40 G-R Th., none of them published later than 1647, may be associated with the project,[2] which was probably abandoned on Langbaine's death in 1658. The librarian, no doubt realizing how huge a task this was, did not become involved.

In April 1654 Barlow received a request from the Lord Protector, Oliver Cromwell, to lend a manuscript to the Portuguese ambassador. The librarian refused, sending a copy of the library statutes to explain why he could not accede to the request. Like Charles I before him, Cromwell praised the founder's foresight and let the matter drop. Indeed, later the same year he presented to the Bodleian twenty-two Greek manuscripts, part of the Barocci collection that the earl of Pembroke had retained when he gave the rest to the library in 1629, and which Cromwell had subsequently purchased. About this time, probably prompted by a request from the lawyer and collector John Selden (fig. 32) to borrow some manuscripts, Barlow prepared for the consideration of the curators a memorandum on lending. In it he rehearsed the library statute of 1610, which unequivocally stated Sir

Fig. 31 **Portrait of Thomas Barlow, Bodley's Librarian from 1652 to 1660.**

Fig. 32 Sir Peter Lely's portrait of John Selden (1584–1654), who bequeathed his Greek and oriental manuscripts to the Bodleian.

Thomas Bodley's own view that 'No book whatsoever can be lent; nor any person whatsoever borrow; nor any caution [money] how great soever be admitted; upon no cause assigned, or pretence whatsoever'.[3] He listed the most eminent men who had been refused loans – the Lord Chancellor (John Williams, bishop of Lincoln and from 1641 archbishop of York) in 1624, the king in 1645 and the Lord Protector in 1654 – and argued that once an exception was made it would cause offence to refuse the same favour to others. Then books that had been intended for everyone to use would be unavailable and at risk of damage and loss. At the same time, observing the statute would encourage more donors 'when they see the sacredness of the place, and from thence be sure, that what they give should be religiously preserved'.[4] Many in the university had doubts about the wisdom of refusing to make an exception for Selden, some of whose collections seemed likely to come to Oxford. Convocation agreed and voted to allow the loan of three manuscripts at a time for a limited period, on Selden's payment of a caution. It is not clear whether or not Selden agreed to this condition.

When Barlow's memorandum was printed in 1670, a lengthy preamble was added, emphasizing that no 'incivility' was intended to anyone whose request to borrow books from the Bodleian was refused:

> It is thought proper to print this Case for the Satisfaction of such Persons, who perhaps, being ignorant of the Force of the *Statute*, may take it as a great Affront, if, upon Solicitation, they be denied any Book out of the *Library*, whereas the *Statute* is so express, that there is no doubt the *University* will never attempt to dispense with it, unless upon Prospect of some such *extraordinary Benefaction* as Mr. Selden's, whose Books were of so inestimable a Value.[5]

As it was, Barlow spent much of his time negotiating the acquisition of Selden's library.

After attending Hart Hall in Oxford, John Selden had been admitted to the Inner Temple in London in 1603 and was called to the Bar in 1612. Lord Clarendon records his 'humanity, courtesy and affability',[6] which no doubt made him a welcome member of London antiquarian and literary circles. He worked throughout his life as a barrister in London and was a member of parliament in the 1620s and again in

Fig. 33 The 'Codex Mendoza', a Mexican manuscript commissioned by the Spanish viceroy in the 1640s, came to the Bodleian in John Selden's bequest.

the Long Parliament of 1640, while pursuing linguistic and historical studies and publishing a wide range of books. He died in November 1654, bequeathing many important oriental and Greek manuscripts to the Bodleian, but leaving his executors to decide the fate of the rest of his huge collection. His bequest included three early Mexican manuscripts, the 'Codex Selden', the 'Selden Roll' and the famous 'Codex Mendoza' – prepared for Antonio de Mendoza, Emperor Charles V's first viceroy of Mexico (fig. 33). Eventually, in September 1659, Barlow succeeded in acquiring for the Bodleian the bulk of Selden's books, about eight thousand volumes, ranging from classics, theology and history to science, law and Hebrew literature. They were placed on the shelves in the western extension of the library which was named Selden End in his honour – a name it retains to this day.

Barlow became provost of his college in 1658, and in 1660, after only eight years in post, he resigned the librarianship on being elected

Lady Margaret Professor of Divinity. Anthony Wood, a shrewd but always highly critical observer of university affairs, thought that Barlow's main reason for leaving the Bodleian was that he did not want to spend his time cataloguing the huge new acquisition of Selden's books. Barlow received further advancement in the Church of England, as archdeacon of Oxford in 1661 and bishop of Lincoln in June 1675, though he was much criticized for remaining in Oxford – Wood noted in July 1678 that the bishop had still not visited his diocese of Lincoln. Just as he had managed, despite his loyalty to the Royalist cause, to remain in Oxford throughout the Protectorate, Barlow was able to accommodate himself to the removal of King James II and the accession of King William and Queen Mary.

The restoration of the monarchy in 1660 left little mark on the Bodleian, but its accounts show that in the following year the curators spent £1 12s. 6d. on removing rust from the king's picture and setting it up again in the library. Barlow's successor as Bodley's Librarian, the 59-year-old Thomas Lockey (fig. 34) himself undertook the cataloguing of Selden's books and planned to have his entries incorporated in a revised general catalogue of all the library's printed book collections. In a project reminiscent of Langbaine's initiative ten years earlier, he intended to recruit fifty Masters of Arts to help with the work of revision, bringing up to date Thomas James's 1620 catalogue with its supplement of 1635. In July 1664 he optimistically wrote to Archbishop Sheldon that their work would be finished by Michaelmas, but there is no documentary evidence of any help being forthcoming. Two slim volumes containing his very imperfect 'Catalogue of Mr. Selden's books in the west end of Sir Th: Bodley's library' survive in the Bodleian's archives. Although an eminent scholar (Hearne recorded that he was 'reckon'd the best in the university for classical learning'),[7] Lockey does not seem to have had the bibliographical skills required for cataloguing. He was a noted connoisseur, tutor and preacher, but offended the Parliamentary visitors by a sermon he preached before the university in January 1651. He was banned from preaching and removed from his tutorship at Christ Church, whereupon he left Oxford, returning only after the Restoration. As Bodley's Librarian he excelled in what we would now call the public relations aspects of library work. A celebrated French physician, Samuel de Sorbière, visited England in 1663–64, and came to Oxford. He was not impressed by those members

Lockey S.T.D. Ædis Christi Canonicus, Protobibliothecarius à XXVIII Sept
CLX, ad IX Decembris MDCLXV, officium Sponte Deposuit.

of the university he met, except for Lockey, 'who had learnt at Court and in France to put on an obliging air and courteous behaviour'.[8] The highly critical tone of his account of his voyage to England (first published in French in 1664) goaded Thomas Sprat, a graduate of Wadham, later bishop of Rochester and dean of Westminster, into publishing a stinging reply in which he described Sorbière's work as 'an insolent libel on our nation'.[9] In 1663 King Charles II and his queen visited the university, accompanied by the duke and duchess of York, and were entertained with a grand banquet in Selden End. The following year Lockey welcomed the earl of Clarendon, the chancellor of the university, and his guest the earl of Manchester, chancellor of Cambridge University, to the Bodleian, giving a speech in Latin. In November 1665 he resigned to become a canon of Christ Church.

It is striking that, while the first Bodley's Librarian was in post for twenty years and the second for thirty-two, the third and fourth covered only thirteen years between them. They maintained the traditional services of the library but, with many offices and interests beyond its walls, they made no attempt to innovate or modernize. With the fifth librarian, the earlier pattern was revived. Thomas Hyde, who had already as an undergraduate at King's College, Cambridge, developed a remarkable aptitude for oriental languages, moved to Oxford and Queen's College in 1654. He graduated MA and was appointed sub-librarian at the Bodleian in 1659. He was much better fitted to the office of Bodley's Librarian than his predecessor and continued in post until 1701. He not only catalogued Selden's library, but also finished a catalogue of all the books in the Bodleian in 1674. In its preface he complains of the difficulty of working in an unheated library in all weathers and of the widespread lack of appreciation of the arduous work involved in producing accurate catalogue entries. He explains that work he had expected to take two or three years had taken much more. Despite the complexity of the task and the unexpected problems he encountered, Hyde introduced real improvements to the general catalogue, standardizing the entries and supplying a wealth of cross references that are still useful in resolving otherwise intractable bibliographical queries. It is a measure of the importance both of the wide range of the Bodleian's holdings and of the quality of Hyde's

Fig. 34 **Portrait of Thomas Lockey, Bodley's Librarian from 1660 to 1665.**

Heore tale þei tolden wiþouten lees
And on heore knees gunne falle.
¶ And seide. Sire þe kyng of Tars
Of wikked wordes. nis not scars.
Heþene hound. he doþ þe calle
And er his douhtur. he ȝiue þe tille.
Þyn herte blod he wol spille
And þi Barouns. alle
When þe Soudan. þis I herde
As a wod mon. he ferde.
His Robe. he rente adoun
He tar þe her of hed. and berd
And seide he wolde hir winne wiþ swerd
Bi his lord. seynt Mahoun.
¶ Þe Table adoun riht he smot
In to þe flore foot hot
He lokede. as a wylde lyon.
Al þat he hitte. he smot doun riht
Boþe sergaunt. and kniht
Erl. and eke Baroun.
¶ So he ferde. forsoþe a pliht
Al a day and al a niht
Þat no mon. miht hym chaste
A morwen whon hit was day liht
He sent his messagers ful riht
After his Barouns. in haste
¶ Lordynges he seiþ. what to rede
Me is don a gret misdede
Of Tars. þe cristene kyng
I bed him boþe. lond and lede
To haue his douhter. in worþli wede
And spouse hire. wiþ my ryng
¶ And he seide. wiþ outen fayle
Furst he wolde me sle. in Batayle
And mony a gret lordyng
Ac certes he schal be forswore
Or to wroþerhele. þat he was bore
Bote he hit þer to bring.
¶ Þerfore lordinges I haue after ow sent
For to come. to my parlement
To wite. of ow counsayle
And alle onswerde. wiþ good entent
Þei wolde be. at his comaundement
Wiþ outen eny fayle
¶ And whon þei weren alle at his heste
Þe Soudan made a wel gret feste
For loue. of his Batayle.
Þe Soudan gedered an ost vnryde
Wiþ Sarazins. of muchel pryde
Þe kyng of Tars to assayle
¶ Whon þe kyng hit herde þat tyde
He sente abouten. on vche a syde.
Alle þat he mihte. of sende
Gret werre. þo bi gon to wake
For þe mariage. ne moste be take
Of þat mayden heende
¶ Batayle þei sette vppon a day
Wiþinne þe þridde day of May
No lengor. nolde þei leende
Þe Soudan com. wiþ gret power
Wiþ helm briht. and fer Baner
Vppon þat kyng. to wende
¶ Þe Soudan ladde. an huge ost
And com wiþ muche pruide and bost
Wiþ þe kyng of Tars to fihte
Wiþ hym mony a Sarazin feer
Alle þe feldes. fer and neer
Of helmes leomede lihte
¶ Þe kyng of Tars com also
Þe Soudan. Batayle for to do.
Wiþ mony. a cristene kniht
Eyþer ost. gon oþur assayle
Þer bi gon a strong Batayle
Þat grislych was of siht
¶ Þreo heþene. aȝein twey cristene men
And falde hem doun. in þe fen
Wiþ wepnes. stif and goode.
Þe stronge Sarazins in þat fiht
Slowe vr cristene men. doun riht
Þei fouhte. as heo weore woode.

¶ Þe Soudan ost. in þat stounde
Feolde þe cristene. to þe grounde
Mony a freoly foode.
Þe Sarazins. wiþ outen fayle
Þe cristene culde. in þat Batayle
Was non. þat hem wiþ stode.
¶ Whon þe kyng of Tars. saugh þat siht
Wod he was. for wraþþe a pliht.
In hond. he hente a spere.
And to þe Soudan. he rod ful riht.
Wiþ a dunt. of muche miht
Adoun. he gon him bere.
¶ Þe Soudan neiȝ. he hedde islawe
But þritti þousent. of heþene lawe
Coomen. him for to were.
And brouhten hit aȝeyn. vppon his stede
And holpen hit wel. in þat nede
Þat no mon. miht him dere.
¶ Whon he was brouht. vppon his stede
He sprong as sparkle. doþ of glede
For wraþþe. and for envye
Alle þat he hitte. he made hem blede
He ferde. as he wolde awede
Mahoun help. he gan crye
¶ Mony an helm. þer was vnweued
And mony a Bacinet to cleued
And sadeles. mony emptye
Men miht se. vppon þe feld
Mony a kniht. ded vnder scheld
Of þe cristene cumpaignye
¶ Whon þe king of Tars. saiȝ hem so ryde
No lengor þer. he nolde abyde
Bote fleyh. to his owne Cite
Þe Sarazins. þat ilke tyde
Slouȝ adoun. bi vche a syde
Vr cristene folk. so fre.
¶ Þe Sarazins þat tyme. saunȝ fayle
Slowe vr cristene. in Batayle
Þat reuþe. hit was to se.
And on þe morwe. for heore sake
Triwes þei gunne to gidere take
A moneþ. and dayes þre
As þe kyng of Tars. sat in his halle
He made ful gret deol. wiþ alle.
For þe folk. þat he hedde I lore
His douhter com. in riche palle.
On knees heo gon. bifore him falle.
And seide. wiþ syking sore
¶ Fader heo seide. let me beo his wyf
Þat þer be. no more strif
Þen hath ben. her bifore.
For me hath be. muche folk schent
Slawen and morþred. and to rent
Alas. þat I was bore
¶ Fader. I chulle hi serue at wille
Erli. and late. loude and stille.
And leeuen on god almiht.
Bote hit be so. he wol þe spille.
And al þi londes. take hym tille
In Batayle and in fiht
¶ Certes I nul no lengor dyre
Þat cristene men. schul for me dye
Þorw grace of god almiht.
Þen was þe kyng of Tars ful wo
Anon he onswerede. þo
To his douhter. briht.
¶ Douhter he seide. blessed þou be
Of god. þat sit in Trinite
Þe tyme. þat þou were bore.
Þat þou wolt saue þi moder and me
Þi presens nolde I graunte þe
Of þat þou bede. bifore.
¶ Fader heo seide. par charite
And for crist. in Trinite
Blyne. þat ich weore þore.
Er eny more sorwe arere.
Þat ȝe. ne my moder dere
For me beo nouȝt forlore
¶ Þe kyng þo. wiþ good entent
In to his chaumbre. hath I sent

After his qween. so hende.
Whon heo was comen. in present.
Dame he seide. vr douhter hath munt
To þe Soudan. for to wende
¶ Dame he seide. counseyle me
Her beoþ no mo. bote we þre.
I comen of cristene kende.
Þe qween onswerde. wiþouten fayle
Þer to schal I neuere. counsayle.
Vre douhter. for to schende.
¶ Þenne was þe douhter. wo
Mercy heo criede. hire moder þo
Wiþ a reuþful steuene.
Moder hit nis not. longe agon.
Þat þer were. for me slon
Þreo þousent men. and seuene.
¶ And certes. I nul no lengor dyre
Þat cristen men. schul for me dye
Þorw grace of god. in heuene
Weore þei wel. weore þei wroþe
Þe douhter dude. ouercome hem boþe
Beo riht reson. and euene
¶ Whon þei weoren. þus at on
Messagers. he sente anon
To þe proude Soudan.
To make frendes. þat weore fon
No mo folk. þei wolde slon
His douhter he graunted him þan
¶ Whon þe messagers. þus herde seyn
Smartliche. þei tornede aȝeyn
To þe Soudan. sterne and wan
Whon he herde. heore lettres rad
Þen was he. boþe bliþe and glad
And murie. as eny man
¶ And seide I chul ben at his wille
Erly. and late. loude. and stille.
And help him. at his neode
No mo folk. nul I nouþe spille.
Þe kyng anon. he sende tille.
And þonkede him of þat dede
¶ Þe kyng and qwene. in chaumbre were þo
In care and sorwe. and muche wo
In stori. as we rede.
Wel hem was. wiþ oute les
Þat þe Soudan wolde make pes.
Wiþ cristen. felawrede.
¶ Þus fel. in a mid somer tyde.
Þe Soudan nolde no lengor byde.
To þe kyng of Tars. he sent.
Wiþ Sarazins. and wiþ muche pryde.
Wiþ mony a Juwel. is nouȝt to hyde
To make hym. a present
¶ Forþ þei went. þat ilke tyde.
To þe kyng of Tars. þei gan ryde
Þat was boþe free. and gent
Þei welcomed. þe messagere.
Of gret þewe. ȝe may here.
Whon þei to chaumbre went
¶ In chaumbre. kyng and qwene was þo
In sorwe and care. and muche wo.
For heore douhter hende.
Heor douhter com bifore hem wende
And bad hem. bi hire counseil do.
To saue cristene kende.
¶ Þe douhter þer. wiþ wordes stille
Brouȝt hem boþe. in betere wille.
And in to halle. gunne wende.
And welcomede þe messagers
Þat come from þe Soudan fers
Wiþ wordes feire. and hende
¶ Þen seide þe qwene. after þan
How farer ȝor lord. þe Soudan
Þat is so noble. a kniht
Þe messagers. onswere gan
He farer as wel as eny man.
And is gor frend. apliht.
¶ Þe qween onswerde. wiþ mylde mod
To þe messagers. þer þei stod.
And seide þenne. anon riht.
Ich fouche saaf. on him my blod.

catalogue that, interleaved and with their own shelfmarks added, it was used by many other libraries, including those of several Oxford colleges and of Lambeth Palace in London, as a guide to their own collections. The Mazarine Library in Paris continued to use an annotated copy of the Bodleian's 1674 catalogue in this way until 1760.

Despite his success in completing the catalogue of printed books, and his own undoubted expertise as an oriental scholar, Hyde was reluctant to undertake the cataloguing of the library's great manuscript collections. He let it be known that he was willing to organize the work of others, but that the failure of the university to reward him for his nine years of gruelling service on the 1674 catalogue of printed books with anything but empty promises of an increase in his salary made him reluctant to take on any further long-term tasks. He preferred to pursue his own research and his work of translating diplomatic correspondence for the government. In addition to being a canon of Salisbury Cathedral and archdeacon of Gloucester, he was appointed Laudian Professor of Arabic in 1691 and Regius Professor of Hebrew in 1697. Fortunately, the Bodleian's manuscripts were included in the union catalogue of English and Irish manuscripts, compiled by several eminent Oxford scholars and edited by Edward Bernard, which was published in 1698. Bernard was an accomplished mathematician and orientalist, a fellow of St John's and Savilian Professor of Astronomy from 1673 to 1691. Writing to the scholar Thomas Smith in June 1694, Bernard reported that Hyde provided no assistance at all to the cataloguing project, refusing even to supply information about the donors of the manuscripts. Bernard regarded the librarian as 'a great enemy' of his catalogue.[10]

The Bodleian's collections continued to grow through generous bequests and judicious purchases funded by the university. Some came as individual items of great importance – such as the late fourteenth-century 'Vernon Manuscript' (fig. 35), named after its donor, Colonel Edward Vernon, who had been a student at Trinity College, had served in the king's army and owned lands at North Aston in Oxfordshire. His gift, which came to the library around 1677, was an enormous volume, weighing over twenty-two kilograms, the largest surviving anthology of Middle English literature. It was described as a 'vast

Fig. 35 **The late fourteenth-century 'Vernon Manuscript' is the largest surviving anthology of Middle English literature.**

Fig. 36 The 'Rushworth Gospels', a ninth-century masterpiece of Celtic
illumination, given to the Bodleian in 1678 by the historian John Rushworth.

massy manuscript' in Bernard's catalogue. Another single manuscript of great importance was given by the historian John Rushworth, who had studied at Queen's College and been secretary to Oliver Cromwell from 1650 and to the Council of State from 1660. In 1678 he gave the library the ninth-century 'Rushworth Gospels', a masterpiece of Celtic illumination, the work of an Irish scribe called MacRegol (fig. 36). Other manuscripts were acquired in larger numbers. The medieval manuscripts collected by Christopher, first Baron Hatton were bought from Robert Scott, the Bodleian's main London agent, in 1671. Hatton, who had served in Parliament and on the Privy Council, was a founder member of the Royal Society and a collector of books and antiquities. His manuscripts included some of the most famous now in the library (among them the oldest surviving manuscript of the Rule of St Benedict, written around the year 700 in southern England, or Mercia (fig. 37); a late ninth-century manuscript of King Alfred's translation of St Gregory's *Pastoral Care*; and a manuscript that had been made for St Dunstan at Glastonbury in the tenth century). These were the first in a decade of major Bodleian acquisitions of importance for studies of Old and Middle English in Oxford. They illustrate the way in which, during Hyde's lengthy librarianship, the Bodleian's acquisition of manuscripts both encouraged and reflected the development of historical studies in Oxford.

Francis Junius, the renowned philologist who had been librarian to the earl of Arundel for many years, often studied in the Bodleian. Towards the end of his life, late in 1676, he moved from Holland to settle in Oxford, close to his friend and pupil Thomas Marshall, who had been rector of Lincoln College since 1672. In July 1677, four months before his death, Junius gave his manuscripts to the Library.[11] They included Old English paraphrases in alliterative verse of parts of the Old Testament, known as the Caedmon manuscript; an early Middle English poem of homilies on the Gospels known as the Ormulum; and a collection of Latin and Old High German texts from the late eighth and ninth centuries, including the Murbach Hymnal. All are of enormous importance for studies of early northern European languages. They reinforced the library's importance as a centre for philological studies, a position further enhanced by the bequest in 1685 of books and manuscripts from Thomas Marshall himself. In his youth a student at Lincoln College, Marshall had served in the

Fig. 37 **The oldest surviving manuscript of the Rule of St Benedict, *c*.700.**

Royalist army during the Civil War and had left Oxford to become
chaplain to the Company of Merchant Adventurers in Rotterdam in
1650. While in Holland and encouraged by Junius, he published his
Latin 'Observations on Two Ancient Gothic and Anglo-Saxon Versions
of the Gospels', which established his reputation as a philologist. His
bequest included many books of Protestant theology, both English and
Continental, and works on Anglo-Saxon, Frisian, Irish, Romanian and
Middle Eastern languages.

A remarkable group of scholars interested in the study of Anglo-
Saxon England developed in the wake of Junius and Marshall, initially
centred on William Nicolson of Queen's College (in 1679 first holder of
the lectureship in Anglo-Saxon studies established there by Secretary of
State Sir Joseph Williamson, who had studied at Queen's in the 1650s).
The group included White Kennett of St Edmund Hall, who had been
taught by Anthony Wood, and Edmund Gibson, whose major work, a
new edition of Camden's *Britannia*, was published in 1695, and Thomas
Tanner,[12] both of Queen's College. All three, like Nicolson himself, were
destined to become bishops in the Church of England. Their studies

gradually moved away from the philological into the historical, and they were all involved in the cataloguing of the Bodleian's manuscript collections. Moreover, their interest in history became increasingly focused on localities rather than on England as a whole.

The bequest by the former Parliamentarian general Thomas, Lord Fairfax, of his own collection of medieval manuscripts and of the papers of the Yorkshire antiquary Roger Dodsworth brought into the Bodleian in 1673 a fine example of a collection inspired by the burgeoning scholarly interest in the charters and muniments that were essential for the study of local history. Assisted by an annuity from Fairfax, Dodsworth had spent much of his life making copies and extracts from original records relating to the history of Yorkshire families and religious houses. The destruction during the siege of York in 1644 of many of the original documents that had been stored there made Dodsworth's transcripts particularly important for later historians. In his *Annals of the Bodleian*, W.D. Macray records that Anthony Wood, realizing that the manuscripts had become very damp and 'were in danger of being spoiled by a wet season',[13] obtained the vice-chancellor's permission to spread them out in the sunshine on the lead roof of the Schools Quadrangle, thus preserving them for future generations.

In 1675 the antiquary and astrologer Elias Ashmole (fig. 38) who, at Thomas Barlow's request, had catalogued the Roman coins in the Bodleian collection, began negotiating with the university about his own collections of natural curiosities, books and manuscripts. He offered to bequeath them on condition that a proper building was provided to house and display them. The university accepted his offer, and by 1683 the original Ashmolean Museum on Broad Street (now the Museum of the History of Science) was completed. The new institution attracted the papers of three of Ashmole's contemporaries – Sir William Dugdale, Anthony Wood and John Aubrey.

John Fell, dean of Christ Church since 1660, bishop of Oxford since 1676 and vice-chancellor of the university from 1666 to 1669, died in 1686, bequeathing several manuscripts to the Bodleian. His interest in manuscripts, like that of Archbishop Laud before him, was closely linked to his determination to establish a scholarly press in Oxford. In 1668 he persuaded Archbishop Sheldon to allow the recently constructed Sheldonian Theatre to be used as a printing house when it was not needed for university ceremonies (fig. 39). Assisted by Thomas

PRÆMIA
NORARIA.

Marshall's contacts in Holland, he imported types and matrices from Amsterdam, and used them to good effect in a series of editions of classical texts published annually. The 1670s witnessed the publication of several scholarly works of more general interest: a Latin translation of Anthony Wood's *History and Antiquities of the University of Oxford* in 1674; a volume of David Loggan's engravings of university buildings, *Oxonia illustrata* in 1675; and Robert Plot's *Natural History of Oxfordshire* in 1677. By 1686, Fell had achieved his ambition – his university at last had its own academic press.

When the celebrated orientalist Edward Pococke, professor of both Arabic and Hebrew in Oxford, died in 1691 the university immediately bought his important collection of Arabic, Hebrew and other oriental manuscripts from his widow for £800. Within a matter of months, they found sufficient funds (almost £1,100) to purchase further oriental manuscripts from Robert Huntington, provost of Trinity College Dublin, who had already given thirty-five manuscripts to the library. The Huntington collection contains many manuscripts of great rarity, mainly Arabic and Hebrew, but also Coptic, Syriac, Samaritan, Persian and Turkish. These were accumulated by Huntington between 1670 and 1681 while – like his teacher Edward Pococke forty years earlier – he was chaplain to the English merchants at Aleppo. The rare book collections were also enhanced by gifts and occasional purchases. Among the latter were many early editions of classical texts with important annotations by eminent European scholars, bought from Edward Bernard's widow in 1697.

These occasional spectacular gifts and purchases masked the difficulties the library faced in trying to maintain a regular intake of recently published scholarly works. Sir Thomas Bodley's agreement of 1610 with the Stationers' Company was largely ignored during the Interregnum. A mere thirty-one books were received in 1650; six parcels of books were sent by the Stationers five years later; and 143 volumes (the publications of sixty stationers) were sent by the warden of the company, George Thomason, in 1657. The principle of depositing all publications in the Royal Library and in the university libraries of

Fig. 38 (opposite) **Portrait of Elias Ashmole by John Riley,** *c.*1681–82.

Fig. 39 (following spread) **Engraving by David Loggan of the Sheldonian Theatre, from** *Oxonia Illustrata* (1675).

CAROLVS II D·G M

Ex solertissimâ designatione Clarissimi Viri D. Christophori Wren L.L. Doct. Professoris Astronomiæ Saviliani, & Coll: omn. Anim: olim socij·Donú ex merito suo, Ædificiorú Regiæ Majtis per Universú Angliam Architecti Generalis.

THEATRI SHELDONIANI, sive fori literarij Universitatis OXONIENSIS, Conventibus
simam juxta & magnificentissimam construxit pariter & dotavit, suis unius impensis, Rev

PAN E T LIB[E]PEX LIONE

Reverendiſsimo in Chriſto Patri
D[no] GILBERTO SHELDON Archiep.
Cantuarienſi totius Angliæ Primati
& Metrop. &c. Theatri hujus Funda-
tori Munificentiſsimo
D.D.C.Q.   Dav. Loggan.

Dav. Loggan Delin. et Sculp. cum Privil. S.R.M.

...blicis, nec non rei Typographicæ uſibus deſtinati, Proſpectus Septentrionalis. Quam molem ornatiſ-
...in Chriſto Pater, GILBERTUS Providentiâ divinâ ARCHIEP. CANTUARIENSIS. &c.

Oxford and Cambridge was revived in the first Press Licensing Act of 1662 and restated in a series of Acts of Parliament from then until 1695. Despite this, the university had already, in 1665, begun to make what were to become regular complaints about the small number of books sent by the Stationers to the Bodleian. In a speech to Convocation in 1674, the vice-chancellor, Ralph Bathurst, complained that to get a book from a bookseller under the copyright regulations was like wresting his club from Hercules. The library's income of rents from the houses in Distaff Lane was disrupted – first by the Civil War and then by the Great Fire of London in 1666 – while its reserve funds had been depleted by the loan to Charles I. To compound the problem, a legal action to regain £450 owed by Sir Thomas Bodley's defaulting executor failed. The university, while generous in funding major purchases, seemed reluctant to subsidize regular book buying, so Hyde arranged a sale of duplicates from the library's collections in 1676 in an attempt to provide funds for purchases. Many of the books sold from the earlier acquisitions had probably been discarded in favour of copies from Selden's collection. This scheme of Hyde's to fund more purchases was temporarily thwarted when the proceeds of the sale (£248) were diverted by the university to the building of the Ashmolean Museum. The money was eventually returned to the library ten years later.

In 1681 the Bodleian played a part in the disputes between the king and Parliament known as the Exclusion Crisis, when the Whigs in the House of Commons attempted to exclude Charles II's Catholic brother James, duke of York, from the succession to the throne. In March that year, the king summoned Parliament to Oxford, with the Commons meeting in Convocation House and the Lords in a room adjoining the Tower of the Five Orders in the Picture Gallery, on the second floor of the Schools Quadrangle. The Commons believed that the desperate state of the king's finances would force him to accept their Exclusion bill in return for their agreement that he could raise more taxes. However, Charles had managed to secure a subsidy from Louis XIV of France, and on 28 March came to the Lords ready to dissolve Parliament. He summoned the Commons, who were debating the Exclusion bill, to attend him. Confident that he was prepared to give way, they began, with the Speaker at their head, to climb one by one the narrow spiral staircase in the Tower of the Five Orders, which provided direct access to the room in which the Lords were assembled. When

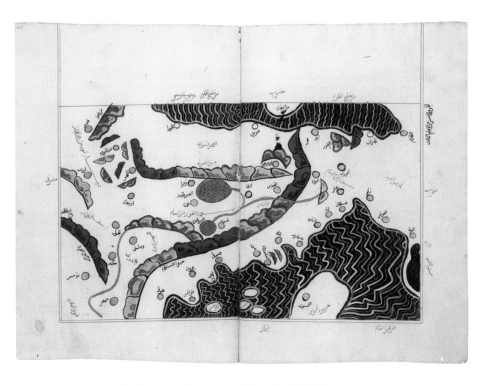

Fig. 40 **Map of Palestine and Syria from al-Sharīf al-Idrīsī's** *Entertainment*, copied 1553, from the Pococke collection.

the first of them entered the room, they saw that the king was dressed in the formal robes required for the dissolution of Parliament, which he had had secretly brought to the library for the occasion. With the required quorum in attendance and before any members of the House of Commons could retreat down the narrow stairs still crowded by their colleagues, Charles was able to dissolve Parliament, and thus to thwart the plan of his opponents in the Commons.

King James II visited Oxford in 1687, two years after he had succeeded to the throne, and was entertained by the university to a sumptuous meal in Selden End on 5 September. The antiquary Anthony Wood gives an account of the food laid out for the king's delectation. It included twenty dishes of sweetmeats and fruit 'piled high', twenty-eight dishes of cold fish and meat, thirty-six dishes of fruit, and hot dishes of mutton, pheasant, partridge and quails. Wood relates that the king did not invite anyone to share the sumptuous fare, though he did

Fig. 41 **Portrait of Humfrey Wanley by Thomas Hill, 1716.**

converse with the librarian about the religion of China and a Chinese scholar he had met in London, who had done some work on Chinese books in the Bodleian. As the king rose to leave, the crowd of courtiers and members of the university, who had been thwarted in their expectation of eating with the king, swooped on the table in a most unseemly way to grab what they could of the largely untouched food, which had cost the university £160.[14]

Finding space to store the growing collections continued to be a problem. In 1691 the former librarian Thomas Barlow bequeathed to the Bodleian the bulk of his large collection, which included many ecclesiastical and political tracts of the reign of Charles I and the Interregnum, along with some fifty-four manuscripts. With all the available shelves filling up, galleries were added above the windows along the north and south walls of Duke Humfrey's Library in the early 1690s. The small and medium-sized books in Barlow's collection were moved into one of these galleries in 1696. The weight of the volumes added to the pressure on the structure of the fifteenth-century building. In 1700 examination revealed that the book presses had moved 3.5 inches away from the walls, that the south wall was 7.5 inches out of the perpendicular, and that the four great arches of the Divinity School below the library room were badly cracked. Another crack, the length of the building, appeared in the ceiling of the Divinity School and some of its ornaments began to fall to the ground. The university hastily sought the advice of the famous architect Sir Christopher Wren, who, while professor of astronomy at Oxford, had supervised repairs to the ceiling in 1669. He confirmed that the library was the cause of the problem, adding the wry comment that the weight of the books had no doubt increased from 'former dayes when learning was less bulky'.[15] His advice (to add buttresses at the ground-floor level; to improve gutters, spouts and drainage to prevent rainwater soaking into the foundations; to drive well-seasoned oak wedges 'at convenient distances … betwixt whole stones' in the crack in the ceiling 'more equably than forcibly' and to fill it with plaster of Paris) was followed throughout 1701 and 1702, and the building was saved. As Wren predicted, it continued 'bewtifull as well as firm for many years' to come.[16]

When we survey the Bodleian in the closing years of the seventeenth century, we see a library with magnificent collections that were for the most part made known to the scholarly world in published catalogues, but with hopelessly overcrowded shelves. The library had all but run out of space. Thomas Hyde, Bodley's Librarian since 1665, had rearranged many of the books in a vain attempt to make room for more, but had kept no proper record of the moves, with the result that scholars found it increasingly difficult to locate the volumes they wanted to consult. Their research was also hampered by the lending of books and manuscripts, which seems to have become a not uncommon occurrence in the second half of the seventeenth century. This development, contrary to Sir Thomas Bodley's specific instructions as enshrined in the library statutes, may well have been the result of Hyde's lax administration, though there is some evidence that for a while there was a recognized procedure for borrowing. In 1679 the curators ordered the return of all books taken out of the library, but as the order was repeated at intervals over the next twenty years, it seems likely either that the removal of books was not checked or that lending was no longer completely prohibited.

By 1697, Thomas Hyde had accumulated an impressive number of offices in both church and university – canon of Salisbury, Archdeacon of Gloucester, Laudian Professor of Arabic, Regius Professor of Hebrew (which made him *ex officio* a curator of the Bodleian) and canon of Christ Church – and, disillusioned by the university's failure to recognize the considerable labour involved in the production of the 1674 catalogue, had long since ceased to be interested in running the Bodleian, concentrating instead on his oriental studies. His history of the religion of the Persians was eventually published in 1700 and became a classic.

Throughout his time as librarian, Hyde's staff consisted only of a sub-librarian and a janitor (sometimes described as an assistant), until in November 1695 the 23-year-old Humfrey Wanley was appointed as an extra assistant (fig. 41). The son of the vicar of Holy Trinity Church in Coventry, Wanley had begun his working life as an apprentice to a draper in his hometown, but by the time he was 19 he was making accurate copies of local manuscripts and had developed an interest in Old English. In 1694 he was busy listing four collections of manuscripts for Bernard's catalogue. A year later he moved to Oxford and matriculated at the university, but his appointment at the Bodleian, giving him access to a wealth of early manuscripts, diverted him from studying for a degree. Instead he produced an index to Bernard's 1698 catalogue of manuscripts, and also added entries to the Bodleian's general catalogue of printed books. Prompted by a suggestion from his patron, Arthur Charlett, master of University College, Wanley was soon writing to friends and acquaintances in Coventry asking for gifts of books for the Bodleian, and he continued to solicit benefactions whenever he was in contact with scholars and collectors. He brought to the Bodleian an enthusiasm and energy that his colleagues lacked, and his relations with Bodley's Librarian, who was thirty-six years his senior, became increasingly strained. When Edward Bernard died in 1696 and the university was keen to acquire books and manuscripts from his collection, it was Wanley (rather than Bodley's Librarian) whom the vice-chancellor commissioned to go to London to survey Bernard's library and to make recommendations for purchase. By June 1697, Wanley had become frustrated with the librarian's neglect (as he saw it) of his duties, and drew up a list of what he considered wrong in the library, criticizing Hyde as 'an antient man, who must needs (not to reflect on his past conduct) labor under the infirmities incident to his age' – Hyde was 61 years old.[17] It is clear that Wanley had ambitions to succeed Hyde as Bodley's Librarian, but without a university degree he was not eligible for the post. When in November 1697, prompted by a raft of complaints about the library from Dr Thomas Crosthwaite, fellow of Queen's College, the curators invited the library staff to offer suggestions 'for the better regulateing any present disorders which may any way concerne the good of the Library',[18] Wanley submitted a detailed memorandum, more circumspect than his earlier one, of the improvements he believed were urgently needed in the administration of the library and in the care and cataloguing of its collections. His recommendations – such as those to secure an Act of Parliament to enforce copyright deposit; to ensure that every book printed by the university press came to the library; to pursue benefactions and to keep the Benefactors' Register up to date; to enter all recent accessions (including Barlow's books) in the general catalogue; and to start work on an appendix to the catalogue, correcting the many errors that had crept into it – were entirely sensible. Others, such as to save space by rearranging the books according to size, to foliate all the manuscripts and to list the contents of each volume, to dust every volume and shelf every year, and to rearrange and catalogue the coin collection, while clearly advisable, were, given the size of the library's staff, very

Fig. 42 'Drake's Chair', given to the Bodleian in 1678, was made from timbers from the *Golden Hind*, in which Sir Francis Drake had circumnavigated the globe.

much a counsel of perfection. There is no evidence that any of his recommendations were implemented. Disillusioned by his experiences in Oxford, Wanley moved to London in 1700, and eventually, as librarian to the earl of Oxford, made his name as one of the great palaeographers and librarians of the age.

Scholars had to be very hardy to contemplate studying long hours in the Bodleian in the seventeenth century, and indeed well into the nineteenth. We have seen how Bodley's Librarian, in his preface to the 1674 catalogue, had complained of the rigours of working in an unheated library in the winter months; but Sir Thomas Bodley's statutes prohibiting the introduction of 'fire or flame' made it impossible to install any heating system. George Hickes, Anglo-Saxon scholar and fellow of Lincoln College until he was deprived as a nonjuror, writing to Wanley in February 1696, warned him of the risks of working in libraries and in particular the Bodleian, which had 'killed many brave men'.[19] He mentioned Gerard Langbaine, provost of Queen's College and Keeper of the University Archives, who had died in 1658 'of an extream cold taken by sitting in the University-Library whole winter Days',[20] and the orientalist Samuel Clarke whose death in his mid-forties in 1669 he also attributed to working in the unheated Bodleian.[21] The Bodleian was not the only library likely to cause illness; according to Hickes, the Cottonian Library in London 'paved all with cold marbell' was equally hazardous during winter.

When the Bodleian was founded there was no public museum in Oxford, and from the beginning the library collected works of art, scientific instruments, natural history specimens, coins, medals and all sorts of curios that learned people were used to having alongside books and manuscripts. Bodley had anticipated that the second floor of the Schools Quadrangle, built over the university's teaching rooms between 1613 and 1618, would provide much-needed storage space for the ever-expanding stock of books, but it soon became a gallery for the display of pictures and objects of interest to visitors, who were for the most part members of the university and their guests. During the reign of Charles II one of the rooms on the first floor (the old Anatomy School in the south-west corner) began to be used to house the curiosities that seem by then to have outgrown the space available in the Picture Gallery. By the end of the seventeenth century, the Bodleian had acquired a considerable number of interesting if very miscellaneous objects. As early as 1601 Captain (later Sir) Josias Bodley, younger brother of the founder, gave the library an armillary sphere and other astronomical instruments, including a beautiful brass quadrant made in 1579. What may well have been the first (of many) architectural models was presented by Sir Clement Edmondes, MP for Oxford, in 1620. In 1658 Major-General John Desborough gave the Bodleian a crocodile from Jamaica, for which the library bought a case at a cost of twelve shillings in 1671. Around 1670 the colleges commissioned portraits of their founders to present to the Picture Gallery.[22] In 1678 the storekeeper at Deptford dockyard, John Davies, presented to the library a chair made from the remains of the *Golden Hind*, in which Sir Francis Drake had circumnavigated the globe in 1577–80. The ship had been kept at Deptford, but by the 1670s its timbers had decayed and it was broken up. The chair has been on display in the Bodleian ever since (fig. 42). Ten years later the library paid fifteen shillings for the carriage of a whale from Lechlade – an unlikely gift from William Jordan, an apothecary of Gloucester. Objects associated with recent history were also on display, among them Guy Fawkes's lantern – the gift in 1641 of Robert Heywood of Brasenose College, whose father had arrested Fawkes in the cellars under the Houses of Parliament in November 1605.

Thomas Hyde resigned in March 1701. Being, as he wrote in a letter to the pro-vice-chancellor 'a little indisposed with gout', he had become 'weary of the toil and drudgery of daily attendance [in the library] all times and weathers'. He wanted to have more time to complete his research on 'hard places of Scripture'.[23] His letter also makes it clear that he had become frustrated by the university's unwillingness to take any notice of his advice on the purchase of books for the Bodleian. Hyde had served as Bodley's Librarian for thirty-six years – longer than any of his predecessors; only two of his successors (John Price from 1768 to 1813 and Bulkeley Bandinel from 1813 to 1860) would serve longer. He died in February 1703, and any assessment of his lengthy librarianship has to balance what the library suffered by his lax administration with what it gained from his reputation as a fine oriental scholar.

The second half of the seventeenth century had seen the Bodleian's collections, especially its oriental and western manuscripts, continue to grow through both generous gifts and judicious purchases funded by the university. With no other library of comparable size in the kingdom, housed in a splendid building in the centre of a famous university that formally and effusively recognized every significant donation, it must have seemed to wealthy owners – and especially to those who had been educated at Oxford – an attractive resting place for their important collections and individual items. It had stood the test of time and, unlike many libraries of the day, was accessible to scholars from all over Europe. From the point of view of the scholarly world, the most significant achievement had been the publication in 1674 of a catalogue of the great collections of printed books. But in the last quarter of the century the shortage of staff needed to catalogue and care for the collections, and of the space required for their storage, became pressing problems, which the ageing librarian was unwilling or unable to tackle.

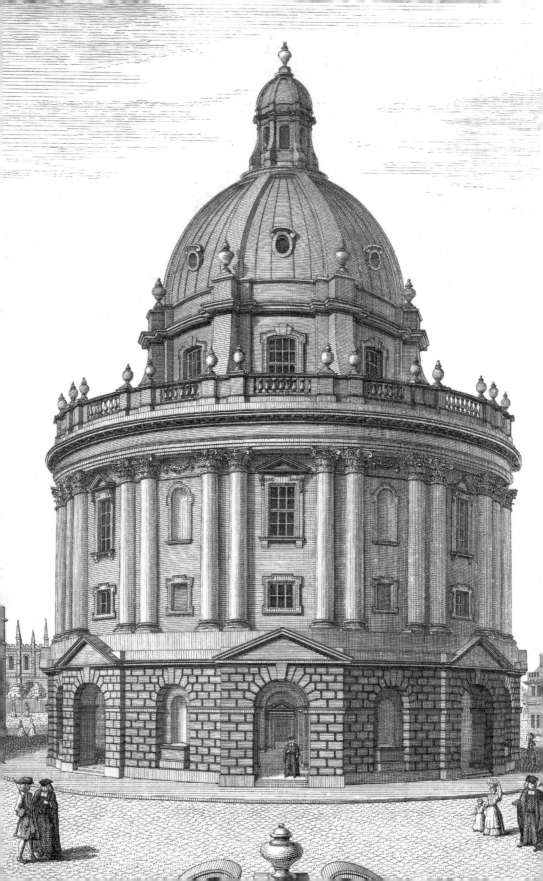

CHAPTER 4

The eighteenth century

FORTUNATELY FOR THE BODLEIAN and its users, Hyde's successor, John Hudson, was a man of considerable energy and useful contacts. He had been a tutor and fellow of University College since 1686. Throughout his time as Bodley's Librarian (from 1701 to 1719), he continued to edit classical texts, and was considered by many to be more assiduous as a delegate of the university's press than as head of its library. He did, however, expend much time and energy in the promotion of the Bodleian's interests. He exhorted the Stationers' Company to honour its old agreement with Sir Thomas Bodley, urged scholars to give copies of their own works directly to the Bodleian and persuaded collectors to part with duplicates from their own libraries. The philosopher John Locke was one of many authors who responded positively to Hudson's request. He wrote to the librarian on 4 March 1703 expressing his respect for the university (from which he had been expelled by royal command in 1684) and his readiness to support its claim for the deposit of newly published English works. He undertook to send copies of his own works, should the booksellers who printed them fail to provide them. The following year he gave his *Essay concerning Humane Understanding* (1690),

Fig. 43 **Engraving of the Radcliffe Camera by P. Fourdrinier after James Gibbs,** *A Perspective View of the Outside of the Radcliffe Library* (1747).

Fig. 44 **Engraving of the Broad Street front of the Clarendon Building from William Combe,** *A History of the University of Oxford* **(1814).**

Some Thoughts concerning Education (1693), several of his writings on money and trade and his letters to Bishop Edward Stillingfleet, together with the bishop's *Reply* (1697) and Stillingfleet's *Vindication of the Doctrine of the Trinity*, which had prompted their controversy. Hans Sloane was one of the collectors who did the same – he gave the library over 1,400 books between 1700 and 1738. Through his college and the university press, and as an author in his own right, Hudson had contacts throughout the university, among them Arthur Charlett, master of University College, who had been mentor to Humfrey Wanley and did much to promote the interests of books and libraries in Oxford. Already in November 1704 Charlett was writing enthusiastically to a friend that the Bodleian 'which for some years had stood still, is now in a thriving condition by the active diligence of Dr Hudson, who spares no author, no bookseller, but solicits all to augment the vast treasure'.

In January 1705 Hudson sent Charlett a list of some of the authors and publishers (including Isaac Newton and John Evelyn) who 'have been very much obliged to the publick Library, but yet none of them has yet learn'd so much gratitude as to make any manner of return'.[1] He intended to approach all of them with requests for their publications, but no evidence survives of any positive response. Hudson was himself a generous donor to the library, giving it some six hundred books. It was during his librarianship that the university built a printing house to the north of the Bodleian. A fine building, looking like a small palace, it was designed by Nicholas Hawksmoor and took four years, from 1711 to 1715, to build. It was financed by the considerable profits the university made from the publication, between 1703 and 1707, of the earl of Clarendon's *History of the Great Rebellion* and so was named the Clarendon Building (fig. 44).

For much of the eighteenth century, Bodley's Librarians had little money to spend on the purchase of recently published books; indeed in its first three years there is no record of any books at all being bought. In the next few years, on average only £9 was spent on books, a sum that rose in 1716/17 thanks to a legacy of £100 from Dr South of Christ Church and a gift of £100 from Lord Crewe. But from 1725 the librarians struggled with totally inadequate funding, and the average expenditure on books in the 1730s was slightly less than £7 a year. This shortage of funds was no doubt a factor in Hudson's enthusiasm for selling duplicates from the Bodleian collections; unfortunately, this became confused with the sale of his own publications and earned him the nickname of 'the Bookseller'. The library's inability to buy books was compounded by the expiry in 1695 of the Press Licensing Act, the last of a succession of Acts of Parliament that had, since 1662, provided for the deposit of all new books in the university libraries of Oxford and Cambridge and in the Royal Library. Hudson, assisted by Arthur Charlett and the library janitor, Thomas Hearne, tried to encourage booksellers to maintain the old system of deposit. But they had limited success: only four London booksellers, all with strong links to Oxford, sent their publications to the Bodleian. The most generous was Richard Sare, who was a frequent visitor to Oxford, a correspondent of Arthur Charlett and a friend of many members of Christ Church. Meanwhile, lobbying for a new Act of Parliament to restore the deposit system proved difficult. In 1707 a bill for the protection of booksellers' copyright in their publications, combined with a requirement for deposit in the three libraries, failed to get through the House of Commons. The libraries had to wait until 1709 for a new Act, and then it was far from ideal. Now booksellers could protect copyright in their newly published works by registering them with the Stationers' Company – though they interpreted the legislation as meaning that only books so registered could be claimed by the libraries. The result was that only a very small percentage of new publications was registered or received by the Bodleian. For the library, this fall in registration and deposit was partially offset by the increase in the number of authors, the most prominent among them Jonathan Swift and Alexander Pope, who, keen to see their books preserved in perpetuity, presented copies to the Bodleian. Pope himself gave the first volumes of his translation of Homer's *Iliad* (published in five volumes between 1715 and 1720) to the library. In 1721 Hudson noticed that the Bodleian lacked the fourth and fifth volumes and asked Pope if he could complete the set. The author duly sent them with a letter (preserved in the Rawlinson collection), thanking the librarian 'for the honour you have done me, in not permitting my books to be imperfect in your library, where it is always an honour to be read'.[2]

It was during Hudson's librarianship, in 1710, that a young German scholar, Zacharias Conrad von Uffenbach, came to Oxford with his brother for a couple of months, and kept a diary of his visit. He was very critical of the tour of the library offered to the general visitor – 'one sees nothing except what the assistant librarians choose to show for an honorarium, only too often all sorts of rubbish, little likely to please anyone who is in search of something more profound'. He had a low opinion of the librarian too, recording how Hudson, 'having boasted they had excellent books in duplicate for sale' showed him and his brother 'into a wretched room in the gallery where about four hundred books were lying around in terrible confusion'.[3] He was irritated by Hudson's haggling: 'he often asked ten shillings for a book which he afterwards parted with for five or six.' He recorded that the librarian's 'erudition is not much thought of, nor did I detect much of it in my intercourse with him'. He conceded that Hudson was 'to all appearances ... very affable', but in the same sentence referred to his 'very disagreeable habit, when he is talking, of crying out every moment "He! He! He!" ... so that it can be heard throughout the library'.[4]

Von Uffenbach was one of many German scholars attracted to the Bodleian as a good place to pursue their studies. In the first ten years of the century the majority of the 143 men described in the admissions register as 'extranei' (not members of the university) who signed in as readers in the library were from Continental Europe, with German scholars far outnumbering those from other countries. There were many too from Scotland, Cambridge and London in the first half of the eighteenth century. As the years passed, the number of visiting scholars declined, with only a handful recorded most years: just nine European scholars in the 1740s and no one at all from outside Oxford in, for example, 1735 or 1738, 1780 or 1782. The record of the books and manuscripts fetched from closed areas of the library shows how assiduously the visitors studied in the early years of the eighteenth century. For instance, of the 317 books and manuscripts ordered by readers in December 1708, 279 (88 per cent) were for seven foreign scholars. But the number of book orders fell dramatically over the years: only 257 for the whole of 1742, compared to 317 on the twenty-three days that the library was open in the month of December 1708. The reduction in the number of foreign readers may well have been due to the difficulties of travel in war-torn Europe at first, and to the opening of the British Museum later, which in 1759 made available to 'all studious and curious persons' the large collections of King George II and Sir Hans Sloane. With the acquisition of the Royal Library, the British Museum gained the privilege of receiving newly published books under copyright legislation, which enabled it to acquire modern publications and to make them available in the heart of London. However, many eminent Oxford scholars are known to have used the Bodleian's collections, especially its manuscripts, throughout the century. The astronomer Edmund Halley was a regular reader from 1709 to 1712 (fig. 45), while the legal writer and judge William Blackstone consulted many works between 1743 and 1762. In the middle years of the century the most assiduous readers were the orientalist Thomas Hunt, Laudian Professor of Arabic and Regius Professor of Greek; his pupil the biblical scholar Benjamin Kennicott, who collated all the library's Hebrew manuscripts of the Old Testament; and the poet and historian Thomas Warton.

Most of the progress made in the listing and cataloguing of the library's collections during Hudson's librarianship was the result of the

work of Thomas Hearne. Born in 1678 in White Waltham, Berkshire, where his father was parish clerk, Hearne, a studious boy, attracted the attention of the Jacobite squire Francis Cherry, who became his tutor and patron and paid for his education, first at school and then at St Edmund Hall. As an undergraduate Hearne proved enthusiastic and reliable, and transcribed Bodleian manuscripts for several established scholars. He graduated BA in 1699 and lived at St Edmund Hall for the rest of his life. Hudson appointed him janitor in 1701, and, recognizing his undoubted bibliographical skills, set him to revise the now very out-of-date 1674 catalogue of printed books. Hearne relished the task, checking every book in the library against its entry in the old catalogue, correcting errors and adding a wealth of useful detail. But Hudson, preoccupied with his own researches, abandoned plans to publish it and the greatly improved catalogue remained available only in two handwritten volumes in the Bodleian. Hearne was indefatigable in cataloguing the library's holdings, compiling all manner of lists – of corrections to Bernard's 1698 catalogue of manuscripts, of books the library wished to acquire, of duplicates to be disposed of and of its collections of coins, pictures, antiquities and curiosities. He was to become a noted antiquarian and his first publication – an edition of the letters from Sir Thomas Bodley to his first librarian, Thomas James (*Reliquiae Bodleianae*, 1703) – is evidence of his passionate interest in everything associated with the Bodleian.

Hearne's salary was meagre, but he was able to supplement it with the fees paid by visitors to view the Bodleian's collection of curiosities on display in the Anatomy School on the first floor of the Schools Quadrangle. His list of the collection of 415 objects, compiled between 1705 and 1713, provides a fascinating insight into the material in what was the oldest museum in Oxford.[5] It included many botanical and zoological specimens (a radish root in the shape of a hand; a 'rose of the valley of Jehosophat, which will open of its own accord'; a monstrous pig, a basilisk and a salamander), as well as very curious items like 'trash out of the stomach of an ostrich' and a mermaid's hand. Among the antiquities were 'an old Danish spur, about six inches long in shank lost when the Danes were in England', a Roman battle axe and

Fig. 45 **Portrait of the astronomer Edmund Halley by Thomas Murray, given to the Bodleian in 1713.**

a Roman urn. Objects of more recent historical interest included a cup made from the walnut tree that was used to blacken King Charles II's face and hands when he was disguised to facilitate his escape from England after the defeat at the Battle of Worcester; a salver made out of the 'royal oak' in which he had hidden; and a 'tobacco stopper' made out of an oak that had grown from an acorn from the royal oak planted by the King in St James's Park but later cut down to make way for the construction of a house in St James's for the duke of Marlborough.

Hudson encouraged Hearne in his scholarly work, contributed to the cost of publishing four editions of classical authors that Hearne completed between 1703 and 1708 and appointed him sub-librarian in 1712. But Hearne's political views as a nonjuror who refused to take the oath of allegiance to the Hanoverian king became an increasing embarrassment to his colleagues both in the library and in the university at large, as were his irascible temper and outspoken attacks on all who disagreed with him. He was finally forced to give up his post in the library he loved in 1716, when an Act of Parliament imposed heavy penalties on all nonjurors who held public office.

Hudson was followed as Bodley's Librarian in 1719 by Joseph Bowles, a 24-year-old, who had graduated BA only in 1717 and had no pretensions to scholarship, but had gained first-hand experience of the practicalities of running the Bodleian since at least 1715. The most pressing problem he faced was the lack of storage space for books – a problem he solved (for the time being) by adding shelves below desk level to the book presses in Duke Humfrey's Library and moving into them the smaller books that had over the years been shelved among the folio volumes. This involved changing the location and therefore the shelfmark of some six or seven thousand volumes. It says much for Bowles's meticulous record-keeping that the operation was successful, with all the new shelfmarks carefully noted in the catalogue so that readers would be able to find the books they wanted in their new places on the shelves. At the time the librarian's labours were not appreciated, indeed were most unpopular with those regular readers who were familiar with the old arrangement and instinctively preferred it to the new one. Thomas Hearne was, as always, highly critical, decrying the 'disorder and confusion' Bowles had brought into a library which, thanks to Hearne's labours over many years, had (in his own opinion) been 'the best regulated library in the world'.[6] Another urgent task for Bowles was bringing the catalogue up to date. He hired young graduates to help with the task of copying out both the old catalogue of 1674 and the handwritten additions to it that were still the only record of books acquired in the last fifty years. Bowles expected the work to take six years, but it was not even half finished when he died in 1729, at the early age of thirty-four.

Robert Fysher, a fellow of Oriel College, succeeded Bowles after a contested election in which he defeated the sub-librarian, Francis Wise, by 100 votes to 85. Fysher has always been a shadowy figure in Bodleian history. We know that he was born in Grantham, Lincolnshire, around 1678, and that he studied first at Christ Church and then at Oriel College. Having graduated BA in 1718 and MA in 1724, he became Bachelor of Medicine in 1725. The great achievement of his librarianship was the publication of the general catalogue of printed books in 1738. With the assistance of his friend Emmanuel Langford, vice-principal of Hart Hall, and building on the work of Hearne and Bowles, Fysher edited the existing catalogue entries into two printed volumes, which remained in use well into the nineteenth century.

It was during Fysher's eighteen years as Bodley's Librarian that the collections of Thomas Tanner came to the library, the first of an impressive number of important acquisitions made in the eighteenth century. Tanner, who was the son of the vicar of Market Lavington in Wiltshire, had been educated at home, and at Queen's College, Oxford, where he met established scholars who encouraged his youthful interest in history and antiquities. He graduated BA in 1693, and in 1695, at the age of twenty-one, he published his first work, *Notitia Monastica; or, A Short History of the Religious Houses in England and Wales.* He was elected a fellow of All Souls the following year, and worked on a variety of projects including a history of his native county and a continuation of Anthony Wood's biographies of Oxford writers. He also contributed descriptions of three Bodleian collections (those of Francis Junius, Richard James and Gerard Langbaine) to Edward Bernard's catalogue of manuscripts. In 1698 he left Oxford to become chaplain to the bishop of Norwich, married the bishop's daughter and lived in Norfolk for many years, receiving a succession of ecclesiastical appointments, the duties of which diverted him from his antiquarian pursuits but not from his interest in collecting books and manuscripts. His appointment as a canon of Christ Church in 1724 renewed his links with Oxford, and in December 1731 he arranged for the removal of his library from Norwich to Oxford. Unfortunately, the barge in which the books were carried sank in the river at Wallingford and some of them still bear the marks of their submersion. Tanner was consecrated bishop of St Asaph in 1732 and died in 1735, bequeathing to the Bodleian his collection of printed books and manuscripts. The former – some nine hundred volumes – were rich in rare examples of English printing of the fifteenth and early sixteenth centuries, and included a copy of the *Bay Psalm Book* (Cambridge, Massachusetts, 1640), the first book printed in North America (fig. 46).[7] His manuscripts included the papers of William Sancroft, archbishop of Canterbury, which he had bought from a London bookseller in 1724, and of John Nalson, Royalist historian and pamphleteer, which he purchased around 1718. Both collections were of considerable importance for the study of seventeenth-century England and included letters of most of the key players in the Civil War, among them Charles I, Prince Rupert, Oliver Cromwell and John Hampden. The interest of contemporaries in the Tanner manuscripts is reflected in the speed with which Fysher dealt with them, and the frequency with which they were fetched for readers to study. They were sorted and arranged into 467 volumes, some of which were sent for binding in 1738 and the whole collection was fully catalogued by the early 1740s.

Another bequest – of around one thousand books from Nathaniel Crynes, fellow of St John's College, who died in August 1745 – was also very quickly catalogued and made available for study. Crynes graduated BA from St John's in 1708, where he had met and become a close friend of Richard Rawlinson,[8] who shared his interest in book collecting. Books from his collection, which included over twenty printed in the fifteenth century and many rare English and European publications of the sixteenth century, were already being consulted in July 1746. Ironically, some of the books that came to the Bodleian in his bequest had been sold to Crynes by the library in the 1720s as duplicates in its collections.[9]

For much of Fysher's time as librarian, the tranquillity of the Bodleian must have been disturbed by the work involved in the construction of the Radcliffe Camera. Dr John Radcliffe had been a student at University College, then a fellow of Lincoln College from

Fig. 46 **The *Bay Psalm Book* (1640), the first book printed in North America.**

THE
VVHOLE
BOOKE OF PSALMES
Faithfully
TRANSLATED *into* ENGLISH
Metre.

Whereunto is prefixed a discourse de-
claring not only the lawfullnes, but also
the necessity of the heavenly Ordinance
of singing Scripture Psalmes in
the Churches of
God.

Coll. III.
*Let the word of God dwell plenteously in
you, in all wisdome, teaching and exhort-
ing one another in Psalmes, Himnes, and
spirituall Songs, singing to the Lord with
grace in your hearts.*

Iames V.
*If any be afflicted, let him pray, and if
any be merry let hins sing psalmes.*

Imprinted
1640

1669 to 1677, and had practised as a physician in Oxford before moving to London, where he made a considerable fortune as a fashionable doctor (fig. 47). Queen Anne was one of his patients. He left £40,000 for a library to be built in Oxford between, on the south, the Church of St Mary the Virgin and on the north, the Schools Quadrangle. The land, with All Souls College to the east side and Brasenose College to the west, was the site of a number of small tenements. Their purchase had to be negotiated with the colleges that owned them and it was not until 1733 that the first of the old houses was demolished. The foundation stone of the new library, designed by James Gibbs, was laid in 1737, and two masons (Francis Smith of Warwick and William Townesend of Oxford) were appointed. Although both masons died within the next two years, building work was continued steadily by their sons until February 1741, when problems with the construction of the dome began to cause delays. The spectacular building (the first circular library in Great Britain) was eventually opened in 1749, with Francis Wise, sub-librarian in the Bodleian, as its first librarian (fig. 48). From its opening it served as a library, but one without any clearly defined purpose. It was only from 1810, with the appointment of the professor of botany, George Williams, as librarian that it began to focus on the provision of books in medicine and natural science and became a significant resource for members of the university.[10] The opening up of what we now know as Radcliffe Square had been suggested 120 years earlier by King Charles I, who, standing on the roof of the Bodleian in 1629, had proposed the clearing of the houses between the church and the library to create a *piazza literaria*; but the estimated cost of the proposal (£1,500) was at that time considered prohibitive.

In 1744 the travel writer and historian Thomas Salmon published *The Present State of the Universities and of the Five Adjacent Counties*, designed as a guide for foreign visitors. He described the Bodleian as 'a large, lofty Structure, built of Stone in the form of a Roman H, said to contain the greatest number of Books of any Library in Europe, except that of the Vatican and that of Paris', and its recently published catalogue as 'a Folio of no mean Size'. He did, however, have reservations about the estimated size of the collections, as 'it is observ'd that there are a great many Duplicates ... which make the Library

Fig. 47 **Portrait of John Radcliffe by Michael Dahl, after Kneller's portrait of 1712.**

appear larger than it really is'. Salmon also recorded some dissatisfaction with the arrangement of the collections on the shelves – 'for the Books of the principal Benefactors having a particular place assigned to each of them, a Student must run from one end of the Room to the other to consult Authors which treat of the same subject', while the chaining of the larger volumes prevented them being brought together for study. The short opening hours (only three in the morning and three in the afternoon) caused much inconvenience to any potential reader, who, moreover, during the winter months had 'to be content to sit without a Fire in a large, cold Room, if he would satisfy his Enquiries'.[11]

Fysher died in 1747 at the age of forty-nine, and was succeeded as Bodley's Librarian by Humphrey Owen, fellow of Jesus College. The son of a gentleman of Meifod in Montgomeryshire, Owen came to Jesus College in 1718, graduated BA in 1722 and MA in 1725, was ordained in 1732, proceeded Bachelor of Divinity in 1733, and was presented to a college living in Worcestershire in 1744. Three years later he was unanimously elected Bodley's Librarian, a post he held until his death in 1768, for the last five years combining it with serving as principal of his college.

As librarian Owen was active in improving the furniture and fittings of the Bodleian, which had begun to look very dated and shabby in comparison with the elegantly refurbished Codrington Library at All Souls, the new library at Christ Church and the impressive new Radcliffe Library. The beautiful dome of the last dominated the view from the south range of the top floor of the Schools Quadrangle – the Picture Gallery. Owen had the Arundel marbles moved to the School of Moral Philosophy on the ground floor and oversaw the redecoration of the gallery, adding elegant wainscoting throughout (paid for by the senior Radcliffe trustee, the duke of Beaufort), and fine plasterwork to the tower room in the east range, echoing the decoration of the Radcliffe Camera. Fortunately, he stopped short of putting a stucco ceiling over Thomas Bodley's panels in Duke Humfrey's Library or replacing the pinnacles around the quadrangle with elegant urns, as advocated by some of the more fashion-conscious members of the university. He did, however, in 1753 superintend the blocking up of two

Fig. 48 **The Radcliffe Camera, built as an independent library in the 1730s and 1740s, was transferred to the Bodleian in 1862.**

of the three west windows in Selden End and the repair of the tracery in the third, no doubt making it darker but gaining space for more bookshelves. In 1756 the library's account book records his purchase of three dozen Windsor chairs (at 8*s*. 6*d*. each) to replace the old benches between the bookcases in Duke Humfrey's Library – an improvement memorably described as 'the first major concession to reader-comfort' in the Bodleian.[12] This was followed, from 1757 to 1761, by the removal of the chains from the larger volumes on the bookshelves, which were probably now considered very unsightly and old-fashioned; they certainly hampered any rearrangement of the books. A blacksmith, Nathaniel Bull, was paid £3 0*s*. 4*d*. for the unchaining of 1,448 volumes in 1760–61. Owen was also much involved in decisions about the replacing of the ceiling in the Convocation House with fan-vaulting, by then very out of date, but perhaps seen as complementing the earlier (and finer) work in the adjacent Divinity School. The reconstruction must have caused much disruption in the library during 1758 and 1759, involving as it did the replacement of the floor in Selden End immediately above. The assistant, John Price (later sub-librarian, and Bodley's Librarian from 1768) was paid an honorarium 'for his extraordinary attendance and work in the Library occasion'd by taking up the floor of that part over the Convocation House'.[13] In addition, several people were paid five shillings each for 'assisting in taking down the books in the Selden Library and carrying them to their places to be put [back] up'.[14]

Owen's period in office saw many significant acquisitions, and there is little doubt that his improvements to the appearance of the library encouraged potential donors, as did his sympathy with their scholarly pursuits. The year 1755 was particularly notable, with the acquisition of the largest collection of manuscripts ever given to the Bodleian by a single donor: a bequest from the topographer and collector Richard Rawlinson (fig. 49). Owen had, in the course of a long correspondence, wooed this most demanding of benefactors and worked hard to secure his spectacular collections. In his first will Rawlinson had divided his collections between the University of Oxford and the Society of Antiquaries, the only institutions that he believed still encouraged the study of history and antiquities. Having

Fig. 49 **Portrait of Richard Rawlinson (1690–1755).**

elected him vice president, the Antiquaries began to have qualms about his Jacobite sympathies and removed him from their society's council. Rawlinson altered his will, bequeathing the bulk of his collections to the Bodleian ('that sanctuary for use and curiosity'), and of his landed property to St John's. He had already endowed a professorship in Anglo-Saxon at Oxford and now also made provision for the salary of the keeper of the Ashmolean Museum.

Rawlinson's manuscripts – numbering over five thousand – include early charters, monastic cartularies, medieval liturgical, biblical and classical manuscripts; an important group of medieval Irish manuscripts (among them the 'Annals of Inisfallen', an account of the history of Ireland from the fifth to the fifteenth centuries); the official papers of John Thurloe as Secretary of State from 1652 to 1660; Admiralty papers of Samuel Pepys; a series of some 250 poetical miscellanies mainly of the seventeenth century; over one hundred volumes of seventeenth- and eighteenth-century literary and scholarly correspondence; and a wide range of manuscripts relating to topography, history and biography, heraldry and genealogy, theology, law and medicine. Rawlinson had a lifelong interest in English history and topography. In 1712, a year after graduating from St John's College, he began a series of extensive journeys throughout England, making notes on antiquities and copying monumental inscriptions. In 1718 he visited most of the parishes of Oxfordshire, intending to compile a history of the county. The history never materialized, but his notes survive among his papers in the Bodleian, as does a fascinating diary of his travels on the Continent from 1719 to 1726, when he visited Holland, France, Germany, Italy, Sicily and Malta and studied at the universities of Utrecht, Leiden and Padua. On his return he settled in London, was admitted a fellow of the Society of Antiquaries, and became a freemason. In 1728 he was consecrated bishop in the nonjuring church, taking 'I collect and I preserve' as his episcopal motto. His collections include a wealth of correspondence, sermons and other papers of nonjurors – those who refused to take the oath of allegiance to the Hanoverian king – including Thomas Hearne's. With the deaths of Hearne and Tanner in 1735, Rawlinson reckoned that antiquarian studies in England were at a low ebb, but this served only to increase his determination to continue collecting books, manuscripts

Fig. 50 **Portrait of St Columba from his 'Life' by Magnus O'Donnell, 1532.**

and historical objects in order to 'provide for posterity without regard to this ungrateful age'.[15] Rawlinson did not confine himself to orthodox methods of purchasing manuscripts from auctioneers and booksellers, but also sought papers of historical interest that had been sold for scrap. He scoured the shops of grocers and chandlers, and bought waste paper by weight, much of which proved to be important archives of the previous century. All the collections that he purchased as discarded bundles of loose papers Rawlinson systematically sorted and had bound into volumes to reduce the risk of their being unwittingly or carelessly thrown away a second time. Alongside books and manuscripts, he collected coins and medals, copperplates (polished plates of etched or engraved copper, used to illustrate many of the finest books of the period) and, most unusually, remarkable specimens of seventeenth- and early eighteenth-century needlework, some by practised needlewomen but also several samplers by girls aged only ten and eleven, all of which he bound into one volume and gave the humorous title of 'Works of Learned Ladies'.[16]

It was difficult to find room for Rawlinson's vast collections in the already overfull Bodleian, and they seem to have been stored all over the place, for the most part unsorted and unlisted. It is clear from the records of items fetched for readers that by 1771 some of the manuscripts had been assigned numbers, and that by 1811 more had been arranged into series; but, according to W.D. Macray, it was not until H.O. Coxe became librarian in 1860 that a concerted effort was made to reassemble and catalogue the collection. Macray gives a graphic account of how a search was made of 'every corner of the Library' and 'cupboard after cupboard was found filled with MSS. and papers huddled together in confusion, while, last not least, a dark hole under a staircase, explored by me on hands and knees, afforded a rich "take", including many writings of Rawlinson's Non-juring friends'.[17]

It took another forty years for a list of Rawlinson's copperplates to be made available. It was compiled by a young graduate of Royal Holloway College, Edith Guest, who described some of the plates as illustrating buildings in Virginia in the mid-eighteenth century. One was later identified as depicting Williamsburg, from 1699 to 1780 the capital of Virginia Colony, and one of America's first planned cities (fig. 51). The copperplate proved particularly helpful during the restoration of the town's public buildings in the early twentieth

Fig. 51 **Eighteenth-century copperplate of Williamsburg, capital of Virginia Colony, from the Rawlinson collection.**

century. This restoration was funded by John D. Rockefeller Jr, whose foundation also made a major grant towards the development of the New Bodleian. The Williamsburg plate was presented to Mr Rockefeller in 1937 as a mark of the university's great regard, and he in turn gave it to Colonial Williamsburg, where it is displayed as the 'Bodleian Plate'.

Other important collections came to the Bodleian in 1755, among them bequests from three antiquaries: George Ballard (1706–1755), Richard Furney (1694–1753) and James St Amand (1687–1754). The son of a chandler of Chipping Campden in Gloucestershire, Ballard had been apprenticed as a tailor and early in life developed an interest in coins and books. He taught himself Old English and Latin, and gradually built up a wide circle of correspondents, including many of the foremost scholars of the day. He met Thomas Hearne in 1726. Sponsored by Lord Chedworth and members of his hunt at Chipping Campden, Ballard matriculated at Magdalen College in 1750, but never took a degree. His principal literary work, *Memoirs of Several Ladies*

of *Great Britain, who Have Been Celebrated for their Writings or Skill in the Learned Languages, Arts and Sciences*, was published in 1752. He bequeathed coins, manuscripts and correspondence to the Bodleian, and his collection of letters – the majority addressed to Arthur Charlett, master of University College – is a rich source of information on the biographical and bibliographical history of the first half of the eighteenth century.

Richard Furney was a Gloucester man, master of the Crypt School in that city from 1719 to 1724, and archdeacon of Surrey from 1725. He bequeathed to the Bodleian a small collection of early editions of the classics, with manuscripts recording his own researches into the history of Gloucestershire, and charters that included three thirteenth-century confirmations of Magna Carta (fig. 52). James St Amand shared Furney's enthusiasm for the classics and worked for many years on an edition of Theocritus, travelling across Europe to collate surviving manuscripts in Holland, Germany, Austria and Italy. On his travels he accumulated a valuable collection of books, manuscript and prints, many relating to the history of the Low Countries, which he bequeathed to the Bodleian.

As Bodley's Librarian Owen was also involved in the early stages of the protracted processes that led to the library's acquisition of the Clarendon and Carte manuscripts. The former were the official papers of the first earl of Clarendon as Charles II's chief adviser in the 1650s and Lord Chancellor in the 1660s; the latter were manuscripts collected by the historian Thomas Carte (1686–1754), which included official papers of Sir William Fitzwilliam (1526–1599) and James Butler, first duke of Ormonde (1610–1688), both of enormous importance for studies of Irish history. Owen's librarianship was marked both by the enhancement of the collections and by a noticeable increase in the number of scholars making use of them.

In the eighteenth century many libraries possessed collections of coins and medals for study alongside their books and manuscripts. The Bodleian's collection had been inaugurated by a gift from Archbishop Laud in the 1630s and had grown as a result of many small donations and a few purchases in succeeding years. During Owen's librarianship it was, like the holdings of books and manuscripts, considerably enhanced

Fig. 52 **One of the four surviving copies of the 1217 reissue of Magna Carta.**

by a succession of major benefactions. In 1750 the sub-librarian, Francis Wise, published a catalogue of the collection which encouraged its use and attracted further additions. Its importance was reflected in the provision of a special 'Coin Room' in the Gallery in 1753.

Humphrey Owen died in March 1768 at the age of sixty-six, and an obituary in *Jackson's Oxford Journal* recorded the respect in which he was held for his 'extensive learning, simplicity of manners, generosity and constant integrity'.[18] He was succeeded by the 34-year-old John Price (fig. 53), one of five graduates of Jesus College and five Welshmen whom Owen had appointed as sub-librarians. The election was closely contested between Price and William Cleaver, a fellow of Brasenose, who each received the same number of votes; but Price, as the senior of the two, was nominated librarian by the vice-chancellor, and Cleaver went on to become principal of his college and bishop of St Asaph. Price, who had been acting librarian from 1765 to 1767, was librarian for forty-five years, without achieving anything of great significance as an administrator. He was a sportsman and a botanist, and his surviving correspondence is as much concerned with gaming licences and plant species as with books or libraries. He also held several ecclesiastical appointments, including two curacies in Oxfordshire between 1766 and 1810. In 1782 and 1798 he was presented by the duke of Beaufort, whom Price regularly visited at Badminton, to two livings, one in Gloucestershire and the other in Breconshire. Given all these outside commitments, it is not surprising that, nineteen years into his librarianship, Price faced public criticism of his administration. Thomas Beddoes, who had been an undergraduate at Pembroke College from 1776 to 1779, and then studied medicine and chemistry at London and Edinburgh, returned to Oxford in 1786. Appointed reader in chemistry, he lectured on both chemistry and geology, but found that his scientific studies were frustrated by the limited collections in the Bodleian and by the difficulties of obtaining access to them when the librarian was not available. In 1787 he circulated a printed *Memorial concerning the State of the Bodleian Library and the Conduct of its Principal Librarian, addressed to the library's governing body of curators*.[19] In it he castigated Price for 'a regular and constant neglect of his duty', for his failure to attend at the library and for lending out books before they were catalogued. Beddoes was particularly incensed by Price's routine absence from the library on

Fig. 53 **Engraving by J.C. Bromley of a sketch, made in 1798, of John Price, Bodley's Librarian from 1768 to 1813.**

Saturdays and Mondays, when he was travelling to and from Wilcote in west Oxfordshire, where he was curate. 'It unfortunately happens', Beddoes complained, 'from the disposition of the Chemical Lectures, that I have scarce any leisure, but on Saturdays and Mondays, to consult such books as may assist me in preparing them.'[20] He frequently had to wait 'half hours and hours' for a Mr Curtis to be called to fetch the books he required, as none of the librarians could find them. Curtis

Fig. 54 **The Auctarium in the 1930s.**

seems to have worked as a cataloguer in the Bodleian, having been
apprenticed to the Oxford bookseller Daniel Prince and employed
by the publisher James Caulfield to transcribe manuscripts in the
Ashmolean. It is ironic that the person Beddoes singles out as the most
helpful member of the library staff was later summarily dismissed,
having been found to have stolen portraits from books in the Bodleian
and several college libraries. Beddoes also voiced a more general
criticism of the library's opening hours: in summer it should have
been open at 8 in the morning, but was frequently opened only after
9. He found fault with the librarian's method of selecting books and

periodicals for purchase, and with his expenditure of limited income on the fitting up of rooms rather than the improvement of the library's meagre collection of modern, especially foreign, publications. It was a comprehensive indictment, to which the curators responded by altering the library regulations, increasing the number of staff to ensure that it was open at the statutory hours, and supervising more closely the response to requests for the purchase of recent publications.

The curators had already, from the late 1770s, begun to take a more active role in library affairs. For most of the eighteenth century the Bodleian's modest income, from the estates with which Sir Thomas Bodley had endowed it, covered only general running costs and part of the salaries of the staff. From 1750 to 1780 a mere £10 per annum (paid from a university fund established with a benefaction from Nathaniel, Lord Crewe, a close friend and adviser of James II, who had been rector of Lincoln College from 1668 to 1672 and bishop of Durham from 1674) was specifically allocated to the purchase of books. The principal acquisitions were gifts – splendid collections in their own right – but ones that reflected the interests of individual donors rather than the needs of scholars in the university. William Scott, Camden Professor of Ancient History (later a renowned maritime lawyer, Baron Stowell, and member of parliament for the university) recognized that, as a result of the inadequate funds for buying books and the failure of London stationers to deposit their more substantial publications, the university was not acquiring the range of modern publications its members needed. In 1779 he circulated a proposal to remedy this sorry, and to him unacceptable, state of affairs. His suggestion was that the Bodleian should receive annual fees from all persons entitled to read in the library, and a share of the fees every member of the university paid on matriculation. This was speedily agreed, for, as the revised statute put it: 'Nothing seems more conducive to the honour of the University, or to touch its utility nearer, than that the ancient renown of the Bodleian Library, so distinguished of yore for the abundance, variety, and choiceness of all manner of literary store, should be kept up and augmented constantly by new accessions.'[21]

From 1780 the Bodleian received around £480 every year in fees, the bulk of which was spent on books, to 'preserve the fame of the Library and facilities to the Students'.[22] The curators, rather than Bodley's Librarian, again took the lead, and published annual catalogues of the books so purchased.

In 1789 the curators became even more involved and organized purchases at the auction in London of the books of the great Venetian collector Maffeo Pinelli, securing for the library an impressive number of early printed books to fill significant gaps in the Bodleian's holdings. As a result, the library accounts showed a deficit of £484 at the end of the year just when it became apparent that another important collection – that of Pierre-Antoine Crevenna – was to be sold early in 1790. The curators again took the initiative, distributing an appeal on 1 December 1789 to members of the university for interest-free loans to enable them to 'make up the deficiencies of the Library' at the forthcoming sale.[23] Colleges and individuals responded so positively that the curators were once again able to buy many early books that the library lacked.

There is no record of the librarian's involvement in this unusual spending spree or of any response from him to Beddoes's criticisms. Perhaps Price was content that assessment of his contribution to the Bodleian should rest, not on his administration, but on the acquisitions that resulted from his cordial relations with historians and men of letters outside the university. John Nichols, the great scholar-publisher of the day, described Price as 'the able pioneer of literature, whose friendly attentions will be recollected by many researchers into the vast treasures of the Bodleian', and extolled his 'obliging and communicative disposition'.[24] Price was a fellow of the Society of Antiquaries in London, sharing the interests and enjoying the friendship and respect of many in the literary world beyond Oxford. Richard Gough's bequest of his topographical collections to the Bodleian was without doubt the result of Price's careful attentions. In these circles Bodley's Librarian was known as 'honest Johnny Price'. He published very little himself, but his help is acknowledged in the prefaces of countless contemporary publications. In many ways he epitomized an old-fashioned style of librarianship that failed to adapt to the business of running a large and ever-expanding library or to meet the needs of a new generation of researchers. Price did, however, in 1789, oversee the annexation by the library of a room in the south-west corner of the first floor of the quadrangle, the university's Anatomy School, which had housed the collection of curiosities. It was transformed into a well-furnished library room, with elegant bookcases specially designed to house the manuscripts and fifteenth-century books then reckoned the most precious in the Bodleian: the Bibles and the Greek and Latin classics, many of them purchased at the Pinelli and Crevenna sales (fig. 54). Thanks both to its curators and to its librarians, the Bodleian ended its second century not only with enormously enhanced collections, but also with a guaranteed income for the purchase of books in the years ahead.

CHAPTER 5

The nineteenth century

L ITTLE CHANGED IN THE BODLEIAN as the eighteenth century turned into the nineteenth. John Price, Bodley's Librarian since 1768, continued in office. A small number of scholars continued to study manuscripts in Duke Humfrey's Library – among them the philologist Samuel Henshall of Brasenose College; Henry Ford, professor of Arabic and principal of Magdalen Hall; and the antiquary Thomas Dudley Fosbroke – while printed books were fetched for a gradually increasing number of recent graduates and college fellows. Major gifts continued to come in: the first, in 1801, a large collection of printed and manuscript music, including many early editions of the works of Handel, Arnold, Boyce and Purcell, bequeathed by Osborne Wight, formerly a fellow of New College, who also considerably left £100 to cover the costs of dealing with his bequest, but forty years passed before his collection was catalogued (fig. 56). Richard Gough, the principal antiquary of the day, died in 1809, bequeathing his vast collections to the Bodleian. He had published three influential works on British antiquities: *British Topography* (1768), a gazetteer of published and unpublished works on British and Irish local history and topography, revised and expanded in 1780; *Sepulchral Monuments* (1786–99), a description of tombs and funeral monuments from the eleventh to the fifteenth

Fig. 55 **Watercolour of the Picture Gallery by Joseph Nash.**

centuries; and an English version of William Camden's *Britannia* (1789), enlarged and reprinted in four volumes in 1806. Gough was director of the Society of Antiquaries from 1771 to 1797 and played a leading role in London's antiquarian circles. He had expected to become a trustee of the British Museum, but not only did the museum fail to appoint him, it was also unable to reach an agreement with him about the storage of his collection of the copperplate engravings from which his works had been lavishly illustrated. The Bodleian proved more accommodating. Price and Gough had corresponded since 1771 and when, in 1799, Gough enquired about the library's policy regarding gifts, Price promptly replied: 'I ... have pleasure to inform you that our worthy benefactors have, and always had, full liberty to impose what conditions they please, with respect to their donations.'[1] But his assurance does not seem to have persuaded the potential benefactor immediately. Two years later, in April 1801, twelve years after the creation of the Auctarium, a letter to Gough announced plans to annex for library use another room on the first floor of the Schools Quadrangle, the Civil Law School in the north-west corner, and to fit it out as 'the Antiquarians' Study'. Separate presses were to be assigned to the collections of Thomas Tanner, Browne Willis, Richard Rawlinson and Roger Dodsworth; and the librarian would 'be very proud to add the name of Mr Gough to the Collection'. Gough was reminded that the Bodleian would agree to any conditions he wished to attach to his gift, and was asked to comment on the plans 'if you can possibly make up your mind to the depositing of your collection in this room'.[2] Gough sent a non-committal reply and it was only after his death in 1809 that it became known that he had bequeathed his enormous and enormously important collections to the Bodleian. Gough's executor, the printer and publisher John Nichols, organized the dispatch of the books, manuscripts, copperplates, prints, drawings and maps to Oxford, where they became the foundation of the library's great topographical holdings. Gough's bequest also included a fine collection of service books of the pre-Reformation English church, and books concerning Anglo-Saxon and Scandinavian literature. The importance of the whole collection was reflected in the speed with which a catalogue was brought out, compiled for the most part by one of the sub-librarians, Bulkeley Bandinel, and published in 1814.

Fig. 56 **Autograph manuscript of Purcell's** *Ode to St Cecilia*, **1692.**

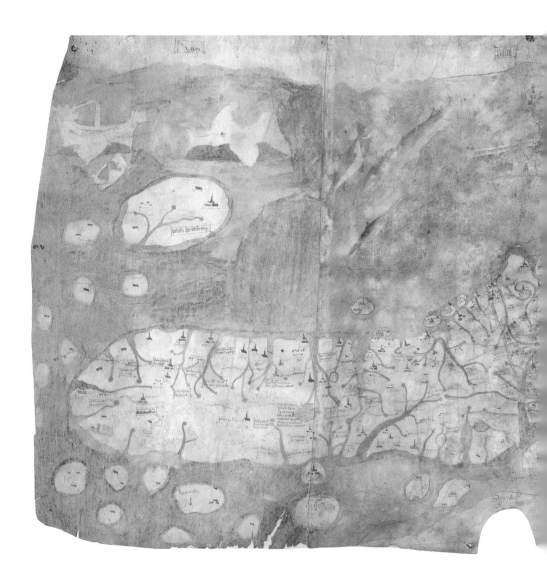

Fig. 57 **The fourteenth-century 'Gough Map',**
the oldest surviving map of Great Britain.

The best-known map in Gough's collection is the oldest surviving map of Great Britain, long known simply as the 'Gough Map' (fig. 57). Dating from the fourteenth century, it depicts almost two hundred rivers and over six hundred towns within a recognizable coastline, albeit with the east coast at the top. A few years before Gough's bequest, around 1800, the library had begun to buy English and foreign maps, and in November 1813 the curators ordered a large table to hold them. In 1801 the Ordnance Survey began to send copies of its maps to the copyright libraries and the Hydrographic Office soon followed suit with Admiralty charts. All these maps and charts seem to have accumulated in enormous piles in one of the first-floor rooms of the Schools Quadrangle, where the young Mary Augusta Ward saw them one morning in 1871 – 'maps innumerable, roll-maps, sheet-maps, bound-maps of every date and every size'.[3] By 1882 the Bodleian was receiving between three and four thousand sheet maps each year, without the resources needed to arrange, store or catalogue them properly. It was only in 1887 that the Moral Philosophy School on the ground floor was fitted out as a map room and a start made on processing the enormous collection.

The acquisition of recently published books continued to pose problems. The deposit of books by publishers under the terms of the Copyright Act did not add significantly to the holdings of modern books – on average only sixty books and sixty smaller publications such as pamphlets are listed as received from this source each year between 1801 and 1805. The regular purchase of recent publications slowed down in the early years of the century, despite the rise in the library's income from its share in university fees from around £450 in 1780 to about £750 in 1813. An average of £500 was spent on books each year from 1800 to 1805, but a mere £200 in each of the following seven years. The curators made good use of the balance that accumulated in the book fund, buying collections of rare books and manuscripts, but not recent publications. In 1805 they were able to spend £1,095 on the purchase of manuscripts and correspondence of the classical scholar Jacques Philippe d'Orville (1696–1751), who had been professor of history, eloquence and Greek at Amsterdam (fig. 58). Four years later they bought the Greek, Latin and oriental manuscripts of the Cambridge traveller and mineralogist Edward Daniel Clarke (1769–1822).

Fig. 58 **Manuscript of Cicero's** *Orationes*, **written by Giovanni Aretino in Florence in 1418.**

John Price died on 11 August 1813 and within a fortnight Bulkeley Bandinel (his godson, who had been appointed sub-librarian in 1810) was elected unopposed to succeed him as Bodley's Librarian (fig. 59). Born in Oxford in 1781, the son of a fellow of Jesus College, Bandinel was educated at Winchester School and became a scholar and later a fellow of New College. He graduated BA in 1805 and was ordained the same year. In 1808 he served as naval chaplain on board the famous HMS *Victory*, at that time the flagship of Admiral Sir James Saumarez, commander of the fleet in the Baltic charged with protecting British trade and blockading ports under French control in those northern waters. The young librarian made an immediate impact. Before the end of 1813 (his first year in office), new library statutes were approved, increasing the librarian's stipend to £400, making provision for two sub-librarians (instead of one) and specifying that one was to be assigned to look after the manuscripts and the other

the rest of the books, while both were to assist in searching for and arranging the books and in cataloguing them. The new statutes also extended the opening hours (now fixed at 9 to 4 in summer months and 10 to 3 in the winter) and provided an additional annual grant from the university of £680 (to pay for the increased staff, work on a new catalogue and much-needed repairs to library buildings). Bandinel lost no time in securing the appointment of two skilled young scholars as sub-librarians. Henry Cotton, then twenty-two years old and a student of Christ Church, was appointed in March 1814, and during his eight years in the Bodleian he listed and catalogued the library's collections of bibles. The 21-year-old Alexander Nicoll of Balliol College came the following month and continued in office until his appointment as Regius Professor of Hebrew in 1822. Already a noted linguist, Nicoll worked on the oriental manuscripts, and in 1821 published one volume of a catalogue that included manuscripts in twelve languages which established his reputation, and that of the library's collections, throughout Europe. His linguistic abilities were phenomenal, and it was said that 'he could travel to the Great Wall of China without needing an interpreter'.[4] A guide to Oxford, published in 1817, noted that a catalogue of the printed collections was in preparation to replace that of 1738, which 'although in two large volumes folio ... is now, through the amazing increase of the Library become of very limited utility', and waxed eloquent about the Bodleian as a 'store house of literature ... in divinity, in classical and critical works it is strong, in early editions of the classics very superior, in oriental manuscripts perhaps unrivalled'.[5]

It was the scale of the acquisitions made when Bandinel was Bodley's Librarian that marked his time in office as one of the greatest periods of expansion of the collections. In 1814, the year following his appointment, a decision in the Court of King's Bench confirmed the copyright libraries' claim to all British publications, not just those registered at Stationers' Hall. As a result of this, and of the subsequent Copyright Act of 1814 which clarified the extent of the publishers' obligations, the deposit of current British publications increased significantly, releasing the library's grant from university funds for other purchases. Bandinel lost no time in spending the grant, both in regular

Fig. 59 **Portrait of Bulkeley Bandinel, Bodley's Librarian from 1813 to 1860, by Thomas Kirkby, 1825.**

purchases from English and foreign booksellers and at auction sales of private collectors' libraries. Thus in 1817 the Bodleian spent £5,444 on the purchase in Venice of the great collection of the eighteenth-century Jesuit Matteo Luigi Canonici, which included Greek and Latin classical and medieval manuscripts, important Italian and Hebrew manuscripts and almost one hundred bibles – among them the 'Ranshofen Gospels' (fig. 60), bound at the Austrian abbey in 1178 and renowned for the depiction of the four evangelists against lavish gold backgrounds. The following year eighty-four volumes of Lutheran tracts of the first half of the sixteenth century were bought for £95, and in 1820 £500 secured fifty Greek manuscripts from the library of the Veronese collector Giovanni Saibante. Throughout the next decade the availability of funds enabled Bandinel to buy enthusiastically at auctions both at home and abroad: a large collection of foreign theological works at the sale of the library of Jona Willem te Water, professor of ecclesiastical history at Leiden, in 1824; many books on foreign history and law as well as patristic and classical manuscripts at the Meerman sale in The Hague in the same year; early works of oriental studies at a sale in Paris in 1825; over forty thousand, mainly German, academic dissertations in 1827; culminating in 1829 with the purchase of the library of David Oppenheimer, chief rabbi of Prague (d.1735) – over five thousand volumes, including 780 manuscripts. These, added to the four hundred or so Hebrew manuscripts already in the library, placed it firmly in the first rank of the world's Hebrew libraries, and immediately brought many eminent Jewish scholars to study in Oxford. In the 1830s acquisitions continued apace, with large purchases of seventeenth- and eighteenth-century plays, pre-1814 booksellers' and auction catalogues, fifteenth-century editions of canon and civil law, and English pamphlets from 1660 to 1820. Meanwhile the holdings of early Bibles, incunabula (books printed in the fifteenth century) and first editions of classical texts (*editiones principes*) – especially Aldines (printed in Venice by Aldus Manutius) – were enhanced by regular purchases whenever the opportunity arose. In the early 1840s the most spectacular purchases were of oriental manuscripts: in 1842 Sanskrit manuscripts were bought

Fig. 60 **The Four Gospels, written and illuminated for Ranshofen Abbey in Upper Austria in 1178, one of many important manuscripts collected by Matteo Luigi Canonici and bought by the Bodleian in 1817.**

Fig. 61 **Qur'ān (c.1709), from the Ouseley collection.**

from Horace Hayman Wilson, professor of Sanskrit, followed in 1843 by Arabic and Ethiopic manuscripts that had been collected by the African explorer James Bruce, and in 1844 by Persian manuscripts collected by the orientalist Sir William Ouseley (fig. 61).

It was not only through purchases that the library's collections were enhanced while Bandinel was librarian. Two major gifts came early in his librarianship. The first was the bulk of the library of the great Shakespearean editor and commentator, Edmond Malone, who had accumulated an impressive collection of over eight hundred volumes of early English poetry and drama, many of them extremely rare. Fortunately for the Bodleian, his collection included a copy of the 1623 First Folio edition of Shakespeare's *Plays*. Malone, while expressing a hope that his collection might eventually be deposited in a public library, left it to his brother Richard, Lord Sunderlin, who (perhaps because he had briefly pursued his studies at Christ Church) bequeathed it to the Bodleian. Lord Sunderlin died in 1816, but, as he instructed, the books remained with James Boswell while he prepared a new edition of Edmond Malone's *Shakespeare*. Malone's collection, when it eventually arrived in 1821, made the Bodleian a centre for studies of Elizabethan literature and encouraged Bandinel and his successors to buy extensively in the same field.

The most spectacular gift of the nineteenth century came during Bandinel's librarianship in 1834 as a bequest from Francis Douce. Born in 1757, the son of a London attorney, Douce had trained as a lawyer but at an early age developed an interest in books and antiquities, and used his inheritance from his father, who died in 1799, to build up a collection of books, manuscripts, coins, medals, prints and drawings, and miscellaneous antiquities. In 1807 he joined the staff of the Department of Manuscripts at the British Museum, became keeper of the department the same year and worked on the catalogues of the Lansdowne and Harleian collections; but at the age of fifty he seems to have found the restrictions of institutional routine irksome. He resigned four years later, in 1811. His two major publications – *Illustrations of Shakespeare, and Ancient Manners* (1807) and *The Dance of Death exhibited in elegant engravings on wood, with a dissertation on the several representations of that subject* (1833) – reflect, as do his extensive collections, his lifelong interest in manners, customs and beliefs down the centuries. Late in life a legacy of about £50,000 from his friend the sculptor Joseph Nollekens enabled him to augment his collections with purchases on a lavish scale. In his *Amenities of Literature*, first published in 1841, Douce's friend, the writer Isaac D'Israeli (father of the future prime minister) gives an account of how he and Douce went on an excursion to Oxford in 1830. Armed with a letter of introduction from Frederic Madden of the Department of Manuscripts at the British Museum, they were cordially welcomed by Bandinel, who showed them around the Bodleian and entertained them to dinner. Disraeli records that:

> Douce contemplated in the Bodleian that arch over which is placed
> the portrait of Selden, and the library of Selden preserved entire; the
> antiquary's closet which holds the great topographical collections
> of Richard Gough; and the distinct shelves dedicated to the small

Shakespearean library of Malone. He observed that the collections of Rawlinson, of Tanner, and of others, had preserved their identity by their separation. This was the subject of our conversation. At this moment Douce must have decided on the locality where his precious collection was to find a permanent abode; for it was immediately on his return home that our literary antiquary bequeathed his collection to the Bodleian Library.[6]

Douce would no doubt have appreciated the sight of his collections as they were eventually housed in the Bodleian – in the spacious first-floor room in the south-east corner of the quadrangle (the old Astronomy School), elegantly fitted out with shelves and cabinets to accommodate his magnificent bequest (fig. 62).

Douce's collection was huge, estimated to be in the region of 44,000 prints, 20,000 books, 1,500 drawings and 430 manuscripts, as well as coins and medals.[7] It brought into the Bodleian many of the medieval illuminated manuscripts that have ever since been counted among its major treasures. They include a gospel lectionary illuminated by nuns at the abbey of Chelles, near Paris, the binding of which incorporates a beautiful ivory plaque, executed in the court workshop of the emperor Charlemagne about the year 800, with a figure of Christ triumphant trampling on a lion and a serpent in the centre, surrounded by scenes from his life. One manuscript of the Apocalypse or book of Revelation, of which there are many in the Douce collection (linked to his interest in the Dance of Death), has long been known as the 'Douce Apocalypse'. It was produced at Westminster around 1270, shortly before the future King Edward I and his wife, Eleanor of Castile, left for the Crusades. The initial on its first leaf incorporates the kneeling figures of Edward and Eleanor and the whole manuscript is illustrated with a series of superb half-page miniatures, many of them intriguingly left unfinished. Another of the many famous medieval English manuscripts in Douce's collection is a psalter written and illuminated in East Anglia around the beginning of the fourteenth century, known as the 'Ormesby Psalter', after the monk Robert of Ormesby, who presented it to Norwich cathedral (fig. 63). Douce's bequest also brought into the Bodleian 379 incunabula, enormously enhancing in new subject areas its already renowned accumulation of books printed in the fifteenth century. Whereas the Bodleian had been building its

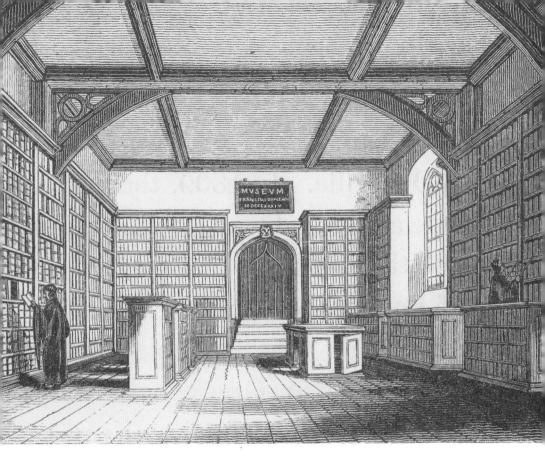

Fig. 62 **The Astronomy School in the south-east corner of the Schools Quadrangle, seen here in an engraving of 1835, was refurbished to house the Douce collection. From James Ingram's** Memorials of Oxford, **vol. 2 (1835).**

holdings of early editions of the classics to support the curriculum of the university, Douce, like many other private collectors of his day, had concentrated on editions of medieval texts – lives of saints, sermons, chronicles, romances and fables – many illustrated with woodcut illustrations. One outstanding volume is a 1476 edition of Pliny's *Historia naturalis*, printed on vellum by Nicolas Jenson in Venice, specially bound and sumptuously illuminated for Filippo Strozzi, a member of the merchant family of Venice (fig. 64). The bills for the work survive and show that it took four years for the artist to complete the illustrations. In marked contrast to this masterpiece is the only known copy of a pocket-sized 1535 edition of Aesop's *Fables* in Latin verse, which aimed to develop English schoolboys' Latin style and to improve their understanding of moral behaviour. Douce also preserved

many fragments of early printing, among them a small document that is reckoned to be the earliest printed advertisement in English, probably from 1479. Its purpose was to let customers know that they could buy a book, the Sarum *Ordinal*, which William Caxton, the first English printer, had just published, 'from his shop in the Almonry Gatehouse of Westminster Abbey'. The Latin formula in the bottom line of the advertisement, requesting readers not to remove the notice, suggests that it was displayed on a doorpost.

Frederic Madden, Keeper of Manuscripts at the British Museum, reckoned that the capacity of the Bodleian staff to catalogue collections lagged far behind Bandinel's ability to acquire them. He was vexed by Douce's bequest of his collections to Oxford and likened it to 'throw[ing] them down a bottomless pit', where they would neither be catalogued nor properly looked after, and would be to all intents and purposes unavailable to scholars.[8] But, for once at least, his criticism was wide of the mark. The Bodleian published annual catalogues of individual purchases between 1780 and 1861, which included some detail on libraries bought en bloc, while work on the large collections proceeded at a reasonable rate. The catalogue of the Gough collection (received in 1809) was published in 1814; the huge collection of foreign dissertations (acquired in 1827) was the subject of a separate published catalogue in 1834, as was Malone's collection of Shakespeareana in 1836. A catalogue of the Douce collection appeared in 1840. Meanwhile the Greek manuscripts acquired earlier in the century were being catalogued by one of the sub-librarians, H.O. Coxe. His descriptions were published in 1853 in the first of what was to be a series of detailed 'Quarto' catalogues (so-called because of the size of the pages, the result of folding each sheet of printed paper into four leaves). The following years of Bandinel's librarianship saw the publication of three more catalogues in the series, of the manuscript collections of Canonici, Laud and Tanner. But for many readers the most useful achievement of his long reign was the completion of a new general catalogue of printed books. When he became librarian, the only catalogue widely available was the one that had been published

Fig. 63 **The lavishly illustrated fourteenth-century 'Ormesby Psalter' was one of the many important medieval manuscripts bequeathed to the library by Francis Douce.**

eighty-five years earlier. Those who came to the Bodleian could use an interleaved copy of the 1738 catalogue, which included handwritten entries for books acquired since then. Work on a replacement started in earnest in 1837 and the new catalogue was published in three volumes in 1843, but it was by then already eight years out of date and was followed by a supplement in 1851.

During the nineteenth century, and especially while Bandinel was librarian, much work was undertaken on the library building. The rooms on the first floor of the Schools Quadrangle, originally designed for teaching and examinations, were gradually taken over by the library and filled with books. The first room, annexed in 1805, was the Civil Law School, designed by John Price as a repository for the library's collections of antiquarians' manuscripts and referred to in Richard Gough's will as the Antiquaries' Closet. Around 1816 more shelving was squeezed in and a number of eighteenth-century manuscript collections joined Gough's and other antiquaries' libraries. In 1821 the Greek School was fitted out to house English and foreign periodicals, and opposite it, in the south range, the Hebrew School was divided into three to house the overflow of folio volumes from Duke Humfrey's Library, miscellaneous western manuscripts and the collections of William Laud and Richard Rawlinson. It was also in 1821 that a first, and apparently ineffectual, attempt was made to introduce some heat into the library in the winter months, with a stove (safely installed outside the library) providing a modest amount of hot air to two small vents in Arts End. W.D. Macray recalled in his *Annals*[9] how the rather frail sub-librarian and Laudian Professor of Arabic, Stephen Reay, would stand by these gratings for half-hours on end in a vain attempt to warm himself. The year 1828 saw the annexation of the east range: the Geometry School to the north of the tower for the great oriental collections (fig. 65) and the Astronomy School to the south for Douce's collection. In 1835 the tower room (originally a study for the Savilian professors) was shelved to house a selection of finely printed and illustrated publications, and in 1841 it was named the Mason Room to commemorate Robert Mason's generous bequest of £40,000. And, finally, in 1835 the staircases in the north-east and south-east corners

Fig. 64 **Pliny's** *Historia naturalis* **(1476), sumptuously decorated for the Venetian banker Filippo Strozzi.**

LIBRO PRIMO DELLA NATVRALE HISTORIA DI .C. PLINIO SECONDO TRADOCTA IN LINGVA FIOREN TINA PER CHRISTOPHORO LANDINO FIORENTI NO AL SERENISSIMO FERDINANDO RE DI NAPOLI. PREFATIONE

ITERMINAI O GIOCONDISSIMO imperadore con epistola forse di troppa licétia narrarti elibri della historia naturale: opera no uella alle muse romane: nata appresso di me nel lultima genitura. Sia adunq; questa prefatióe uerissima di te métre che gia inuecchia nel grá dissimo tuo padre: per che usando el uerso di Catullo mio compatriota tu soleui pure stima re qualche chosa le mie ciácie. Tu conosci que sta castrense & militare parola. Et lui chome tu sai mutando le prime syllabe si fece alquanto piu duro che non uolea essere stimato da tuoi familiari & serui. Per questo adunq; dittermi nai scriuerti: & áchora per che le nostre chose apparischino & sieno manifeste p questa mia audacia maxime dolédoti tu che pel passato non lhabbi facto in una altra nostra procace epistola. Et accio che tutti glhuomini sappino quanto di pari lomperio techo uiua: Tu elquale hai triomphato & se stato censore & sei uolte cósolo & participe del la tribunitia potesta: Se stato prefecto del pretorio: ilche hai facto piu nobile che tutti glaltri magistrati: perche per piacere a tuo padre & allordine equestre lacceptasti: Et tutte queste cose per rispecto della republica hai facto: Et me chome nel contubernio castrense tractasti: Et certo niéte ha mutato inte lamplitudine & grandezza della tua fortuna: se non che tanto piu possi & uogla giouare: quáto quella e maggiore. Adúq; béche a tutti glaltri huomini sia aperta la uia a impetrare ogni chosa da te uenerádoti: Niente di meno solo laudacia fa che io piu familiarmente te honori. Questa audacia adunq; imputerai a te medesimo: & a te medesimo nel nostro fallo perdonerai. Io mi stroppicciai la faccia: & niente di meno nessuno proficto ho facto: perche per unaltra uia mappanisti grande: & di lontano mi rimuoui con le faccelline del tuo ingegno. Et certo in nexuno piu sfolgora quella: laquale piu ueramente e decta in te che in altri for za deloquentia. In te e quella facundia che alla tribunitia potesta si conuiene: Con quáta risonantia tuoni tu le laude paterne? Có quanta (non sanza amore) dimostri quelle di tuo fratello? Quanto se excellente & sublime nella poetica faculta? O gran fecondita danimo. Certo hai trouato inche modo possi imitare tuo fratello. Ma queste chose chi potrebbe sanza paura considerare: hauendo a uenire al giudicio dellongegno tuo: maxime essendo quello dame prouocato? Certamente non sono in simile conditione quegli che publicano alchuno libro: & quegli che ate glintitolano. Impero che se io lo publicassi & non lo intitolassi ate: potrei dire perche leggi tu queste chose o imperadore: lequali sono scripte albasso uulgo & alla turba de glagricultori & de glar tefici & a quegli che cósumano elloro otio negli studi? Perche adunq; ti fa tu giudice: concio sia che quando io scriuuo questa opera: non thaueua posto nella tauola doue sono descripti egiudici: Et eri di tanta excellentia: che non stimauo che tu ti degnassi scendere si basso? Preterea quando bene non fussi in si excelso grado: niente dimeno gli scriptori comunemente fuggono el giudicio de docti? Questo fa Cicerone: elquale e di tanta eloquentia: che puo sottomettere longegno al giuocho della fortuna: & quel

Fig. 65 **The former Geometry School was refurbished in 1828 to house the oriental collections, photographed c.1940.**

of the quadrangle were removed and each of the towers altered to house three small rooms.

The additional weight of the books on the first floor exacerbated the problems associated with the weakness of the building's structure. In 1825 the Oxford architect Daniel Robertson was commissioned to report on its state. He confirmed earlier opinions that the structure was defective in design, but saw no cause for immediate alarm, except in the tower, where the side walls were cracking. He suggested that the building, which he considered exceedingly plain, would be much improved if its facades were decorated. The university did not follow his advice, and instead, four years later, commissioned plans and estimates for the repair or replacement of the roof and ceiling of the Picture Gallery. The architect, Sir Robert Smirke, supervised a major renovation of the gallery in 1830 and 1831. A new floor was laid, and windows on the north side of both the north and south ranges were blocked up to facilitate the installation of new wall bookcases. All the wainscoting and the bookcases were painted green, the colour made by mixing 'the best Oxford ochre, Turkey umber and Prussian blue'.[10] The lead roof was replaced with copper in order to reduce the pressure of its weight on the walls, and, for the same reason, Smirke advised that the original painted ceiling panels be replaced with plastered deal. Perhaps because this would be cheaper than restoring the old panels, or because the panels were too decayed to be preserved, his advice was followed. The richness of the original decoration can be seen in the twelve panels, salvaged by Bandinel, which spell out 'THOMAS BODLEY'.[11] The carpenter's bill records that he charged £40 more than his estimate for doing the work on the ceiling, to cover the extra care needed to preserve some of the panels as instructed by the librarian. It was during this renovation that the original frieze of painted heads which decorated the walls immediately below the ceiling was plastered over and remained hidden until 1949. A watercolour by Joseph Nash (1809–1878) records the appearance of the gallery after Smirke's renovations (fig. 55).

In 1845 the old Logic School, in the south-east corner of the ground floor, was assigned to the library and fitted out with double-sided cross-cases to maximize its storage capacity. Its cupboards had long been used to store sheet music acquired under copyright. The music remained in piles until, in 1845, Henry East Havergal, chaplain at New College and Christ Church, sorted it into separate sequences of vocal and instrumental music, and arranged each series alphabetically by composer. The same year saw the introduction of steam heating in Duke Humfrey's Library, by means of pipes running along the walls below the windows; but the room remained very cold in winter. In his memoirs Friedrich Max Müller, who first visited Oxford in 1847 and settled there the following year, recalled among his first impressions how the Bodleian seemed 'perfect paradise for a student'. But he revised this opinion when he

> had to sit there every day during a severe winter without any fire, shivering and shaking and almost unable to use my pen, till kind Mr. Coxe, the sub-librarian, took compassion on me and brought me a splendid fur that had been sent him as a present by a Russian scholar, who had witnessed the misery of the librarian in this Siberian library.[12]

The sub-librarian H.O. Coxe frequently noted in his diary the low temperatures in the library: often around freezing point in January

1841, and on one day in March 1845 only 12° F at 7 in the morning. Not surprisingly he found his own solution to the dreadful cold, recording in January 1842 that with 'a new spencer' he felt very comfortable.[13] Inevitably, the installation even of rudimentary heating led to concerns about the risk of fire, concerns that intensified as other libraries began to install supposedly fire-proof iron bookstacks. One expert after another was consulted for advice on how best to strengthen the structure, to expand its capacity for book storage, to improve its heating and to reduce the risk of fire. One after another they warned of the extreme flammability of its ancient wooden floors, ceilings, staircases and bookshelves packed full of books. One calculated that the whole building would burn down within thirty minutes of a fire breaking out. All advocated drastic alterations, none of which was pursued. Instead, in 1856 the curators took the simple step of resolving not to use the heating system. The following year the heating pipes were insulated in slate troughs to prevent contact with the dry timber floors, and iron doors were fitted at both entrances to Arts End to isolate Duke Humfrey's Library from the rest of the building.

By 1850 Bandinel was approaching seventy and his health was failing. He had been absent from the library for all of the winter of 1846–47, and on one day in February 1849 Coxe reckoned that the librarian was close to death. Bandinel rallied, but thereafter played scarcely any part in the running of the Bodleian. The year 1850 was marked by the appointment of a Royal Commission of inquiry into the university, its governance and teaching, which recommended considerable reforms. Its *Report*, published in 1852, provides interesting evidence of how members of the university regarded the Bodleian. There were inevitably complaints about the low temperature in the library in the winter. One senior member recalled how as a young graduate he had been romantic enough to think of working in the Bodleian; but, despite wearing so many layers of warm clothing that he could scarcely move, he still found it too cold to work there for more than two hours at a time. Many considered that the usefulness of the great collections was circumscribed by the library's limited opening hours. College tutors in particular, who were busy teaching students every morning and afternoon in term time, were frustrated by the library closing at 3 in the winter months and at 4 in the summer; but Sir Thomas Bodley's injunction that no 'fire or flame' should be brought into the library was

Fig. 66 **Panel from the original ceiling of the Upper Reading Room with a portrait of Sir Thomas Bodley.**

still adhered to strictly, so no artificial light could be used. The short opening hours led many to suggest that another of Bodley's regulations – the prohibition on the lending of books – ought to be relaxed in order to overcome the inconvenience it caused to many members of the university. In his observations submitted to the commission, Bandinel reported that the librarian of the Advocates' Library in Edinburgh reckoned that between six and seven thousand books had been lost from his library as a result of the facilities afforded to borrowers. It is interesting to contrast the views of Oxford men with those of many foreign scholars who said that 'of all the great libraries of Europe the Bodleian is the most convenient and generally useful'.[14]

Despite failing health and increasingly frequent and lengthy absences from the library, Bandinel clung to office for another ten years, retiring only in 1860. He had proved a formidable Bodley's Librarian, enormously enhancing the library's collections, but his staff had not found him an easy taskmaster. Even the library's governing body of curators were said by one of their number – the Sanskrit scholar Friedrich Max Müller – 'to tremble before him when he told them what had been the invariable custom of the Library, and could not be altered'.[15] Müller also commented in his autobiography on Bandinel's selective courtesy to visitors and on the language in which he gave orders to his staff, including the sub-librarians – 'such as would not now be addressed to any menial'.[16] Bandinel's tendency to lash with his tongue may well have been learned on the quarter-deck of HMS *Victory*, and it was the opinion of Sir Edmund Craster, writing in 1952, that 'other librarians since his day have been as autocratic, none so terrifying'.[17] W.D. Macray, who had been a member of Bandinel's staff for twenty years, passed a very similar verdict on the librarian's character, admitting that Bandinel sometimes lacked 'the general courtesy which should be exhibited to all duly qualified readers alike. The library too often seemed to be regarded as a rich preserve for favoured students, while the unfavoured were viewed somewhat jealously, not to say suspiciously. And all the staff trembled at Jupiter's nod.'[18]

Henry Octavius Coxe, sub-librarian since 1839 (fig. 67), had been impatient for Bandinel to retire but had continued the systematic cataloguing of manuscripts as his principal task. For the last ten years or so he had been regarded by the curators as to all intents and purposes in charge, but, with Bandinel still in post, he had been unable to implement any much-needed reforms. Born in 1811, the eighth son of the Revd Richard Coxe, he was educated first at Westminster School, then by his brother who was curate at Dover. He came to Worcester College, Oxford, and on graduating joined the staff of the Department of Manuscripts at the British Museum in 1833. He was ordained the same year and held a succession of curacies, first in London, then in Oxford diocese – at Culham, Tubney, Yarnton and Wytham –becoming rector of Wytham in 1868, where the parsonage provided a welcome country residence. He was unanimously elected Bodley's Librarian in November 1860.

Whereas Bandinel's reputation rests on his skill in enormously expanding and enhancing the Bodleian collections for the use of established scholars, Coxe's librarianship was most notable for the means by which, in keeping with the recommendations of the Royal Commission of 1850, he made the library more accessible to the university at large. Macray considered Coxe to have been the ideal man for the job – 'one who with the knowledge of the wants of the new time, possessed respect for and sympathy with the arrangements of the old, and so was best qualified to act the part of the true reformer, constructive and not destructive'.[19] As we have seen, the library's limited opening hours significantly reduced its usefulness. An opportunity to solve this major problem arose when the Radcliffe Library of scientific and medical books was transferred from the magnificent domed building just to the south of the Bodleian to the new University Museum in the Parks in 1861. The Radcliffe Trustees offered their beautiful eighteenth-century building to the university for use as a second Bodleian reading room, and their offer was immediately accepted. At the end of December 1861, the move from the overcrowded rooms in the Schools Quadrangle of those modern publications most in demand began, and the Radcliffe Camera became a Bodleian reading room on 27 January 1862, from the outset – thanks to its gas lighting – open for twelve hours a day. Arranged on the shelves by subject, the modern books were immediately available for study, alongside periodicals and reviews. Over twenty years later, Macray applauded the achievement of making separate provision for both traditional and more up-to-date readers: 'the old room [Duke Humfrey's Library] remained consecrated to the study of the Past, and the new [the Radcliffe Camera] was given to the Present'.[20] The university was persuaded to make an annual grant to help finance the new operation: £200 in 1861, increased to £300 four years later. However, general Bodleian funds had to cover the remainder of the cost, chiefly the wages of the staff required throughout the long working day (three or four assistants and a janitor). The building itself remained the property of the trustees, who continued to be responsible for its maintenance. In 1863 the ground floor of the Camera – until then an elegant ambulatory open to the public – was enclosed and the outer arches converted into windows. The walls in the new room were lined with bookshelves and the Bodleian thus acquired an additional 20,000 metres for the storage of its ever-expanding collections of books.

Before becoming librarian, Coxe had proposed a new system of cataloguing the library's books as another significant means (alongside longer opening hours) of making its collections more readily available, especially to those members of the university who were not established scholars, and whose interests had been neglected under the old regime. The published catalogue of 1843 and its supplement of 1851 had not included the large collections of Francis Douce and Richard Gough, while current acquisitions (those most likely to be required by younger members of the university) were recorded only in a card index. Work on the new catalogue began in 1859, adopting the 'moveable slip' method of the British Museum. Each catalogue entry was written on a slip of paper, which was pasted onto a page in a book of blank leaves from which it could be lifted and re-pasted when the insertion of further entries made re-spacing necessary – a process that continued in use until the 1980s. The catalogue for the entire collection of printed books was completed in 1879, and thereafter new accessions were incorporated as they came in.

This major undertaking needed many more staff. At first one member of the existing establishment (Alfred Hackman) was assigned to it, with the assistance of three new recruits, but by 1862 the complement had to be doubled to two teams of four cataloguers. From 1865 to 1879 the university made an annual grant of £500 towards the cost of producing the catalogue, but by 1875 the wages of the cataloguing staff had risen to £1,133, and the balance had yet again to be met from general library funds. The library's income came from three sources: the regular grant from the university (which rose from £850 in 1856 to £2,800 in 1861, and to £3,350 in 1876), investments in government funds (consols), and rents from houses in London and land in Berkshire. By 1861 the library's deficit was almost £1,500, and the curators attempted to remedy this with the sale of duplicates from the collections. A five-day sale at Sotheby's in May 1862 realized £766 and a second in April 1865 made £750; but these could only provide short-term relief.

In these straitened circumstances, it is not surprising that Coxe was unable to make any spectacular purchases. Indeed, the annual expenditure on books and manuscripts had fallen to around £1,000

Fig. 67 **Portrait of H.O. Coxe, Bodley's Librarian from 1860 to 1881, by George Frederick Watts, 1876.**

by 1879. The most significant acquisitions during his librarianship were transfers to the Bodleian from other institutions: Elias Ashmole's books and manuscripts (fig. 68), and those of his fellow antiquaries William Dugdale, Anthony Wood and John Aubrey from the Ashmolean Museum; oriental manuscripts from the Radcliffe Trustees, and the records from the registry of the archdeaconry of Oxford. Shortly after he became librarian Coxe lost a potential acquisition that would have put Bandinel's in the shade, but the negotiation had begun years earlier – in 1827 – when the omnivorous collector Sir Thomas Phillipps had offered to sell his manuscripts to the Bodleian on condition that he would have sole management of them during his lifetime. The curators declined the offer, no doubt wary of this sort of commitment to a man who was only thirty-four years old. (Their caution was justified, for Phillipps lived to the ripe old age of eighty.) He reopened negotiations in 1851, with an offer to deposit his manuscripts temporarily but with no promises about their ultimate destination. By 1856 Coxe thought he had managed to clinch a deal that involved the gift of the collection, with Phillipps as its custodian; but the owner withdrew as the offer of accommodation in the vice-chancellor's rooms in the Clarendon Building was for a limited period of two years. Two years later another agreement was almost reached, this time involving the housing not just of the manuscripts but also of their owner in the Ashmolean Museum building in Broad Street. Once again Phillipps drew back, changing his proposed gift to 2,000 manuscripts – only one twentieth of his collection. The Radcliffe Camera, assigned for use by the Bodleian in 1861, seemed a better location, although Phillipps was concerned that it lacked a bed. As an alternative he offered to give the whole of his collection to the library, on condition that he was made Bodley's Librarian, with (he magnanimously suggested) Coxe 'of course becoming second'. It says much for the patience and courtesy of Coxe, who had been in office only for a few months, that he allowed Phillipps the last word in their lengthy correspondence – a diatribe on the theme of Bodley's Librarian being too concerned about his own personal dignity to value 'the glory and honour of acquiring for Bodley such a collection as mine'.[21]

Fig. 68 **The library's medieval holdings were enhanced by the transfer of Elias Ashmole's manuscripts in 1860, including the early thirteenth-century 'Ashmole Bestiary'.**

ditur: a dinsu ipeti ab ecthre libratur. s; p appetitum
uentris iram expetit seseq; a sublimbus repente de or
sum fundit. Sic sic humanum genus in parente pmo
a dma desublimibs errurt. op nimirum condicionis sue
dignitas in racionem excelsitudinem. op in aeris libta
te suspenderat; S; op contra preceptum cibum comitig.
p uentris concupiscenciam a dterras uenit. z op p uola
tum cartuibz pascitur. quia illa libera contemplacio
nis inspiracula pdidit. z deorsum corporeis uolupta
tibz letatur. Item de aqla. Renouabitur ut aquile
iuuentus tua. Solet de aquila dum senectute pmit.
op rostrum illius adunccetur. ita ut sum ere cibum
nequeat s; macie languescat; y euens ad petram
rostrum accuit. z sic cibum capiens. z iterum iuuenes
cit petra est xpc aquila quilibet iustus. qui ad petram
rostrum accuit. dum seipm xpo p bonam opera cione
conformem reddit.

Apes dicte.
ul op sepe
ditz alligerit. us
p eo op sine pedi
bus nascuntur.
s; am postea z
pedes z pennas
accipiunt. he sol
lertes in generan
di mellis officio
assignatas in eo
lunt sedes. domicilia inennarabili arte componunt.

Fig. 69 **The basement of the Radcliffe Camera, *c*.1940.**

Much of Coxe's term of office was taken up with a protracted debate within the university about the use of the library and the Schools with which it shared the quadrangle. As we have seen, the library had between 1789 and 1845 gradually taken over all the rooms on the first floor and the Logic School on the ground floor, filling them with books and manuscripts. The allocation of the Radcliffe Camera postponed the Bodleian's need for further expansion in the Schools Quadrangle and, although it had been agreed that the library would eventually take over the rest of the rooms on the ground floor, the university continued to use them for lectures and examinations. Between 1860 and 1875 potential sites and designs for a new building to house the Schools were investigated, but no consensus was reached, and in the course of the discussions it was proposed that it would be better to move the Bodleian to a new building on a site that allowed for expansion. The library's governing body of curators was divided on the issue, but, to the librarian's great relief, eventually voted against the proposal in 1875. The following year the university accepted the plans of the architect T.G. Jackson for the building of new Schools on the High Street, and there was at last a reasonable prospect of the ground-floor rooms of the Schools Quadrangle being released for library use.

Meanwhile it had become clear that the fifteenth-century building housing Duke Humfrey's Library and beneath it the Divinity School was in need of major repair. During the long vacation of 1876 the lead roof over Arts End, Duke Humfrey's Library and Selden End was replaced with copper, both to reduce its weight and to eliminate the risk of it dropping molten lead on the library should fire ever break out. To facilitate work on the roof, the seventeenth-century galleries above the windows on the north and south walls of Duke Humfrey's Library were removed and their contents transferred to the Picture Gallery. After the renovation they were not returned, because it was thought that the weight of the books was contributing to the stress on the structure. Their removal left expanses of blank wall which were filled with a series of portraits of founders of colleges, painted (perhaps around 1670) as gifts to the Bodleian. These had originally hung in the Picture Gallery, but in the mid-nineteenth century were to be seen on the staircase.[22] At the same time work on the floor necessitated the removal of Sir Thomas Bodley's book presses. Extraordinary though it seems to us today, some of the curators opposed their replacement, and advocated stripping and modernizing the reading room. Fortunately, they were outvoted. The quiet of the library continued to be disturbed for many years as the external stonework was gradually refaced, and pinnacles, windowsills and mullions replaced.

For most of his life Coxe was physically robust, and an enthusiastic rider, but as he approached fifty-five his health began to fail. After an operation in the autumn of 1874 he referred frequently in his diary to his 'malady'. At Michaelmas 1880 he was taken gravely ill and died on 8 July 1881. Accounts of his character are remarkably consistent. J.W. Burgon, in his *Lives of Twelve Good Men*, described Coxe at the time of his death as 'perhaps the most generally known and universally beloved character in Oxford'.[23] Contemporaries refer to his kindliness, courtesy and charm, which inspired respect and affection in everyone he met. His skill as a mimic and storyteller made him excellent company. Archdeacon Edwin Palmer's verdict was that Oxford would find it difficult 'to get so good a librarian as Coxe ... as loveable a librarian it is out of the question to expect'.[24]

An influential group of the curators (the committee of thirteen senior university men, including the vice-chancellor, the proctors and the Regius professors, who formed the library's governing body) thought that what the library needed was someone to undertake a thoroughgoing modernization, and so they departed from the tradition of appointing fellows of Oxford colleges who were established scholars and chose a young man, Edward Williams Byron Nicholson, who had spent the last eight years reviving an almost moribund institution, albeit one much smaller than the Bodleian – the London Institution (fig. 70). Nicholson came from a background unlike those of any of his predecessors. Born in 1849, the only child of a sailor and an actress, he was educated at a village school in north Wales, then at Tonbridge School in Kent, where, as school librarian, he compiled and published a catalogue of its books. He won a classics scholarship to Trinity College, Oxford, in 1867 but switched from classics to law and modern history, in which he achieved only a third-class degree in 1872. Meanwhile he had been a founder member of the University Chess Club (where he was renowned for his bizarre opening moves), and librarian and treasurer of the Union, for which he produced a cogent report on the inadequacies of its library (among them shortage of space, an inappropriate classification system and an unusable catalogue).

After a short spell teaching at the Rookery School in Headington, Oxford, Nicholson moved to London on his appointment as librarian of the London Institution, where he thoroughly overhauled its programme of lectures and its lending library. He was also the prime mover in the organization of an international conference of librarians in London in 1877, at which the United Kingdom Library Association and the Metropolitan Free Libraries Committee were formed. But over the next few years his outspoken and controversial comments on public library matters came to be increasingly resented by colleagues, who, unlike Nicholson, worked in the public sector. His failure to consult added to the problems and in 1881 he resigned from the association's council – impatient of its failure (as he put it) 'to instigate one single improvement however trifling in library-management or library-appliances'.[25]

Immediately on his appointment Nicholson set about the modernization of the Bodleian. Keen to make the library more accessible to members of the university and to alert them and others to developments, he wrote 'Bodleian Notes' for the *Oxford Review* from

Fig. 70 **Photograph of E.W.B. Nicholson, Bodley's Librarian from 1882 to 1912.**

1885 to 1887. In these chatty columns he explained policies, answered complaints, gave an account of purchases and donations, joked about the odd forms of address foreigners used in writing to the Bodleian and its librarian, and reported news such as the deposit of college manuscripts. He also had an ulterior motive: 'to give the University a much better idea of the work done for it by the Library – [for] no work is less obvious to the casual observer than the bulk of that done in libraries, none is less demonstrative of its own amount, its difficulties, or the high pressure at which it often has to be executed'.[26] In 1888 there followed a much more substantial publication, a sixty-six-page report on the Bodleian from 1882 to 1887, prepared 'for the information of members of the university and of other persons who may be interested in the Bodleian' – another example of Nicholson's awareness of the importance of good public relations. He summarized his first five years in office as 'a time of transition and reorganization' and was able to report significant progress on many fronts.[27]

The library's chronic shortage of storage space had begun to be alleviated. After the completion of the university's new Examination Schools in the High Street in the summer of 1882, additional space had become available on the ground floor of the Schools Quadrangle and between 1883 and 1890 the rooms had been fitted out with bookshelves. The traditional wooden bookcases around the walls were supplemented with fifteen-foot-high cross-cases, which had the added advantage of giving some support to the sagging floors above them. Nicholson brushed aside concerns about the hazards of fetching books from these double-decker bookcases, asserting that 'librarians no more mind going up a ladder than sailors mind going up rigging'.[28] The basement of the adjacent Sheldonian Theatre had in 1887 been converted into a bookstack for newspapers and other little-used printed material. The storage capacity of the shelves throughout the library was gradually being increased by the introduction of classification (and thus storage) of volumes by size. The number of days each year when the Radcliffe Camera was closed had been reduced and its opening hours extended.

The lamentable shortage of staff had been alleviated without crippling the library's finances by the employment of boys to undertake routine library tasks, freeing up the time of the more senior assistants for cataloguing. 'Since the beginning of 1883,' Nicholson reported, 'there have been employed never less than six boys, and sometimes as many as ten.'[29] They were divided into two groups: the younger, lower-paid boys doing the fetching, and the older ones the replacing of the books required by readers (fig. 71). If they had sufficient knowledge of Latin and modern European languages, boys were also employed in revising the catalogue slips. Nicholson saw school leavers not simply as cheap labour, but as a pool of recruits who could be trained for eventual promotion to more senior permanent posts. In the early years he devoted

Fig. 71 **Photograph of 'Bodleian under-assistants', also known as 'Bodley boys', 1906.**

an inordinate amount of his time to teaching and examining them in the private studies they were required to pursue outside their working hours. Always concerned for their welfare, Nicholson even insisted that all the boys should learn to swim – this was after one of them had drowned in the River Cherwell. Some senior staff and curators were less enthusiastic about having boys between the ages of fourteen and eighteen let loose in the library. The sub-librarian Falconer Madan considered the boys unreliable and inaccurate, and the classical scholar and curator Henry Chandler, parodying Nicholson's constant complaints about the Bodleian being undermanned, described it as 'considerably overboyed'. A further economy in staffing costs achieved by Nicholson was in the transcription of the catalogue slips. (Three copies were needed: one for the main catalogue in Arts End, one for the catalogue in the Radcliffe Camera and the third for use in the projected subject catalogue.) In 1884 the rate of pay was halved (from twopence to a penny a slip), and the task taken from the boys and given to girls who did no other work in the library and were prepared to work at the lower rate. The first to be recruited were two daughters of a former assistant and the sister of another. Nicholson went on to recruit many women to the extra staff, drawing on the increasing number of women who had followed degree courses, and using their newly acquired skills to calendar charters, list early books and, from 1907, revise the general catalogue. In this, as in so many other library matters, he introduced innovations that, though criticized at the time, developed into standard practice.

Nicholson's report of 1888 drew attention to an anomaly that had crept into the library statute in the course of revisions in 1856 and 1873, and summarized the course of events. The first statutes of 1610 had, in line with Sir Thomas Bodley's wishes, explicitly forbidden the lending of any item from the collections. This prohibition had been criticized from time to time by succeeding generations, and matters came to a head with the Royal Commission of 1850. Many members of the university argued that the Bodleian's limited opening hours hampered their research and that lending would be a sensible way to make the collections more useful. Others vehemently opposed this break with tradition, citing the loss of books from lending libraries and the inconvenience to other scholars when the book they wanted to consult was not available in the library. The commission's report recommended that if the library had more than one copy of a book, the duplicate

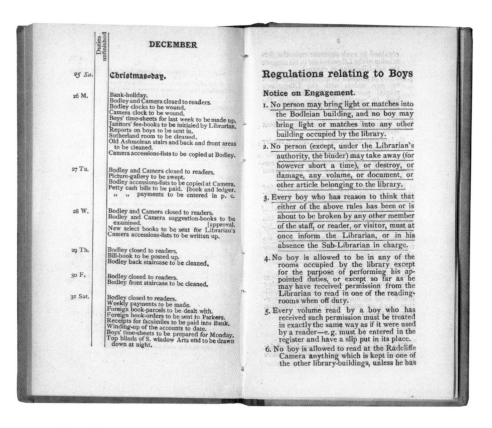

Duties unfinished

25 Su. | **Christmas=day.**

26 M.
Bank-holiday.
Bodley and Camera closed to readers.
Bodley clocks to be wound.
Camera clock to be wound.
Boys' time-sheets for last week to be made up.
Janitors' fee-books to be initialed by Librarian.
Reports on boys to be sent in.
Sutherland room to be cleaned.
Old Ashmolean stairs and back and front areas to be cleaned.
Camera accessions-lists to be copied at Bodley.

27 Tu.
Bodley and Camera closed to readers.
Picture-gallery to be swept.
Bodley accessions-lists to be copied at Camera.
Petty cash bills to be paid. [book and ledger.
  „   „   payments to be entered in p. c.

28 W.
Bodley and Camera closed to readers.
Bodley and Camera suggestion-books to be examined.   [approval.
New select books to be sent for Librarian's
Camera accessions-lists to be written up.

29 Th.
Bodley closed to readers.
Bill-book to be posted up.
Bodley back staircase to be cleaned.

30 F.
Bodley closed to readers.
Bodley front staircase to be cleaned.

31 Sat.
Bodley closed to readers.
Weekly payments to be made.
Foreign book-parcels to be dealt with.
Foreign book-orders to be sent to Parkers.
Receipts for facsimiles to be paid into Bank.
Winding-up of the accounts to date.
Boys' time-sheets to be prepared for Monday.
Top blinds of S. window Arts end to be drawn down at night.

Regulations relating to Boys

Notice on Engagement.

1. No person may bring light or matches into the Bodleian building, and no boy may bring light or matches into any other building occupied by the library.

2. No person (except, under the Librarian's authority, the binder) may take away (for however short a time), or destroy, or damage, any volume, or document, or other article belonging to the library.

3. Every boy who has reason to think that either of the above rules has been or is about to be broken by any other member of the staff, or reader, or visitor, must at once inform the Librarian, or in his absence the Sub-Librarian in charge.

4. No boy is allowed to be in any of the rooms occupied by the library except for the purpose of performing his appointed duties, or except so far as he may have received permission from the Librarian to read in one of the reading-rooms when off duty.

5. Every volume read by a boy who has received such permission must be treated in exactly the same way as if it were used by a reader—e.g. must be entered in the register and have a slip put in its place.

6. No boy is allowed to read at the Radcliffe Camera anything which is kept in one of the other library-buildings, unless he has

Fig. 72 Regulations relating to 'Bodley boys', in Nicholson's *Staff Kalendar* (1904).

should be available for loan. There is no evidence that this was followed up, but when the library statutes were revised in 1856, the clause forbidding lending was quietly dropped. By the late 1860s the curators were regularly authorizing loans of books and manuscripts for senior members of the university to use in their college rooms. In 1873 they delegated decisions on applications to borrow to the librarian. Coxe had been less liberal than the curators, but an increasing number of readers, and university institutions such as the Clarendon Press and the Ashmolean Museum, came to be recognized as legitimate borrowers. Nicholson was keen to have the policy on lending clarified and codified, and a committee of the curators set about drafting new statutes. When they were presented for endorsement to Congregation (the body of senior members with ultimate responsibility for university legislation) in 1887, opponents of lending took the opportunity to propose an amendment that deprived the curators and librarian of the power to grant loans without the authorization of Convocation (then the main governing body of the university) in each instance. It was passed by 106 votes to 60, and routine lending came to an end.

By 1910, Nicholson had brought about many improvements in the library. First, storage space had been further increased by extending the shelving on the ground floor of the Radcliffe Camera, by fitting out the large History School on the north side of the ground floor of the Schools quadrangle with iron stacks along the lines of recent installations in the British Museum and the Public Record Office, and by securing the allocation to the Bodleian of the basement of the Old Ashmolean (in 1895) and of a large cellar under the new Examinations Schools (in 1904). Then in 1909 excavations began prior to the construction of an underground bookstore immediately to the north of the Camera – an idea Nicholson had first put forward in the mid-1890s. Constructed of brick, iron and concrete, it was fire-proof, divided by an open iron grating into two storeys and fitted out with iron shelving that pulled out endways. The design of the shelving is attributed to William Gladstone, who, on a visit to the Bodleian in April 1888, sketched out the design on the back of an envelope that survives in the Bodleian's archives. The new bookstore had an enormous capacity – optimistically estimated as sufficient for the library's needs for at least fifty years. It was not, alas, completed in Nicholson's lifetime, but was one of the most important achievements of his librarianship.

Facilities for readers were also much improved in Nicholson's time. In 1888 the gallery in the Camera Reading Room was fitted out with thirty-six more readers' places, and easier access to the gallery was provided by the installation of two spiral iron staircases. In 1905 electric light was introduced throughout the Camera, giving much better illumination for reading than had been possible with the old gas lamps, which dated back to the 1830s. Even more significant for future developments in the Bodleian as a whole was Nicholson's idea of transforming the Picture Gallery on the top floor of the Schools Quadrangle into a reading room, which later came to be known as the Upper Reading Room. He had first articulated the idea as early as 1884, and further developed it in 1892. It was only in 1902 that the proposal for the new reading room was formally adopted by the curators and in 1907 that the north range and half of the east range were equipped with readers' desks. The windows that had been blocked during Smirke's reconstruction in 1831 were uncovered, heating was installed and the shelves were filled with the learned periodicals that were increasingly in demand. He also introduced a 'reserve counter' – now a standard feature in all Bodleian reading rooms – which made it possible for readers to reserve books for their own use without unduly inconveniencing others. So far as many readers were concerned, Nicholson was definitely making improvements. Indeed, Sir Edmund Craster, in his *History of the Bodleian Library*, estimates that the number of readers increased by 150 per cent during Nicholson's period of office.

Nicholson made less progress on the cataloguing front. His ambitious plans for the revision and printing of the general catalogue of printed books were not realized – partly through his decision to continue the subject catalogue and his insistence on over-elaborate cataloguing, and partly through lack of funds. But when money at last became available, a start was made on revision in 1907 and also on many separate projects, such as the calendaring of charters and the cataloguing of incunabula, music and maps. Meanwhile the two sub-librarians, Falconer Madan and Adolf Neubauer, produced published catalogues of a substantial part of the western and Hebrew manuscript collections, and a start was made on cataloguing the last forty years' acquisitions of printed, mainly sheet, music which had come under copyright. Early in Nicholson's librarianship, in 1885, the music collections were greatly enhanced by the transfer of the library of the university's Music School. The school had been established with an endowment from William Heather in 1627 in a small room on the first floor of the Schools Quadrangle, to provide training in the theory and practice of music. It moved to more spacious accommodation on the ground floor in the south-east corner of the quadrangle in 1656, when John Wilson, formerly musician to Charles I, became professor. Wilson had many of the school's instruments (an organ, a harpsichord and four viols) repaired, and began building up its collections of music. Under the care of a succession of professors it came to be regarded as the university's principal resource in its field. This was no doubt the reason why Richard Rawlinson, while bequeathing the bulk of his great collections to the Bodleian, left his printed and manuscript music to the Music School. The material transferred to the Bodleian in 1885

included some 880 manuscripts, mainly works of English composers, among them John Taverner, William Lawes and William Boyce.

The number of permanent regular staff increased very little under Nicholson: in 1882 it stood at eighteen and it was still only twenty-one in 1911. What did substantially increase was the number of 'extra staff' – a combination of the boys (fourteen in 1911), the catalogue revisers (ten since 1907) and seventeen part-time and/or temporary employees, many of them women, who together brought the staff complement to sixty-two.

Nicholson's undoubted administrative skills are illustrated in his *Staff Kalendar*. It began as a carefully thought-out work schedule for each member of staff, to enable them to perform their allotted tasks without frequent instruction and constant supervision. It developed into a comprehensive plan for the day-to-day running of the library.

It was published annually and has come to be recognized as the precursor of library management manuals throughout the western world. Late in his career, Nicholson pioneered another development in the staffing of the Bodleian, with the appointment in 1910 of the first woman to the permanent staff. Although this now seems unremarkable, in 1910 none of the major libraries in the United Kingdom had employed women on anything but a casual basis, and the appointment of Frances Underhill (fig. 73), who later became superintendent of catalogue revision, was a remarkable Bodleian first. It does no credit to the curators or to sub-librarian Madan that Nicholson had to battle to make this breakthrough.

One significant purchase made during Nicholson's term in office attracted no opposition in or outside the university. Early in 1905 a young graduate of Magdalen College sought advice from the library on how to repair a dilapidated copy of the First Folio edition of Shakespeare's plays, published in 1623, which had been in his family for generations. Examination of the book by Strickland Gibson, who had been recruited to the library by Nicholson in 1895 as an assistant and was already developing his skills in bibliography and early bindings, revealed not only that it had been bound in Oxford in the early seventeenth century, but also that it was the copy that had originally belonged to the Bodleian and, presumably, been discarded when superseded by the third edition of 1664. The fascinating and most unusual history of this copy of the First Folio made it a particularly interesting item and led Henry Folger, the great American collector, to offer the owners £3,000 for it. Nicholson promptly appealed to all members of the university, past and present, for help to match this offer and to buy it for the Bodleian. With the deadline for raising the necessary sum fast approaching, Sir William Osler, Regius Professor of Medicine at Oxford and a curator of the Bodleian, appealed for help from his fellow Canadian Lord Strathcona, a noted philanthropist. With Lord Strathcona's generous contribution the required sum was raised and the library was able to restore to its shelves the copy of the most famous book published in England in the early seventeenth century. It was then by far the most expensive book or manuscript the library had ever bought.

One of the many, and in this case unjust, criticisms of Nicholson was that he was not interested in augmenting the library's manuscript

Fig. 74 'St Margaret's Gospels', eleventh century.

collections; but it was he who in 1887 placed a speculative bid of £10 on a manuscript described in Sotheby's sale catalogue as a fourteenth-century manuscript of the Gospels. No one else was interested in buying the little volume and the Bodleian acquired it for £6. Falconer Madan immediately recognized it as dating from the eleventh century and in the course of cataloguing was able to identify its owner as Margaret, granddaughter of the Saxon king Edmund Ironside, who married Malcolm Canmore, king of Scotland in about 1067. A Latin poem in the manuscript recounts, as does St Margaret's biographer, how this her favourite Gospel book had been lost on one of her journeys and found only hours later at the bottom of a stream she had forded. When recovered it proved by a miracle to be undamaged despite its immersion. To this day, the outer leaves of the manuscript may possibly show signs of damp (fig. 74).

Unfortunately, despite his many achievements, there was a downside both for Nicholson personally and for the institution to which he was devoted. In 1882 he was a young man in a hurry and within a few years he had managed to alienate his senior staff and many of the curators who had appointed him. Henry Bradshaw – librarian of Cambridge University – had warned him 'not to despise the traditions of a place where good traditions are of such vital importance if that aroma is to be preserved which gives a charm to the Bodleian and places it at the head of all the libraries in Europe'.[30] By 1889 Nicholson himself was regretting that he had failed to follow this advice. In an extraordinary report to the curators that year he advised that any new librarian 'coming, as I did, into the Bodleian from elsewhere [should] … give himself plenty of time to acquire sympathy with all that deserves perpetuation in the system and spirit of the library; and, before deciding on anything new, will try to realize and give full weight to all objections to it'.[31] But Nicholson was, alas, incapable of following his own advice, and seems to have learned nothing from the experience of his first seven years. His relations with the senior sub-librarian, Falconer Madan, rapidly deteriorated after the first eighteen months or so. Madan made inspections of the library whenever Nicholson was away and began to keep a record of every mistake Nicholson made and to report to the curators behind Nicholson's back. Before long Bodley's Librarian and the man who should have been his second in command were not on speaking terms, and communicated with each other only in writing. Each kept the other's letters and they make unedifying reading. When in 1890 they clashed publicly over Madan's proposal for a summary catalogue of the manuscript collections, the curators sided with Madan and adopted his scheme, despite Nicholson's vehement opposition. Thenceforth Madan concentrated on cataloguing manuscripts and took no part in library administration. Nicholson battled on alone, trying to run a huge library which, as he put it in a letter of 1895, was 'under-roomed, under-monied and under-manned, with only the rudiments of organization, with mountains of arrears of work inherited from previous generations',[32] and with what seemed like a regular supply of elected curators whose only aim was to 'fetter' him. The number of committees set up by the curators to discuss the minutiae of a wide variety of library matters does now seem to justify Nicholson's complaints of undue interference.

It is small wonder that Nicholson's health suffered. As early as 1889, the Regius Professor of Modern History, Frederick York Powell, one of the *ex officio* curators, writing to him in May, suggested that he take a rest from the library 'now that the weather is improving and there is no

Fig. 75 **The Proscholium, Bodley's 'vaulted walk', 1903.**

immediate pressure ... *Don't pitch this letter away, without thinking of it again.*'[33] Nicholson did keep the letter, but there is no evidence to suggest that he followed Powell's wise advice. He continued to work relentlessly, refusing to delegate any but the simplest of tasks, and had a serious breakdown in health in 1902 from which he never fully recovered. On his return to work after that illness, he discovered that bicycle racks had been placed in the Proscholium, which was then the entrance to the Divinity School and, so far as Nicholson was concerned, hallowed as Thomas Bodley's 'vaulted walke' (fig. 75). He immediately went into battle to save it from what he considered sacrilege. In so doing he was taking on the vice-chancellor and the curators of the University Chest, but he kept at it for three years and finally, after an impassioned letter addressed to all resident senior members of the university, he managed to get the vice-chancellor's formal proposal defeated in a vote in Convocation. It is in many ways an amusing story, with Nicholson himself physically removing the offending racks time and again, and the vice-chancellor having them replaced, but his campaign must have made him more enemies throughout the university and reinforced the widely held view that he was an outsider who would never understand Oxford ways. In March 1912 he was persuaded to take a year off work for the sake of his health. Within a week he died, on 17 March. It was not until 1979 that the university next appointed a professional librarian to head the Bodleian.

The account of Nicholson's funeral in the *Oxford Times* noted the attendance of junior library staff – the boys, assistants and catalogue revisers, whose confidence and respect he enjoyed, in marked contrast to his strained relations with senior staff and curators. The newspaper published on the same day an obituary appreciating Nicholson's remarkable record as Bodley's Librarian, rehearsing in some detail the achievements of the last thirty years. R.H. Hill, who had been a graduate assistant in the Bodleian from 1908 and rose to be its first secretary (that is, chief administrator), addressed the Library Association in 1940 on 'The Bodleian since 1882', with the express intention of remedying the 'scant justice ever done' to Nicholson.[34] Strickland Gibson, the first Keeper of Printed Books in the Bodleian, who had started his distinguished library career under Nicholson, published 'Some Impressions' of him in 1949, on the centenary of his birth, endorsing the view that Nicholson was 'a great librarian' and recalling how in his later years his staff referred to Nicholson as 'the Great Man'.[35] G.W. Wheeler, superintendent of the Radcliffe Camera, and expert on Bodleian cataloguing and classification, who had known the library before Nicholson arrived, wrote in 1940: 'I have always regarded him as almost the re-founder of the Library.'[36]

The 1800s were for the library, as for the university, a century of growth and change. The collections grew in spectacular fashion through both gifts and purchases, and significant progress was made with the cataloguing that advertised them throughout the scholarly world. In the second half of the century the Bodleian came to be regarded as an essential resource for the whole university, as the acquisition of the Radcliffe Camera enabled it to extend its opening hours and to provide facilities for an increased number of readers, including undergraduates and college lecturers, not just for the small group of eminent scholars who used the manuscript and rare book collections in Duke Humfrey's Library. Edward Nicholson, despite opposition from many in the university who disliked his enlightened changes, succeeded in modernizing the Bodleian and preparing it for the years ahead.

MADAN
ÆT LXIX

CHAPTER 6

A new century
and a New Bodleian,
1912–1945

I N JUNE 1912 FALCONER MADAN was unanimously
elected to succeed Nicholson as Bodley's Librarian (fig. 76). Born
in April 1851, the fifth and youngest son of George Madan, vicar of
Cam in Gloucestershire, Madan was educated at Crewkerne Grammar
School and Marlborough College, and in 1870 won a scholarship to
Brasenose College, where he studied *Literae Humaniores* (classics,
philosophy and ancient history). He was elected a fellow of Brasenose
in 1876; although his fellowship lapsed on his appointment as sub-
librarian at the Bodleian in 1880, it was renewed in 1889 (when he
was also appointed university lecturer in palaeography, a post he held
until 1913). Madan was sixty-one years old when he became Bodley's
Librarian and had served on the staff for thirty-two years. He had
already made a major contribution to the Bodleian – his cataloguing
of the western manuscript collections. Three volumes of the *Summary
Catalogue of Western Manuscripts*, all entirely his work, had been
published in 1895, 1897 and 1905, making known to researchers
throughout the world the great collections acquired by the Bodleian in
the eighteenth and nineteenth centuries. He had begun to catalogue the
manuscripts acquired in the first half of the seventeenth century, when

Fig. 76 **Portrait of Falconer Madan, Bodley's Librarian from 1912
to 1919, by Percy Bigland, 1920.**

his appointment as librarian brought his scholarly work temporarily to a halt. To this day Madan's descriptions of the manuscripts are regarded as models of their kind, distilling his wide knowledge and his grasp of minute scholarly detail into entries that are entirely accurate and admirably succinct. His classical training was also put to good use in the cataloguing of printed books (including early editions) in Latin and Greek. In the course of this work he developed an interest in printing and the book trade, and in 1895 published the first volume of *Oxford Books* – a monumental work comprising a full-scale bibliography of books printed in Oxford up to 1680 as well as of works relating to the city and university. The second volume followed in 1912, but the third had to await his retirement and was eventually published in 1931.

It now seems ironic that when he became librarian Madan, having vehemently criticized – publicly as well as privately – most of Nicholson's decisions on library matters, should have continued almost all of his predecessor's policies, albeit in a calmer and more measured way. Both Nicholson and Madan opposed all suggestions that, in order to relieve Bodley's Librarian of some of the day-to-day responsibilities involved in running a rapidly expanding library, specialist departments should be established, with the sub-librarians in charge of administering the collections (which hitherto they had only been responsible for cataloguing). Both were determined not to delegate any powers, preferring to oversee every aspect of library administration personally. Both were hampered by a chronic shortage of funds, which prevented spectacular acquisitions and thwarted any plans they might have formed for reorganizing or extending the library. Madan's term of office was, moreover, dominated by the First World War.

Nicholson had, as we have seen, begun the enormous task of revising the general catalogue of printed books in 1907, with a view to its publication, and had appointed women to do the work. Unfortunately, he was by then already a sick man and the cataloguing revision staff lacked the leadership and supervision that such a complicated task required. On becoming librarian in 1912, Madan immediately appointed a superintendent of the nine revisers and the work proceeded more surely, although not as swiftly as the librarian and curators might have hoped. By 1915 only one quarter of the catalogue had been dealt with and it was decided to revise in a more summary fashion. The drain of regular staff into the armed forces as the war progressed necessitated the transfer of the women cataloguers to fill their places and revision of the catalogue ground to a halt in 1916.

In January 1915 Madan reported that sixteen members of his staff of sixty-eight were absent on military service; a year later the number had risen to twenty-two and by February 1917 to thirty. In March of that year the first of the two members of the Bodleian staff who lost their lives during the war was killed in action – Lieutenant R.A. Abrams of the Sherwood Foresters – at the age of twenty-eight. He was followed in November by Lieutenant H.J. Dunn of the Royal West Kent Regiment, who was also twenty-eight years old and had joined the library staff at the age of fourteen. Both were commemorated, together with 137 other librarians who had lost their lives in the war, on the Librarians' Memorial Tablet, unveiled in the British Museum in 1924. The senior sub-librarian, Arthur Cowley, too old for active service, nevertheless volunteered to work with the Red Cross ambulance service in France and was away from the library from December 1916 to July 1917. The junior sub-librarian, Edmund Craster, was absent from March 1917 to February 1919, serving as a lieutenant on the General List, while Strickland Gibson, the secretary of the library, was on active service for three years from March 1916, returning in March 1919. The women on the staff at first contributed to the war effort from home by organizing a scheme to send a parcel (containing 'cigarettes, assorted edibles and other comforts'[1]) once a month to every colleague on active service; but they were themselves gradually drawn into service abroad – in 1916 both Miss Underhill and Miss Dixon of the catalogue revision staff went to Malta to work at the Imtarfa Hospital. Use of the library was much reduced during the war, as more and more students and fellows joined the armed forces. In October 1914, reporting the drain of the war on the regular staff, Madan commented that the number of readers had also declined, alleviating the usual pressure on the reading rooms in term time 'except at the Camera, where the women-students are as numerous as ever'.[2] Accessions of books and periodicals from the Continent also declined during the war, reducing the work required to record and catalogue them.

It was feared that Oxford would suffer aerial bombardment. In July 1915 Madan reported that the most valuable manuscripts and printed books had been removed from the exhibition cases to a safer place. For obvious reasons he did not at the time specify their new location,

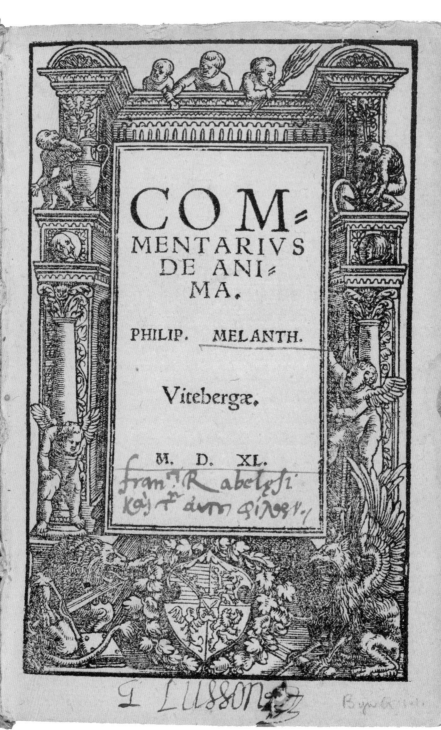

COM=
MENTARIVS
DE ANI=
MA.

PHILIP. MELANTH.

Vitebergæ.

M. D. XL.

fran̄ Rabelesi
καὶ τῶ αὐτῶ φίλωϛ·

J. Lusson

but we now know that the treasures were stored in the south-west corner of the new underground bookstore between the Camera and the Old Library, surrounded by sandbags. At the same time existing fire extinguishers had been tested and new ones purchased, and a voluntary fire brigade had been organized. Three times in March and April 1916 these volunteers were alerted to approaching Zeppelins and assembled in the quadrangle ready to deal with any fire, but fortunately there were no bombing raids and the Bodleian, like the rest of Oxford, survived unscathed.

Madan inherited from Nicholson an accumulated deficit on the library's general fund of well over a thousand pounds. With an income of £11,700 and annual expenditure of £12,000, as noted in the library's annual report for 1913, it was clear that there were not enough regular funds to cover day-to-day running costs. In June 1914 a major public appeal was launched, with the aim of raising £50,000, a capital sum that was to be invested to provide a regular income. But the timing was far from auspicious; when war broke out two months later, in August 1914, only £1,400 had been raised, and the appeal had to be suspended. Madan, by careful management and assisted by a significant reduction in the availability of books for purchase in Continental Europe, was able in the annual report for 1915 to register 'a most welcome change from a debit to a credit balance',[3] but there was no money to spend on spectacular purchases of books or manuscripts. Indeed, the annual expenditure on manuscripts hardly ever came to as much as £100 a year.

The collections were, however, enhanced with some judicious purchases, such as, in 1912, the broadside ballads that had belonged in the eighteenth century to the antiquary Thomas Hearne, and in 1916 the letter-books of George, Lord Macartney, as governor of Madras from 1780 to 1786. Madan's scholarship, combined with his courteous assistance to all scholars, students and visitors, attracted many donations, large and small. In 1914 the classical scholar Ingram Bywater, Regius Professor of Greek and *ex officio* a curator of the Bodleian from 1893 to 1908, bequeathed to the library some four thousand volumes, illustrating the history of classical learning and including many choice copies of the works of sixteenth- and early

Fig. 77 (opposite) Melancthon, *Commentarius de anima* (1540), with the signature of François Rabelais.

Fig. 78 **Drawing of Minster Lovell by Francis Grose in Percy Manning's Oxfordshire collections, *c.*1770.**

seventeenth-century humanists. Back in 1879 Bywater had been appointed sub-librarian in the Bodleian by H.O. Coxe, but within a matter of weeks he had resigned, 'not the man to submit to the drudgery and hackwork of the class catalogue, or to long hours of enforced seclusion in the library'.[4] In 1912 the Dante scholar Paget Toynbee presented to the library his collection of editions of works of Boccaccio printed in Florence and Venice in the sixteenth century, the first of many gifts of early books that culminated in the bequest of his entire collection in 1932. Two major collections of prints, drawings and manuscripts relating to Oxford and Oxfordshire came as gifts. The first was the collection of a local antiquary and painter, Herbert Hurst, given by his son and daughter in 1913. It included many drawings of old buildings in and around Oxford, among them his forty-four drawings of the church of St Peter in the East in 1891. Hurst, who graduated as a non-collegiate student at the age of forty-eight in 1886, was probably best known to contemporaries for his *Rambles and Rides around Oxford*, published by Shrimpton's of Broad Street in 1873, with a second edition in 1885. He also revised the popular *Pictorial and Historical Gossiping*

Guide to Oxford, which reached a sixth edition in 1897. The gift of Hurst's manuscripts was followed by Percy Manning's bequest of 1917. Manning, the son of a wealthy railway engineer, matriculated at New College in 1888. His interest in Oxfordshire antiquities, archaeology, customs and folklore may well have interrupted his academic studies, as he did not graduate until 1896. By then he had begun to amass a wealth of artefacts, books and manuscripts, which includes drawings by J.B. Malchair, J.C. Nattes and Joseph Fisher. His bequest greatly enhanced the Bodleian's local collections. Madan was himself a generous donor to the Bodleian while he was librarian, presenting a large number of books printed in Oxford in the seventeenth century, including a collection of tracts published during the Civil War, and in retirement his collection of seventy-two editions of the Eikon Basilike, a devotional work popularly attributed to King Charles I.

In April 1914, on Madan's initiative and with him as editor, the first issue of *The Bodleian Quarterly Record* was published, with the aim of providing, four times each year, lists of the library's most important recent acquisitions, an account of library-related activities (in a section of 'Notes and News'), reports of significant discoveries made in the library collections by staff and researchers (in 'Documents and Records') and a forum for discussion of how best to improve the library's services to its users. Over the next few years Madan received many welcome letters of approval from readers who found the lists of acquisitions useful, the notes informative and the documents interesting. He also initiated an expansion into the Picture Gallery of the display of library treasures for visitors, which until 1912 had been restricted to a couple of exhibition cases in Arts End, and in 1916 began what was to become a regular and popular series of special exhibitions with a very successful Shakespeare Centenary Exhibition.

Madan resigned from the post of Bodley's Librarian on 14 April 1919, his period in office having been dominated by the war. Despite this he had significantly improved the administration of the library, reduced its deficit and organized a systematic arrangement of its archive. In retirement he continued to be a regular and welcome presence in the library, resuming his own research on Oxford printing and seeing his work on the western manuscript collections acknowledged and published in volumes 2 (part 1) and 6 of the *Summary Catalogue of Western Manuscripts* in 1922 and 1924.

The publication in 1931 of the final volume of his *Oxford Books* was followed by the award of the gold medal of the Bibliographical Society. He died at home in May 1935, and a curator of the Bodleian wrote: 'We cannot expect to see his like again … After a lifetime spent in the unostentatious service of learning … he has left to all who were connected with him a memory of single-minded devotion, of courtesy, of Christian faithfulness, which we shall not cease to honour.'[5]

In June 1919 the curators unanimously elected the senior sub-librarian, Arthur Cowley, to succeed Madan as Bodley's Librarian. The fourth son of a customs house agent, he had been educated at St Paul's School, London, then at Trinity College, Oxford, where he was an exhibitioner and, like Madan, graduated in *Literae Humaniores*. After university he spent two years in Switzerland studying French and German, then in 1885 became a schoolmaster, teaching modern languages first at Sherborne School and then at Magdalen College School. In 1896 he was appointed an assistant sub-librarian in the Bodleian to help the elderly sub-librarian Alfred Neubauer in his work on the library's oriental collections. With Neubauer he also published two works on the surviving Hebrew texts of Ecclesiasticus, and in 1898 he produced a revised edition of G.W. Collins's translation of Wilhelm Gesenius's *Hebrew Grammar*, which became the standard work of reference for English students. The following year he succeeded Neubauer as sub-librarian and in 1902 was elected a fellow of Magdalen College. The year 1906 saw the publication of his work with A.H. Sayce on Aramaic papyri, and of the second volume of the catalogue of the library's Hebrew manuscripts, compiled by Cowley and Neubauer. When he became Bodley's Librarian in 1919, at the age of fifty-seven, he was an established Hebraic scholar, an honorary DLitt of the university, and a fellow of the British Academy. Throughout his time in office he pursued his academic research alongside his duties in the Bodleian. He also continued to catalogue, eventually publishing his *Concise Catalogue of the Hebrew Books in the Bodleian Library* in 1929. On his appointment as librarian, he broke with tradition by abandoning the librarian's study in Duke Humfrey's Library and moving to a separate room off the Picture Gallery, where he could work without the constant interruptions of a reading room. To maintain contact with his staff he had an internal telephone system installed, and opened direct links to the outside world with a Post Office telephone. In the same year, 1919, he 'instituted a short hand writer' and bought 'a typewriting machine' for the library.[6]

The financial position of the library continued to be a matter of grave concern. In the post-war years there was no possibility of relaunching the general appeal for funds that had come to a halt in August 1914, and Cowley hoped that the University Commission of 1920 might recommend a substantial increase in the Bodleian's grant, to enable it both to meet the needs of the university and to maintain its position as one of the greatest libraries in the world. In the event the immediate problem was solved by a number of donations and legacies. The most spectacular came in 1920 – a magnificent benefaction of £50,000 (precisely the sum the library had sought in its ill-timed appeal in 1914) from Walter Morrison, a Balliol graduate then in his eighties, who specified that the money was to be invested and the income used for any purposes the librarian thought fit. It was immediately used to increase staff salaries and to buy more books published abroad. At about the same time, part of the government grant to the university began to be allocated to the Bodleian.

It was Morrison's gift, at that time the largest the Bodleian had received from a single donor, that prompted the librarian to set up a memorial to library benefactors. A handsome marble tablet, designed by Sir Reginald Blomfield in Jacobean style and honouring thirty-five major benefactors, from Humfrey, duke of Gloucester, in 1439 to George Bodley in 1921, was placed at the top of the main staircase of the Old Library in 1923. The tablet followed the tradition set by Sir Thomas Bodley, who believed that the public recognition of benefactors would serve not only to record their generosity, but also to encourage others to follow their example. Two years later, in June 1925, largely at the instigation of Sir Michael Sadler, a new body, the Friends of the Bodleian, came into being, 'with the object of providing ... an income for the purchase of rare and desirable books and manuscripts' that the library could not otherwise afford. Through judicious purchases from booksellers and at auction sales, the Friends filled many gaps in the library's collection of eighteenth- and early nineteenth-century English literature, including first editions of works by Swift, Pope, Sterne, Smollett, Scott, Wordsworth, Coleridge and Keats. They also gave a wide range of literary and historical manuscripts, among them fragmentary manuscripts of the Northamptonshire poet John Clare, notebooks of Christina Rossetti, working papers of Anthony Trollope and Jane Austen's 'Volume the First', containing copies she made around 1793 of her earliest writings (fig. 79). Many contemporary authors and composers gave manuscripts through the Friends: T.S. Eliot gave five volumes of drafts of a variety of works, John Buchan the manuscript of *The Massacre of Glencoe*, and Walter de la Mare a draft of *Memoirs of a Midget*, while Gustav Holst gave the vocal score of *A Choral Fantasia*. In 1930 a more unusual volume came from Sarah Angelina Acland, daughter of the Regius Professor of Medicine Sir Henry Acland; she gave an album of photographs she had taken in the 1890s of her father with a variety of distinguished friends and visitors to their Oxford home in Broad Street (fig. 80).

The production of a catalogue of its enormous collections of printed books continued to challenge the library. Within two years of his appointment, Cowley had decided to abandon the revision of the unwieldy transcribed catalogue, which had been started in 1859 with a view to its publication as a replacement for the catalogue printed in 1843. Work started on a new catalogue for books published after 1919, continuing the 'moveable slip' system introduced in 1859, but with the entries printed (rather than handwritten). This reduced their length and made the new catalogue much easier to consult, but it involved the momentous decision to abandon the plan of publishing the general catalogue in its entirety, and had the added disadvantage of splitting it into two – the pre-1920 'transcribed catalogue' and the '1920 catalogue'. It was recognized at the time as a far from ideal solution but the most practicable one, given the insurmountable cost of revising and publishing the whole of the old catalogue.

Cowley, unlike his two immediate predecessors, recognized that the library had become too large to be directly administered by one man. He advocated the establishment of departments within the Bodleian, and of libraries physically separate from the main library, each to be managed by an expert in the field of study represented in its collections. These departments and dependent libraries would, Cowley maintained, bring the Bodleian into closer contact with the modern educational demands of the university, as studies became more specialized and work in every branch of them became more intensive. The dependent libraries, housed off the cramped central site, would be able to make books more readily accessible to students and to provide space for

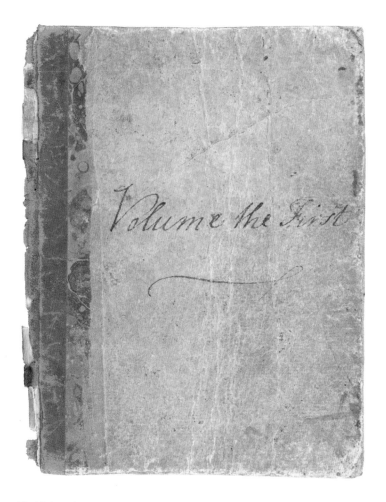

Fig. 79 Jane Austen's 'Volume the First', 1793.

teaching alongside the reading rooms. Bodley's Librarian would
continue to be responsible to the university, through the curators, for
the administration of the whole institution. This process began with the
creation of a law departmental library in the Examination Schools in
1923, housing all the Bodleian's legal books in a reading room that was
open for seven hours each day and available for teaching and discussion
in the evening. The Law Faculty clearly found this a good arrangement,
for two years later the Corpus Professor of Jurisprudence transferred
to the Bodleian the Maitland Memorial Library of legal and social
history, so that it could be merged with the law departmental library.

Then long negotiations with the Radcliffe Trustees culminated in 1927 in the transfer to the university of their natural science library – the building and all its contents – and to the establishment of the Radcliffe Science Library as a dependent library under Bodleian management (fig. 81). All the Bodleian's recent scientific books were transferred to it. In the same year the curators took over the administration of the Indian Institute Library, which had been founded in 1880 as a centre for Indian studies in Oxford. A third dependent library was added in 1929, differing from the others in that it was a new foundation. Rhodes House was established by the university as a centre for the study of the political, social and economic development of the British Empire and of the United States of America, and was named in honour of Cecil Rhodes, who had bequeathed his vast fortune to Oxford. Rhodes House was to include a library, to which the Bodleian's books (some 25,000) relating to the empire and the United States were transferred (fig. 82). Meanwhile, to provide better facilities for the increasing number of students of English language and literature in the university, the southern end of the east range of the Picture Gallery was in 1929 converted into a reading room, with seats for forty-eight readers and the books most frequently required in their studies immediately available on the shelves around its walls.

Cowley's term in office also saw the gradual improvement of the central buildings: in 1922 and 1923 the unblocking of the two large windows on the ground and first floor of the Old Library that looked onto Exeter College garden were restored to their Jacobean splendour; in 1925 a thorough clean and redecoration of the reading room and staircase in the Radcliffe Camera revealed the splendour of the original ceilings; in 1926 the ceiling in Duke Humfrey's Library, which had become badly damaged by worm and rot, was repaired; in 1928 a lift in the north-west stairwell of the Bodleian building was installed; and, finally, electric light was introduced, which extended the hours the library was open to readers by two hours every day in the summer months and by four in the winter – a revolution memorably reported in the *Oxford Mail* on 4 October 1929 under the headline 'Pandemonium at the Bodleian: Famous Library to Work at Night'.

Like so many of his predecessors, Cowley was faced with the problem of finding space for the ever-expanding library collections. In 1923 the lower deck of the underground bookstore was fitted with

Fig. 80 **Sarah Angelina Acland's photograph of her father, Henry Acland, with John Ruskin in 1894.**

shelves, and the growing runs of foreign periodicals were moved there from the old building. The transfer of the bulk of the library's collections of engravings to the Ashmolean Museum and of the Evans collection of scientific instruments to the Old Ashmolean (now the Museum of the History of Science), both in 1924, released some space, as did the transfer of books to the new dependent libraries; but much more was needed. In 1925 Cowley warned the curators that the Old Library was to all intents and purposes full and that there was room in the underground bookstore for only ten years of normal accessions. In their turn the curators warned the university's Council that extension of the Bodleian on a very large scale was absolutely essential. The debate about how best to achieve this expansion dominated the rest of Cowley's term of office, indeed of his life. Many different solutions were put forward, all of them strongly advocated by some members of the university and vehemently opposed by others. They included disposing of non-academic books in the library, both by weeding the existing collections and by drastically reducing future acquisitions under the

Fig. 81 **Second-floor reading room in the new extension to the Radcliffe Science Library, 1930s.**

copyright privilege; excavating to the north and south of the Bodleian to provide more underground storage; fitting the ground-floor and first-floor rooms of the Schools with modern stack shelving, and roofing over the quadrangle; and (following the example set by Cambridge University) building an entirely new university library, perhaps in the University Parks. As early as 1921, in a paper on the recent history of the Bodleian read to the Library Association, Cowley had insisted that abandoning the original library building was not an option:

> The spirit of Bodley is in the place. The old reading-room, full of history, from its panelled wooden ceiling down to its old oak desks, the beautiful rooms downstairs, the quadrangle with a sermon in every stone – it has all been the stately home of learning since the fifteenth century, and it is no mere fancy to say that it fosters learning as no modern setting possibly could. We cannot give it up.[7]

Eventually two proposals were put to Congregation in May 1928, but both were rejected. In March 1930 a commission was appointed, under the chairmanship of Sir Henry Miers, to advise the university on the best means of developing library provision in Oxford to meet modern requirements. It reported in 1931, and its recommendations – that a supplementary library building along more modern lines should be constructed on the north side of Broad Street, capable of holding some five million books, and extending at the librarian's discretion the privilege of access to the bookstack, while the Old Library was converted into reading rooms with shelves housing at least 100,000 volumes that would be immediately available to readers – were adopted without opposition. The proposals stressed the need for the rapid delivery of the books housed in the new building to the reading rooms 'by mechanical means through a tunnel', and for provision to be made for advanced teaching and research alongside the library's collections in the ground-floor rooms of the Old Library. They also endorsed the continued use of the Camera as a reading room for undergraduates, who had been using it in increasing numbers from the 1870s, the development of the existing system of 'subsidiary special libraries under the control of the Faculties', the preparation of a new working catalogue for the Bodleian and an improvement in the salaries of Bodleian staff.[8]

By the time a decree embodying the Commission's recommendations was passed in Congregation, in May 1931, Cowley was in hospital and seriously ill. He resigned in July, a month after the conferment of a knighthood – he was the first Oxford librarian to receive that honour. He died in October, aged sixty-nine, bequeathing his estate in trust to the university for the benefit of the Bodleian. P.S. Allen, president of Corpus Christi College, wrote an appreciative obituary in *The Bodleian Quarterly Record*, summarizing the many tangible achievements of Cowley's twelve years in office, adding (with a reference to 'the charm and urbanity of his welcome to foreign scholars'): 'Perhaps the Bodleian is most indebted to him for the success with which he upheld its tradition of being the pleasantest of all the great libraries of Europe and the easiest to work in.'[9]

Some readers did not find the Bodleian an easy place in which to study. They were particularly discouraged by the low temperatures in the reading rooms. The circulation of the report of the Commission on Library Provision in Oxford prompted the publication in the *Oxford Magazine* on 28 May 1931 of verses headed 'Small Things', in which a 'humble reader' recorded his disappointment that the commission had not been concerned with such important matters as conditions for students who were chilled to the bone in winter or suffocated in summer, and throughout the year disturbed by the conversations of the library assistants:

I who had felt the chill of tombs
(Though sometimes I was suffocated),
Dreamt hopefully of reading rooms
Perfectly warmed and ventilated.
...
Time has flown by on rapid wing,
And the report at length is out,
And this is not the sort of thing
That the Commission cares about.

The curators unanimously elected the senior sub-librarian Edmund Craster, who had acted as librarian during Cowley's illness, to succeed him (fig. 83). Craster, with an established reputation as archaeologist and historian of his native Northumberland, had been a fellow of All

Fig. 82 **Reading room in Rhodes House Library, 1930.**

Souls since 1903 and sub-librarian in the Bodleian since 1912; he was awarded a DLitt in 1916, and in 1927 was promoted to the newly created post of Keeper of Western Manuscripts. As sub-librarian and keeper, his principal task was the cataloguing of the western manuscript collections, work that bore fruit in the publication of three volumes of the *Summary Catalogue of Western Manuscripts*, in 1922, 1924 and 1937. He regularly contributed short pieces to *The Bodleian Quarterly Record* on the interesting discoveries he had made in the course of this work. Now, despite the fact that his own preference throughout the protracted debates on the future of the Bodleian had been for an entirely new library on an extendable site, as Bodley's Librarian his principal task was to implement the plans agreed by the university for a new library building on the north side of Broad Street and the development of the old building to provide more reading rooms and space for administrative staff. Edgar Lobel, junior sub-librarian since 1919, became senior sub-librarian and Keeper of Western Manuscripts,

Fig. 83 **Portrait of Sir Edmund Craster, Bodley's Librarian from 1931 to 1945, by Augustus John, 1944.**

and Strickland Gibson, who had been on the library staff since 1891, was appointed junior sub-librarian. The oriental department was created, with Thomas Gambier Parry as its first keeper. By 1938, the curators had agreed in principle to the creation of a third department, of printed books, though this became a reality only in 1942, when the completion of the new library building made it possible to concentrate in one large room the staff responsible for accessioning and cataloguing the current intake of printed books. Strickland Gibson was then appointed the first Keeper of Printed Books. In his *History of the Bodleian Library, 1845–1945*, published in 1952, Craster recorded, clearly with some satisfaction, that from 1942 the librarian had the support of three sub-librarians, each in charge, as keeper, of a particular department – a noticeable improvement on the old system when the activities of the two scholarly sub-librarians were for the most part confined to cataloguing the collections.

Stanley Gillam, who joined the staff as a Bodley boy in August 1931, recorded his recollections some sixty years later of the Bodleian during the first decade of Craster's librarianship.[10] Contrasting the library as it was then with the library he knew in the 1990s, he commented on the limited accommodation for staff, the small number of reading rooms and the desperate need for more book storage space. His account gives a graphic picture not only of the Old Library, room by room, but also of its staff. Among them he recalled W.H.B. Somerset, the senior assistant in charge of Duke Humfrey's Library, 'a genial figure of military bearing with a martial air, a captain in the First World War and a member of the Home Guard in the Second. He could be very firm with both readers and junior staff when occasion demanded'; Edgar Lobel, a 'tall and impressive man, immersed in Greek Papyri, totally remote and aloof'; Thomas Gambier Parry, superintendent of the Upper Reading Room and Keeper of the Oriental Department, 'small in stature … but could be very fierce'; E.O. Windstedt, Parry's deputy, 'a detached, bearded figure with a very high-pitched voice [who] rarely seemed to talk to anyone'. Gillam provides insights into the difficulties of fetching books for readers from the various storage areas. The rooms on the first floor of the Old Library were almost entirely devoted to book storage, but they did not have electric light, and the fetching involved 'moving and ascending very tall, heavy ladders, at the same time clutching one or more readers' order-slips and, on dark days, an electric torch as well'. The basement of the Examination Schools, 'poorly ventilated and in places almost without lighting', housed fiction and other little-used classes of books. Fiction was fetched only for readers of MA status and above. Books were fetched daily and returned weekly on Mondays, 'loaded into baskets which were placed in the library handcart and, covered with a waterproof sheet', then wheeled carefully down the High Street. The basement of the Old Ashmolean, equipped with moveable shelving, was 'a slightly less disagreeable place in which to work than the Schools Basement, but far, far worse than either was the Sheldonian'. Here large volumes of bound newspapers were stored on rough wooden shelving, with extremely narrow gangways between. 'Very little daylight penetrated the small subterranean windows and there was no artificial lighting whatsoever. The enormous volumes had to be found by the light of an electric torch which, if dropped, probably meant that one had to find one's way out in almost complete darkness.'

Craster's librarianship was dominated by the planning and construction of the new building. Before becoming librarian, he had the reputation of a meticulous but retiring scholar and was not well known in the university beyond his own college; he also suffered from a severe speech impediment. Faced with the major project of library extension, he proved the ideal man for the job – mindful of the need to consult all interested parties, he did so within a carefully constructed framework of committees and informal meetings, devised and adhered to strict schedules, and was able to reach a consensus within the university on the complex range of related issues. The first hurdle was to find funding, a task made infinitely easier in May 1932 by the generous offer of the trustees of the Rockefeller Foundation to contribute up to three fifths of the estimated total cost of £400,000,[11] on condition that the university find the remainder within four years. In the event, the university needed only one year to raise the required sum. Decisions on the future use of the Old Library, a necessary prerequisite to planning the allocation of rooms in the new building, were made by May 1934 and an architect, Sir Giles Gilbert Scott, was appointed. In July the architect and Bodley's Librarian together visited some of the great libraries of Continental Europe, and in September the librarian and the secretary of the library toured more modern libraries in the United States. A small planning subcommittee of the building committee of the curators then settled to the task of framing instructions for the architect. These were completed

Fig. 84 **Houses in Broad Street demolished to make way for the New Bodleian Library, 1936.**

and accepted in June 1935. Primarily intended for the storage of books, the square core of the new building was to be eleven floors of bookstacks, each of the three below ground covering the whole one-acre site, the top two set well back so as to be scarcely visible from the street, and the intermediate six encased by three stories of outer rooms, separated from the bookstack by corridors. With each floor just over seven feet (about two metres) high and fitted out with steel shelving, the total capacity of the stack met the specified requirement of storage for some five million books. In order to transfer the books speedily to readers in the Old Library, a tunnel was to be driven under Broad Street.

In December 1936 the local firm of Benfield & Loxley was contracted to do the building work, and the houses on the site began to be cleared before the end of the year (fig. 84). Some of them were found to have, behind their Victorian exteriors, interesting architectural features of the seventeenth century, and these were carefully recorded. Throughout the excavation for the basement of the new building, a careful watch was kept, on the librarian's instructions, for objects of archaeological interest. In the event a mass of medieval pottery was recovered, as well as three mammoths' teeth. Then, as the mechanical excavators reached down to the last foot or so of gravel, water began to pour through at the rate of 2,000 to 3,000 gallons an hour, which made it necessary to encase the excavated area in iron sheeting. Fortunately, beneath the gravel was a solid layer of blue Oxford clay which provided firm foundations.

On 25 June 1937 Queen Mary laid the foundation stone of the new building (fig. 85). Throughout the next year work, first on the structural steel frame and then on the floors and outer walls, proceeded, and by the summer of 1939 the staircases were in place, the walls and ceilings had been plastered, the heating was operational and the drying-out process had begun. Arrangements for a royal opening in June 1940 were in hand, but on 3 September 1939 war was declared, and the official opening was postponed. The building, however, gradually came into use, with two reading rooms (one for students of politics, philosophy and economics, and the other for the consultation of maps), a room for the study of practical bibliography, two exhibition rooms (the only part of the building open to the public), one large room for cataloguing and another for the reception and processing of new accessions, a bindery and repair room, a photographic studio, and a canteen and common room for the library staff.

Throughout the Second World War, mainly in the university vacations, the Bodleian's collections of books and manuscripts were gradually transferred to their new home in the spacious bookstack from the overcrowded first- and second-floor rooms in the Old Library, the cellars of the Examination Schools and the basements of the Camera and the Old Ashmolean. All the old books from Duke Humfrey's Library and Arts End were also, though only temporarily, moved to the New Library, where they would be much better protected in the event of enemy action. The most precious items were placed in a specially constructed brick chamber two floors below ground. For the first time in its long history the library had more than enough storage space, and it began to take in temporary deposits from Oxford

Fig. 85 **Queen Mary laying the foundation stone of the New Bodleian, 1937.**

colleges and institutions for safe keeping. Most of the deposits were of books and manuscripts, but other treasures also arrived, including the medieval stained glass from New College and Merton College chapels; masterpieces from Christ Church picture gallery; portraits from Balliol, Exeter, University and Corpus Christi colleges; the finely carved reredos from Trinity College chapel; type plates and matrices from the Clarendon Press; cabinets of coins from the Ashmolean Museum and of seeds from the Botany Department. Later, seeds from the national collection at Kew and botanical specimens from the Natural History Museum were also deposited for safe keeping. Among the archives were those of Oxford City Council and of the university itself – the latter transferred from the top floors of the tower of the Old Library in June 1940. When the bombing of London began in September that year, many institutions in the capital were desperate to find safer places

Fig. 86 **The Broad Street frontage of the New Bodleian.**

to store their collections. Thus it was that books and archives from the University of London Library, the Science Museum, the Natural History Museum, the British Drama League, the Mineralogical Society, the Linnaean Society, the British Museum, the London School of Economics, the Oxford and Cambridge Club, the Victoria and Albert Museum, the Royal Geographical Society, both Houses of Parliament, the General Register Office at Somerset House, the Royal Society, the Royal Statistical Society and the Geological Society spent the war years in the bookstack of the New Bodleian, as did a consignment from Eton College.[12]

Although so many collections had been moved there from London, Oxford was not expecting to be immune from aerial attack. As Craster wrote in his *History of the Bodleian*: 'Librarianship in time of war is an affair of stirrup-pumps and sandbags, of static water-tanks and trailer-pumps, and of the many activities that go by the name of A.R.P.'[13] Air-raid precautions for the Bodleian were at first provided by library staff who formed a volunteer fire brigade, taking it in turns to keep watch every night. From 1941 they were reinforced by teams of undergraduates, and in 1942 it became standard practice to have thirty persons on duty in the library overnight, all trained in firefighting. It is an indication of how concerned Oxford was about the threat of bombing that the lowest floor of the new bookstack was converted into a public air-raid shelter, with accommodation for 1,100 people, and put at the disposal of the City Council. Fortunately, it never needed to be used. Meanwhile the outer rooms were used by bodies engaged in a variety of war work, among them naval intelligence departments of the Admiralty, regional offices of the British Red Cross Society, the Blood Transfusion Service, the Women's Voluntary Services and the Royal Observer Corp, the Royal National War Libraries and the Educational Book Section of the Prisoners of War Department.

Craster's time in office also saw improvements in staff salaries and numbers, largely as a result of the recommendations that arose from his systematic analysis of what was needed. In 1927 there had been sixty-two people on the staff; by 1938, partly as a result of the absorption and creation of dependent libraries and the resumption of catalogue revision, the number had increased to 107; and by 1951 it had reached 147. The war years significantly altered the composition of the staff, bringing to an end the recruitment of the boys on whom the Bodleian had come to depend for the delivery of much of its day-to-day service, a situation 'saved', as Craster explained in his *History of the Bodleian*, 'by the employment of female labour'.[14] Many of these women, initially hired (from 1933) to work on the revision of the catalogue of printed books, had to be transferred to general library duties as regular staff were recruited into the armed forces, bringing their cataloguing work to a temporary halt – repeating, during the Second World War, the experience of the First. Meanwhile, detailed cataloguing of the manuscript collections continued, and bore fruit in the publication in 1932 of a fourth volume in the *Calendar of the Clarendon State Papers* (the first volume had appeared in 1869, and the last was to be published in 1970). This important collection of official papers of the seventeenth century had come to the library in the course of the eighteenth century, and the example set by the Royal Commission on Historical Manuscripts in the nineteenth century had inspired a project to provide a description of every document in the collection.

Fig. 87 **Book conveyor station and pneumatic tube delivery point in the bookstack of the New Bodleian, 1942.**

The high cost of publishing such detailed catalogues led, as a more cost-effective alternative, to the production of in-house card indexes to other collections, including eighteenth-century English correspondence, topographical prints and drawings of Oxford, and first lines in English verse in Bodleian manuscripts.

Craster's careful attention to the management of the library's finances saw the budget brought back into balance, both by reduction in day-to-day expenditure and by the introduction of more rigorous procedures for the authorization of extraordinary expenditure. Several generous bequests were made to the library between 1931 and 1941, among them one from Kenneth Grahame, author of *The Wind in the Willows*, who in 1933 bequeathed, subject to life interests, the residue of his estate, which included the royalties in all his writings; and another from Craster's predecessor, Sir Arthur Cowley, who bequeathed the reversion of his estate to the Bodleian. Craster retired in 1945 and was knighted the same year. In retirement he was librarian of the Codrington Library at All Souls College, and wrote histories of both the Codrington and the Bodleian.

The development of departments and dependent libraries in the first half of the twentieth century had laid the foundations for future developments, while the construction of the New Library had solved for the time being the perennial problem of finding storage space for the collections. The library had survived two world wars and, despite financial difficulties, had maintained acquisitions and adapted its staffing structure to the changing labour market. Most significantly, the foundation of its Friends' organization had paved the way for the substantial fund-raising that was to become an essential feature of the second half of the century and beyond.

CHAPTER 7

Post-war expansion and modernization

C RASTER WAS SUCCEEDED AS Bodley's Librarian by Harry R. Creswick, a Cambridge graduate, who had been appointed to the newly created post of deputy librarian in the Bodleian in 1938, having been assistant under-librarian in charge of incunabula and early printed books at Cambridge University Library. During his brief spell as Bodley's Librarian the New Library recovered from its wartime service as a safe repository for the collections of other institutions. Most of the deposits were swiftly returned and gradually the outer rooms became available for library and university use, as the organizations and government departments that had been based there during the war departed. The New Library was officially opened by King George VI on 24 October 1946, an occasion that has entered Bodleian folklore because the beautifully designed silver ornamental key that had been especially made for the ceremony broke in the lock (fig. 89). A great deal of pushing and pulling failed to solve the problem and, just when the embarrassed chancellor of the university was on the point of conducting the royal couple to another door, the Bedel of Arts, G.W. Beesley, managed to turn the shank of the key with his fingers and open the huge ceremonial doors.

Fig. 88 **Blackwell Hall in the Weston Library, opened to the public in March 2015.**

205

In 1946 the photographic studio, which had been established in
1891 at the west end of the north range of the Picture Gallery, moved
into more spacious quarters on the top floor of the New Library. Run
by Oxford University Press, it enjoyed a monopoly of the photographic
reproduction of Bodleian books and manuscripts, coming under the
administrative control of the library only in 1975. There was also
generous accommodation for the bindery on the ground floor of the
New Library. Provision had first been made for an in-house binder in
the Old Library in 1864, but the facilities there were quite inadequate to
meet the needs of the rapidly expanding and heavily used book stock. In
its larger and better equipped quarters, the bindery could take on much
more of the work involved in both the binding of periodicals and the
repair of monographs. It was also nominally responsible for the repair
of manuscripts. By the early 1960s it was apparent that continually

Fig. 89 (above) **Ceremonial key for the official opening of the New Bodleian in 1946.**

Fig. 90 (opposite) **Portrait of J.N.L. Myres, Bodley's Librarian from 1947 to 1965,
by Anthony Morris, 1967.**

increasing use of the manuscript collections demanded more focused attention, and a start was made with the appointment of the library's first paper conservator, Maureen Vaisey, in 1963. A separate document repair room was set up on the top floor of the New Library in 1972, with facilities for three conservators. Five years later what was by then known as the conservation unit transferred to specially equipped accommodation in the Clarendon Building, the fine early eighteenth-century building to the north of the Old Library that had been allocated to the Bodleian in 1975. Major restructuring of library services in 1978 led to the creation of a new post of head of conservation, to which Michael Turner was appointed, with overall responsibility for the welfare of the collections and specifically for the bindery, bookstack, photographic studio and paper conservation unit. With Chris Clarkson, an already well-established conservator, as his deputy, Turner created a new department with a strong emphasis on preservation, while funding from the Mellon Foundation provided for a completely redesigned and re-equipped bindery.

By the beginning of 1947 the stack housed only Bodleian books and manuscripts. With both of its reading rooms open to readers and the staff canteen fully operational, the new building was at last functioning simply as a library. The reading rooms proved extremely popular with the growing number of students, and within twelve years the Map Room was extended into an adjacent room and more desks were squeezed into the annexe of the Politics, Philosophy and

ETE BIBLIOTHECAE
PVS INIQVA MANVS
PIETATE REPICTAS
EXHIBET EFFIGIES

Fig. 91 **Section of the Upper Reading Room frieze with the medallion portrait of Roger Bacon and the inscription added on its restoration in 1954.**

Economics Reading Room. By the early 1960s, with the development of their own buildings, the university faculties began to vacate the rooms around the bookstack that had been designed for seminars and research projects, and plans were afoot to transform them into reading rooms or additional work space for library staff.

Creswick resigned in 1947, planning to have more time to pursue his academic research, but he returned to library work on being appointed university librarian at Cambridge in 1949 (a post he held for twenty years). His successor in the Bodleian was J.N.L. (Nowell) Myres, who had been a Student of Christ Church from 1928, dividing his time between the teaching duties of that post and a series of archaeological excavations. Librarian at Christ Church since 1938, he must have seemed to the curators a natural choice to head the Bodleian. He had also proved an able administrator during his war service in the Ministry of Food, where his experience and enthusiasm as a vegetable gardener had proved extremely useful.

Myres's eighteen years at the Bodleian were to a large extent dominated by reconstruction work on the Old Library, a project he directed with consummate skill and attention to detail. Work on the south range facing the Radcliffe Camera had begun in 1946 and took five years to complete. The old wooden beams had rotted and were replaced with steel girders to support new fire-proof floors. Much of the external stonework was refaced and new mullions inserted in many of the windows. Work on the inside walls of the upper floor revealed in 1949 the frieze that Bodley's first librarian, Thomas James, had designed to decorate the Picture Gallery (fig. 91). Painted along the top of the walls, the frieze consisted of some two hundred portrait heads of writers whose works were then, and mostly still are, on the shelves in Duke Humfrey's Library. The frieze was described by the antiquary Thomas Hearne in a published list of 1725 but had been plastered over in the course of Robert Smirke's replacement of the original roof and ceiling in 1830–31. It was thought to have been painted on canvas that had rotted over the years, but the newly discovered portraits were found to have been painted directly onto the stone walls. They had been damaged in the course of plastering, but were now carefully restored and repainted, with the illegible parts of the inscriptions around the portrait heads supplied from the wording recorded in Hearne's list. The continuity of the frieze had been broken by the construction of a partition at the west end of the north range in 1831. This partition wall was now decorated with a four-line Latin inscription devised by Bodley's Librarian celebrating the careful restoration of the frieze, cunningly containing a double chronogram: the letters painted red reading MDCXVIII to record the approximate date of 1618 for the original frieze, and those painted blue MCMLIIII, the date of the completion of its restoration in 1954. A band on either side of the inscription, linking it to the frieze on the north and south walls of the reading room, contains on the left Sir Thomas Bodley's arms and initials, with the initials of Thomas James, the designer of the frieze, displayed on some of his books, and on the right the initials of J.N.L. Myres, his family crest and motto and the initials of Clive Rouse and his two assistants, Janet Lenton and Helen Watson, who had repainted it.[1] The 1954 addition is very much in the style of the original frieze, an impression strengthened by the portrait of Bodley on one of the original painted ceiling panels that hangs below the inscription.

Work in the tower room in the centre of the east range revealed, under the elaborate eighteenth-century plaster ceiling, the moulded beams and painted panels of the original ceiling as well as an undamaged section of the frieze, both of which were permanently uncovered, and the plaster ceiling carefully transferred to the upper

Fig. 92 Statue of William Herbert, third earl of Pembroke, by Hubert Le Sueur, in the Schools Quadrangle.

room of the University Archives in the tower. The appearance of the tower room was further altered by the removal to the quadrangle of Hubert Le Sueur's bronze statue of William Herbert, earl of Pembroke (fig. 92), who was chancellor of the university from 1617 to 1630. It had been given to the university by the seventh earl in 1723 and is the subject of an amusing anecdote recorded by the sub-librarian John Walters,

Fig. 93 **Law books being transferred from the Radcliffe Camera to the Old Library, 1955.**

a scholar of Jesus College, in 1780. Two members of the university, having dined with the earl at his country seat in Wiltshire, and secured a promise from him that he would present the statue to Oxford in memory of his great uncle, are said to have returned with the removable head of the statue to ensure that the earl did not change his mind.[2]

In 1950 work on the south range of the Old Library was complete, with two reading rooms the first floor providing on open shelves much consulted works on classics, theology and oriental studies, and the room above housing the huge catalogue of printed books, accompanied by a run of general reference works. On the ground floor, the School of Natural Philosophy was refurbished and opened as an entrance hall to the library. Reconstruction of the north range began the following year and work continued on the Old Library for another four years. In September 1955 the whole of the Upper Reading Room was opened, with the number of desks for readers increased from 64 to 160, to serve students of modern history, English language and literature, bibliography and modern languages. In November the law collections were moved from the ground floor of the Radcliffe Camera into the Lower Reading Room (fig. 93). The Bodleian's *Annual Report* for the academic year 1955/56 could rightly claim that the Old Library was now a building worthy of its splendid heritage.

Duke Humfrey's Library also needed attention. New heating was installed in 1953; then, in order to facilitate major building work, the reading room was moved to the New Bodleian in 1959–60, when a survey by Robert Potter, architect to Salisbury Cathedral, had revealed not only that the walls of the fifteenth-century building were unstable but also that its floor was resting directly on the vault of the Divinity School, which was not designed to be load bearing. The walls were stabilized by the insertion of concrete uprights into the seventeenth-century buttresses and new concrete floors were constructed. A generous benefaction from Donald F. Hyde, a New York lawyer and literary scholar, covered the cost of cleaning and repairing the painted roof timbers and ceiling panels in Duke Humfrey's Library and Arts End. Selden End was transformed by the insertion of four new staircases, providing easy access for readers to reference works in the galleries; and, with the financial help of many well-wishers, new tables and chairs were provided to make it an extension of the reading room in Duke Humfrey's. Its appearance was greatly enhanced by a ceiling of fifty-two panels discovered during the recent restoration of the Old Library at Christ Church, and transferred to the Bodleian by the college. The panels had been painted at the same date and by the same artists responsible for those in Arts End, which had been commissioned by Sir Thomas Bodley in the early seventeenth century. To facilitate the major work of renovation, all the furniture was removed from Duke Humfrey's Library and the outlines of the medieval lecterns (long covered by Thomas Bodley's book presses) were revealed between the windows on the north and south walls (see fig. 6). By April 1963 the whole of Duke Humfrey's Library was reopened as a reading room, and a celebratory concert devised and presented by Bodleian staff was held there on 18 May, with music by Monteverdi, Byrd, Haydn and Orlando Gibbons.

The eighteenth-century Radcliffe Camera did not require such major work as Duke Humfrey's Library, but the building continued to need attention. Additional tables on the ground floor doubled the accommodation for students in its lower reading room in 1946–47, and twelve years later the lighting and ventilation there were much improved by the insertion of new aluminium-framed windows behind the iron grilles. In 1968–69, its upper reading room and grand staircase, which

Fig. 94 (opposite) **The ceiling of the upper reading room in the Radcliffe Camera, redecorated in 1968–69.**

Fig. 95 (above) **The Indian Institute at the east end of Broad Street.**

had last been painted in 1925, were redecorated. This, with improved lighting, revealed the glories of the decorative ceilings for the first time in generations (fig. 94). The lead covering of the dome and lantern needed replacing in 1971–72. In the course of this work a glass bottle was discovered, placed there by six employees of the local firm of Holywell Contractors, who had been doing similar work in the summer of 1867.

It was a dispute about another building, the Indian Institute in Broad Street, that made the Bodleian headline news in 1964 and 1965. The university's proposal to demolish the imposing nineteenth-century institute (fig. 95) in order to make room for much-needed office accommodation for its central administration prompted acrimonious discussion, especially about a new location for the library it housed. The library in the Indian Institute had been a dependent library of the Bodleian since 1927. Myres was determined that it was not in the Bodleian's interest to relinquish any space on its cramped central site and opposed the university's proposal to rehouse the Indian Institute Library in an extension to be built on the roof of the New Bodleian. But he failed to convince the curators, who agreed to the plan in June 1965. Bodley's Librarian immediately tendered his resignation and left office at the end of the year. In the event, members of the university voted against the demolition of the institute, which still dominates the east end of Broad Street, but an extension to house its library was built on the top of the New Bodleian and opened in 1968.

In the years after the Second World War, the number of undergraduates studying at the university increased substantially. In the 1930s and 1940s this growth had not been anticipated. It had been expected that the Radcliffe Science Library, the Radcliffe Camera and the Politics, Philosophy and Economics Reading Room in the New Bodleian would together meet their needs, and that the Old Library could be developed as a series of reading rooms for research. By 1957 it had become apparent that this was a miscalculation. Despite being open until 10 p.m. in term time, the rooms designed for undergraduates were often full to capacity, while those in the Old Library were being increasingly used by undergraduates pursuing the wider range of first-degree subjects that had become available, seriously inconveniencing research students and senior members of the university. While alerting the university to the need for further expansion, the Library's *Annual Report* for 1957/58 could note with some satisfaction that over three hundred additional reader spaces had been provided in the last ten years, bringing the number of readers the Bodleian and its dependent libraries could accommodate at any one time to 1,117 (a larger number than any other British university library).

By then, congestion in the Radcliffe Science Library had prompted discussion about how best to provide for the increasing number of students and the expanding collections. The ideal solution was thought by many in the university to be a completely new science library to house a million books and 550 readers, but it proved impossible to find

Fig. 96 **The Law Library, St Cross Building, completed in 1964.**

a suitable site for such a large building, and the alternative of expanding the existing library was reluctantly accepted. Shortage of funds delayed progress for over a decade and it was only in 1975 that an underground extension was completed, with a reading room for physical sciences accommodating 276 readers over a bookstack with 87,500 feet (26,670 metres) of shelving. Meanwhile, in 1970 a science lending library (the Hooke Library) was established, primarily for undergraduates, and administered within the Radcliffe Science Library.

The Law Faculty was also rapidly outgrowing the library provision made for it in the Lower Reading Room of the Old Library, and by 1960 it had been agreed that a new law library should be established, as a dependent library of the Bodleian, on a site the university was developing a little to the north and east of the city centre on Manor Road, near the parish church of St Cross. In September 1964 the law collections some 111,000 volumes were transferred to the new St Cross Building, designed by Sir Leslie Martin, where there was sufficient storage for expansion to 450,000 volumes (fig. 96). Of more immediate importance was the provision of desks for over 160 undergraduates and some eighty research students.

Oriental studies were provided with greatly increased accommodation in 1966 when their reading room was transferred from cramped conditions in the Old Library to a spacious room on the ground floor of the New Bodleian that had originally served as an exhibition room. The space thus vacated in the Old Library made it possible to increase the number of desks and of books on the open shelves for classics students. With the opening of two more reading rooms in the New Bodleian in the 1970s (one for music in 1973 and the other for the consultation of modern manuscripts and the John Johnson Collection of printed ephemera in 1976), all available space in the building had been converted for use by readers.

The need for more reading rooms is graphically demonstrated in the increasing number of readers admitted to use the library: from around 2,500 in the academic year 1952/53 to over 12,600 in 1992/93. This rapid rise was only partly due to the growth of the university. These four decades witnessed a great change in the nature of the readership. Whereas three quarters of the new readers in 1952/53 were members of the university, in 1992/93 only one third were. Sir Thomas Bodley's intention that his library should be of use not just to his own university but to the whole 'republic of the learned' had been amply realized. As a national and international research library the Bodleian was serving scholars from all over the world.

It was not only the number of readers that increased; the library's holdings also grew at an amazing rate. In 1951 it was estimated that the total number of volumes in the Bodleian was two million; by 1986 this had risen to almost five million, and by 2002 to seven million. The rapid growth was mainly the result of the increase in the number of books published in the United Kingdom, all available for acquisition under the copyright privilege, but also of the purchase of more foreign publications required by the expanding university. By the year 2001/2002 the accessions of current printed books and periodicals filled almost two miles of shelving. The earlier printed holdings also grew significantly, with the acquisition of a succession of large collections. The largest, the John Johnson Collection of printed ephemera, was transferred from the University Press in 1968 and filled two rooms in the New Library. The most varied and important collection of its kind in the British Isles, it was formed by John de Monins Johnson, printer to the university from 1925 to 1946, to illustrate the history of non-book printing, and came to be recognized as an important source for the study of social history from the seventeenth to the twentieth

Fig. 97 **Writing Blank (or school piece)** of 1808 entitled *Adventures of Franklin*.

Fig. 98 **First edition of songs from the film of** *The Wizard of Oz.*

centuries. With well over 1.5 million items, arranged by subjects devised for the most part by Johnson himself, it includes all manner of everyday printed material produced for short-term use, material that was usually thrown away once it had served its original purpose advertisements, ballads, bill headings, bookplates, cigarette cards, greetings cards, menus, paper bags, playbills and theatre programmes, postcards, trade cards and the like. In 1974 the enormous collection of opera scores and English, American and French popular songs accumulated by Walter Harding, a music hall pianist and cinema organist in Chicago, arrived in the Bodleian. Harding was born in south-east London, just off the Old Kent Road, in 1883 and moved to the USA when his parents emigrated to Chicago four years later. He never returned to England, but in 1950, when he began to consider what to do with the great collections he had amassed, he wondered if they 'should not go back to the land from whence they came and to the people that wrote the songs they contain. The Bodleian might be the library in which my stuff could fill a proper niche though a small one.'[3] Learning in the course of correspondence with Bodley's Librarian about the library's interest in music, he decided to donate his collection to the Bodleian, and confirmed the gift in 1963. In 1970 his name was inscribed on the Benefactors' Tablet.

The western manuscript collections also grew rapidly in the post-war years during the keepership of Richard Hunt. A graduate of Balliol and Senior Scholar at Christ Church, he had for eleven years been lecturer in palaeography at Liverpool University before he returned to Oxford on his appointment as Keeper of Western Manuscripts in 1945. He was the ideal man for the post, combining a well-established reputation as a medieval historian and classicist with extensive knowledge of manuscripts and an enthusiasm for making them more widely available. In 1953 his introductory volume to the *Summary Catalogue of Western Manuscripts* (alongside an index volume by P.D. Record) provided an indispensable guide to the Bodleian collections, and insights into the history of the library. He appointed specialist staff to the department, and directed the production of a succession of catalogues of the collections, some published and many more made available in Duke Humfrey's reading room in typescript form. He spent much of each day in the reading room, where over the years his willingness to discuss their research with readers made Duke Humfrey's a renowned centre for manuscript studies.

In 1955 the archaeologist and philanthropist Alexander Keiller gave the Bodleian his collection of over fifty manuscripts of the eighteenth-century antiquary William Stukeley, best known nowadays for his work on Avebury, Stonehenge and the Druids. The library had been collecting Stukeley material since 1924, when it purchased twenty volumes of his diary and antiquarian notes, which included accounts

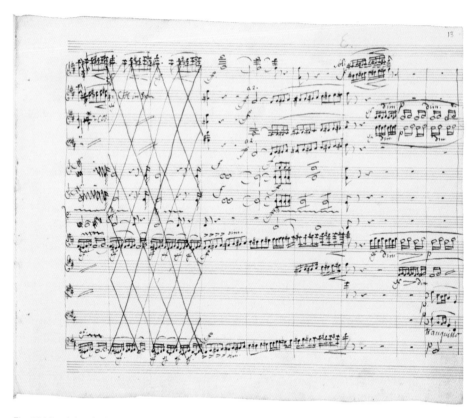

Fig. 99 **Mendelssohn's autograph score of** *The Hebrides* **overture, 1832.**

of the proceedings of the Royal Society. The collection grew over the
years through both donations and purchases. Keiller's gift doubled
the size of the collection, adding a wealth of important manuscripts,
among them Stukeley's drawings and plans of Avebury, Stonehenge
and Roman antiquities throughout Britain, and his *Liber amicorum*,
an autograph album containing the mottoes and signatures of a
host of eminent contemporaries in London society, the majority of
them physicians, antiquaries and members of the Royal Society,
but also including artists and engravers such as Godfrey Kneller,
John Talman, George Vertue and Michael Van der Gutch. In 1958
the antiquarian booksellers Lionel and Philip Robinson gave to the
library the topographical manuscripts that had been collected by the
nineteenth-century antiquary and bibliophile Sir Thomas Phillipps,
with all his personal correspondence and papers a collection of almost
two thousand volumes and boxes, a major source for studies of this
eccentric collector's life and work.

From 1973 the Bodleian became one of the foremost centres in the world for the study of the life and works of Felix Mendelssohn Bartholdy, thanks to the acquisition of a magnificent collection that includes manuscripts, drawing books, correspondence and printed scores from his library (fig. 99). It came directly and indirectly from descendants of the composer through the generosity and initiative of Margaret Deneke of Lady Margaret Hall. In 1978 Paul Mellon, having already donated several manuscripts of the seventeenth-century philosopher John Locke to augment the collection purchased by the Bodleian in 1947, presented over eight hundred books from Locke's library, which he had bought in 1960 from the descendants of Locke's cousin and legatee Peter, Lord King. In the same year the early records of the Conservative Party came to the Bodleian another huge collection and one that would grow over the years. Financed by private donations, it preserves documents dating from 1867 to the present day and is a major source for historical and political studies. It joined a growing number of collections of the private papers of politicians of all three major parties (including many cabinet ministers, and Prime Ministers Disraeli, Asquith, Macmillan, Wilson, Heath and Callaghan), as well as public servants (especially diplomats) and officials who worked in the United Nations organization.

In the course of the 1980s, large collections of the papers of Oxford scientists began to be acquired through the good offices of the Contemporary Scientific Archives Centre, among them those of Sir Rudolf Peierls, theoretical physicist; Charles Coulson, theoretical chemist; and William Hume-Rothery, chemist and metallurgist. Then in 1985 manuscripts from the library of St Michael's College, Tenbury Wells, including such treasures as Handel's own conducting score of *Messiah* (fig. 100), came as a gift. Five years later 4,500 printed items from Tenbury's collection were purchased, among them seventeenth-century musical treatises, French and Italian opera scores of the seventeenth and eighteenth centuries and many fine editions of major nineteenth-century works.

The collections at Rhodes House Library were expanded in 1986 by the deposit of the archive and historical section of the library of the Society for the Propagation of the Gospel, a major source for studies of Christian missions from the eighteenth century onwards. Iona and Peter Opie's great collection of children's literature was acquired in 1988, half

Fig. 100 **Handel's conducting score of** *Messiah*, 1743.

of it generously given by Mrs Opie and half purchased as the result of a public appeal. There are about twenty thousand items in the collection, accumulated in the course of their pioneering work on nursery rhymes and the lore, language and games of childhood. It contains all kinds of books for children, from grammars to colouring books, catechisms to comics, ranging in date from the sixteenth to the twentieth centuries. Acquisition of their collection was followed by the gift of the Opies' working papers. In 1988 the library's cartographic holdings were also augmented by the generous gift of Mr and Mrs H.M. Allen, who presented a fine collection of antiquarian maps and atlases of the British Isles, ranging in date from the sixteenth to the early twentieth centuries, which had been collected by G.E.H. Allen, and included material accumulated by Hugh Todhunter. The Todhunter Allen collection filled many gaps in the Bodleian's holdings: of the over one hundred county atlases dating from 1617 to 1885, forty-five were not already in the library, and the remarkable series of large-scale county maps and of maps of the whole of England and Wales (among them eighteenth- and nineteenth-century maps of canals, roads and railways) included a large proportion that were new to the Bodleian.

Space in the bookstack of the New Library was rapidly being used up by these acquisitions, and in 1966 the air-raid shelter on its lowest (L) floor was demolished; then, over the next thirteen years, as funding permitted, the whole of the large area (equivalent to the size of a football pitch) was gradually fitted out with compact mobile shelving. In 1975 it became apparent to the fire-prevention authorities that the original, unsophisticated air circulation system in the stack, which from the 1930s had kept it at an acceptable temperature for the storage of books, would, in the event of a fire, spread the fire all too rapidly from floor to floor. Fire-resistant walls were built around the stairwells and the shafts for the lifts and book conveyor. A smoke detection system was installed four years later. New environmental controls were then gradually introduced. Meanwhile, the storage capacity of the central Bodleian was increased by the installation of compact mobile shelving to house around one million more volumes on the lower floor of the underground bookstore between the Radcliffe Camera and the Old Library in 1995. It had, however, long been clear that books would have to be stored outside Oxford, and in 1974 planning permission was obtained for the construction of ten storage modules on university land adjacent to the Harcourt Arboretum at Nuneham Courtenay, about eight miles to the east of the city centre. The first was immediately constructed and gradually filled with books. In 1981 a second module was needed, but permission to build was withdrawn by the new planning authority. After protracted negotiations, including a ministerial inquiry, the university was granted permission to erect seven of the ten intended modules, and the second was completed in 1984, to be followed by the remainder over the next fifteen years. By 2005 the bookstack in the New Bodleian was filled to capacity with 3.5 million volumes, while 1.3 million books were housed at Nuneham Courtenay, where no further expansion would be possible. As a temporary measure, inconvenient and expensive commercial storage in the West Country and Cheshire had to be used.

The substantial increase in both the use of the library and the demand for the purchase of books published abroad coincided with a prolonged period of financial difficulty and of debate within the

Fig. 101 **Old Mother Hubbard from** *The Fairies Playtime* **by Clifton Bingham, c.1899.**

university about the role of the Bodleian. In 1968 the *Annual Report of the Curators*, while giving the good news that the year had ended with a favourable balance in the accounts, drew the university's attention to the need for significantly increased financial provision if the library was to maintain its current levels of service and acquisition, let alone explore new developments or make the major purchases that are an essential element in building up a library's reputation and usefulness.

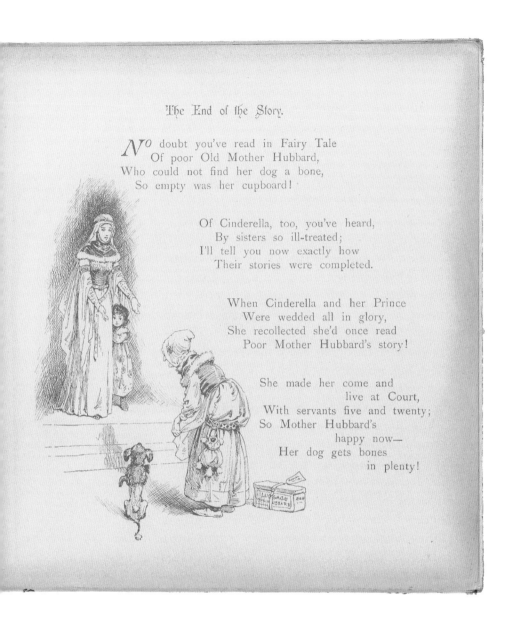

The End of the Story.

NO doubt you've read in Fairy Tale
Of poor Old Mother Hubbard,
Who could not find her dog a bone,
So empty was her cupboard!

Of Cinderella, too, you've heard,
By sisters so ill-treated;
I'll tell you now exactly how
Their stories were completed.

When Cinderella and her Prince
Were wedded all in glory,
She recollected she'd once read
Poor Mother Hubbard's story!

She made her come and
live at Court,
With servants five and twenty;
So Mother Hubbard's
happy now—
Her dog gets bones
in plenty!

After a brief respite in 1971/72, the financial situation worsened for the rest of the decade and persisted for the rest of the century. Staff posts were not filled when they became vacant, and budgets for the purchase of books and periodicals published abroad were cut, while inflation led to unexpected increases in expenditure on lighting and heating throughout the library's many buildings. Then, during the summer of 1978, the conveyor that since its installation had been the principal means of carrying books and manuscripts from the bookstack in the New Bodleian to the reading rooms in the Old Library suffered a series of breakdowns, unfortunately damaging a number of items. It was clear that a complete (and expensive) overhaul of the machinery was required. The university was unable to fund this essential work, and the cost (over £250,000) was met from the library's endowments, substantially reducing its income from trust and special funds. In their *Report* for the years 1980–85, the curators again made it clear that the library's major concern had been its finances, with what had by now become regular difficulties exacerbated by the fall of sterling against other currencies, especially the American dollar. The attempt to economize by reducing opening hours throughout the Bodleian was blocked by opposition within the university. Despite economies such as extending the moratorium on filling vacant staff posts and cutting expenditure on cleaning and maintenance to what many considered an unacceptable level, the library ended the year 1984/85 with a deficit of almost £55,000, which by 1993 had risen to £76,000.

In 1980 the reduction in the number of specialist staff in the Department of Western Manuscripts prompted its withdrawal from its role as an archive training establishment, a role it had first taken on in 1947, at the instigation of the Regius Professor of Modern History, Sir Maurice Powicke. He was keen to see the Bodleian's collections and the expertise of its staff used to help satisfy the demand for archivists in the burgeoning local authority record offices when no formal training courses existed. The Bodleian course was firmly based on practical work: listing, cataloguing and indexing; providing help to students in the reading rooms; and dealing with the many and varied queries which in those days came by post or telephone. By 1980 fifty archivists had been trained in the Bodleian, many of whom went on to become leaders in their profession, some as county and city archivists, one (Brian Smith) as secretary to the Historical Manuscripts Commission, and another (David Vaisey) as Keeper of Western Manuscripts and then Bodley's Librarian. One member of the Bodleian staff, Dr Molly Barratt, played a major part in the training course throughout its thirty-three years. She joined the library staff in 1947, while a postgraduate student at Somerville College researching for a DPhil on the condition of the parish clergy from the Reformation to 1660, and became an expert in the local ecclesiastical records deposited in the Bodleian. She retired at the end of 1983, and the following year the Bodleian relinquished its role as Diocesan Record Office, transferring the bulk of the records to Oxfordshire County Record Office and smaller quantities of Berkshire and Buckinghamshire archdeaconry and probate records to the record offices in Reading and Aylesbury.

In the 1960s two committees produced reports that prompted further discussion about the Bodleian's role within the university and the United Kingdom. The first was concerned with library provision in Oxford. It was chaired by Robert Shackleton, university reader in French, fellow and librarian of Brasenose College and a curator of the Bodleian, who was elected in February 1966 to succeed Nowell Myres as Bodley's Librarian. His committee reported later that year. Its major recommendation the establishment of a libraries board, to be charged with the coordination of the many libraries in the university (though not the college libraries) and with responsibility for advising the central administration on library matters was implemented in October 1967. All university funding for its libraries (including the Bodleian) was channelled through the new board. The second committee, the National Libraries Committee chaired by F.S. Dainton, had a nationwide remit, and reported in 1968. It spelled out how the larger university libraries including the Bodleian were discharging national library functions as a result of the strength of their collections, the quality of their staff and their services to international scholarship. The difficulties for the Bodleian of combining these dual roles as the major library for Oxford University and a national library (in the UK second only to the British Library) became increasingly apparent, especially when funding was not sufficient to meet either. When the university statutes were revised in 1971, it was made explicit that the libraries board, in allocating the university's grant between the libraries, was to 'have regard to the obligation of the University to maintain the Bodleian as a national and international as well as a university library',[6] while the curators were to be responsible for maintaining its importance in all three arenas. The response of the curators to the report of yet another university committee on library provision (the Nicholas Report of 1987) stressed the importance of the Bodleian as 'by far the largest, oldest, and most important of the University's libraries', while committing themselves to finding ways of making it more responsive to the university's needs. The main recommendation of the Nicholas Report was that Bodley's Librarian should become librarian to the university, with responsibility for the management of the majority of the university's many libraries. The suggestion was not new. It had first been made in 1877 by a fellow of All Souls College, but was at that time rejected out of hand. In 1987, in association with a host of other radical recommendations, it was put on hold.

The 1966 report of the Shackleton Committee analysed the potential of applying computer technology to the cataloguing of printed books throughout the university's libraries. A new sub-librarian post of Keeper of Catalogues was created in the Bodleian, and work began on the conversion of the pre-1920 transcribed catalogue into machine-readable form, as the first stage in what would be the long process of automating the Bodleian's general catalogue of its great collections of printed books. Technical problems and shortage of funds considerably delayed progress, and it was only in 1994 that the catalogue of all the pre-1920 books in the Bodleian became available worldwide, in the form of a CD-ROM published by Oxford University Press.

Robert Shackleton had been Bodley's Librarian for thirteen years when, in 1979, he resigned on his appointment as Marshal Foch Professor of French Literature. His successor, Richard Fifoot, after service with the Coldstream Guards in 1943–46 when he was awarded the Military Cross, had had a distinguished career in the university libraries of Leeds, Nottingham and Edinburgh. The fact that he had begun his library career in 1948 as a temporary junior assistant in the Radcliffe Science Library was fondly remembered, but his return to the Bodleian thirty years later was at a very difficult time. The post of deputy librarian had recently been abolished, so the librarian had no immediate source of independent advice on how best to implement the drastic cuts in library activities required by university retrenchment. His health soon began to give way under the strain and he retired in 1981 at the age of fifty-seven. He was succeeded by John Jolliffe, an expert in the use of computers in the cataloguing of early books, who had been Keeper of Catalogues since 1970. His term of office as Bodley's Librarian was characterized by the rigorous and expert way in which he brought the library's finances under control. It was brought to an abrupt end by his untimely death in March 1985.

During Jolliffe's years in the Bodleian the foundations were laid for the huge task of automating the cataloguing of the current intake of printed books. The library's idiosyncratic cataloguing rules and its nineteenth-century classification system were finally abandoned in September 1988 when online cataloguing to national and international standards began. The following April the first records became available to the public as part of a university-wide catalogue. Thereafter it became possible to catch up on the backlog of uncatalogued books and, assisted by cooperative cataloguing agreements with the other copyright libraries, to have information about newly acquired books available within a matter of weeks, even days. During the 1990s the catalogue of the library's holdings of books published between 1920 and 1988 was gradually converted into machine-readable form and by the end of the century the academic community worldwide could access online bibliographical records for the bulk of the Bodleian's printed collections. This improved access was one factor in a steady increase throughout the 1990s in the number of requests for books to be fetched from the bookstack in the New Library to the reading rooms in the Old. In the early months of 1995 the system for book delivery almost ground to a halt, and additional staff had to be recruited to maintain the service.

David Vaisey was appointed to succeed John Jolliffe as Bodley's Librarian and took up office in April 1986 (fig. 102). He had trained as an archivist in the Bodleian in 1959–60, after graduating in modern history at Exeter College. After three years at Staffordshire Record Office he returned to the Department of Western Manuscripts in 1963, was Deputy Keeper of the University Archives from 1966, and from 1975 Keeper of Western Manuscripts. The year 1986 proved a particularly onerous time to take the helm of the Bodleian. The chairman of the standing committee of the curators wrote that shortage of money had made the last few years difficult ones for the Bodleian, and forecast: 'It is not likely that things will get better quickly and the immediate outlook is in fact bleak, with the prospect of further cuts in income over the next few years.'4 How right he was! By the end of 1987 the financial situation had worsened. Thirty-three staff posts were vacant, and were left unfilled as an economy measure, while others had been abolished; book-purchasing budgets had been reduced; and, in accordance with university policy, the library had to cut its expenditure by a further 11 per cent in the next four years. Meanwhile, the number of readers, from within the university and beyond, continued to increase and there was no reduction in the need for library support of teaching

and research. Only by seeking new sources of funding could the library hope to maintain its great collections and to meet some of the demands for the introduction of more facilities, especially those associated with the new technology. David Vaisey as Bodley's Librarian proved the ideal person to revive Sir Thomas Bodley's tradition of 'stirring up other men's benevolence'.

In July 1988 the Bodleian combined celebration of the five-hundredth anniversary of the completion of Duke Humfrey's Library with the launch of a fund-raising campaign at a dinner in the Radcliffe Camera. One of the most glittering events in the history of the library, it was attended by 245 guests, with the Prince of Wales as guest of honour. The only other time a meal had been served in the Camera's splendid upper room was in 1814, when the Prince Regent had presided over a banquet there, to celebrate the defeat of Napoleon (prematurely as it turned out) with the king of Prussia and the tsar of Russia. The campaign launched in 1988 aimed to raise £10 million in five years, and, thanks to donations large and small from all over the world, especially from North America, the target was reached. Many donations were earmarked for the conservation of the collections that were deteriorating through overuse, others to supplement book-buying budgets in specialist areas or to assist both with the cataloguing of recent acquisitions and the improvement of older catalogues. A donation of £1 million from the publisher Paul Hamlyn enabled the library to fill, on a temporary basis, many of the staff posts that had had to be frozen. In recognition of his generous gift, the keepership of printed books was named after him. Other donors specified that their gifts should be used for the maintenance and enhancement of library buildings. Fund-raising had become an essential part of the library's and especially the librarian's work, and continues to be so to the present day.

The campaign had both benefited from and contributed to the development of associations of Friends of the Bodleian, which provide a network of international friendship and support for library acquisitions, cataloguing and conservation. To the original Friends of the Bodleian, established in 1925, were added, first, Bodley's American Friends in 1957, then groups of Canadian and German Friends in 1983 and 1988

Fig. 102 **Portrait of David Vaisey, Bodley's Librarian from 1986 to 1996, by Paul Brason, 1996.**

respectively, followed by Japanese Friends in 1990 and South African Friends in 1994. All these groups have bought important items to add to the library collections, often in collaboration. For example, the Friends of the Bodleian and Bodley's American Friends combined to purchase a collection of notebooks of two Oxford tradesmen Henry Hinton, an ironmonger (1749–1816) and James Hunt, a chemist (1795–1857), which are of great interest to historians of Oxfordshire and Berkshire, as they provide a wealth of information about churches, their furnishings, fittings and monumental inscriptions before so much was lost in the restoration work later in the nineteenth century. Of national importance was the purchase, assisted by Bodley's American Friends, of the only known autograph manuscript of a poem by John Donne, his 'Epistle to Lady Carew' (fig. 103). In 1993 the Friends and American Friends together filled a significant gap in the library's holdings with the purchase of a copy of the first edition of Mary Shelley's *Frankenstein*. Throughout the 1980s and 1990s, the pump-priming contributions of its Friends organizations facilitated the library's applications to national fund-giving bodies for the purchase of a wide range of important books and manuscripts.

A major exhibition on *The Bodleian Library and its Friends* was displayed in the USA (in Washington, Chicago and Los Angeles) from December 1969 to May 1970 as an expression of the library's gratitude for the generous assistance of American Friends. Exhibitions had long been recognized as an important means of making the collections known to a wider audience. In 1965 part of the agreement associated with the move of the Indian Institute Library was that the Bodleian could use the Divinity School as an exhibition room (thus freeing up much-needed space in the New Bodleian that had originally been designated for exhibitions) and of the Proscholium as an entrance to the Old Library. Three years later the Bodleian took over responsibility for both the Divinity School and the Proscholium. The combination of magnificent fifteenth-century architecture with changing displays of a wide range of books and manuscripts from the library collections proved a tremendous attraction. In the first year 64,000 people visited the exhibition in the Divinity School; by 1985 the number had risen to an astonishing 400,000, and the Old Library had become firmly established as a high point on the Oxford tourist route. Many of the visitors were interested in seeing something of the library itself, but

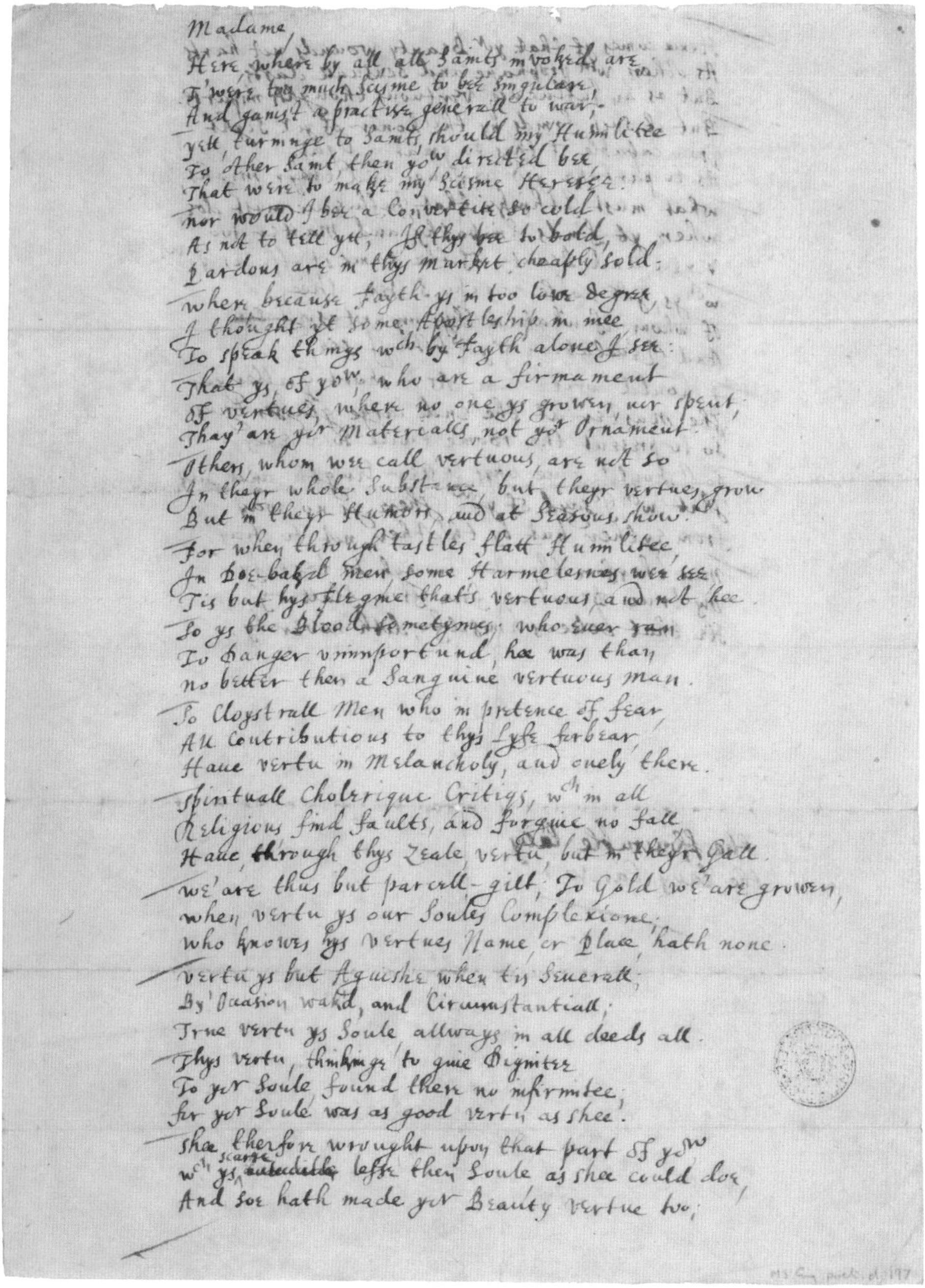
Madame,
Here where by all all Saints invoked are,
T'were too much Scisme to bee singulare,
And gainst a practise generall to warr,
Yett turninge to Saints, should my Humilitee
To other Saint, then yow directed bee
That were to make my Scisme, Heresee.
Nor would I bee a Convertite so cold
As not to tell ytt; If thys bee too bold,
Pardons are in thys market cheaply sold.
Where because fayth ys in too lowe degree,
I thought ytt some Apostleship in mee
To speak things wch by fayth alone I see:
That ys, of yow, who are a firmament
Of vertues, where no one ys growen, nor spent,
They'are yor Materialls, not yor Ornament.
Others, whom wee call vertuous, are not so
In theyr whole Substance, but theyr vertues grow
But in theyr Humors, and at Seasons show.
For when through tastles flatt Humilitee
In doe-bak'd men some Harmelesnes wee see,
'Tis but hys flegme that's vertuous, and not hee.
So ys the Blood sometymes; who ever ran
To danger vnimportun'd, hee was than
No better then a Sanguine vertuous man.
So Cloystrall Men who in pretence of fear
All Contributions to thys Lyfe forbear,
Haue vertu in Melancholy, and onely there.
Spirituall Cholerique Critiqs, wch in all
Religions find faults, and forgiue no fall
Haue, through thys Zeale, vertu, but in theyr Gall.
We'are thus but parcell-gilt; To Gold we'are growen,
When vertu ys our Soules Complexione;
Who knowes hys vertues Name, or Place, hath none.
Vertu ys but Aguishe when tis Severall;
By'Occasion wak'd, and Circumstantiall;
True vertu ys Soule allwayes in all deeds all.
Thys vertu, thinkinge to giue Dignitee
To yor Soule found there no infirmitee;
For yor Soule was as good vertu as shee.
Shee therfore wrought upon that part of yow
Wch ys scarse lesse then Soule as shee could doe,
And soe hath made yor Beauty vertue too;

Fig. 103 **Autograph manuscript of John Donne's 'Epistle to Lady Carew', 1611–12.**

Duke Humfrey's Library had been closed to the general public since 1979, as a result of concerns about security and disturbance to readers. In response to demand, and in the hope of generating much-needed income, a programme of tours conducted by volunteer guides was introduced. It was an enormous success and continues to provide a glimpse of the oldest parts of the Bodleian to thousands of visitors every year. Meanwhile income generation through commercial operations, originally centred on the library shop, expanded through publications and sales by mail order; in the year 1996/97 the turnover of the marketing and publications division was just short of £450,000. The fine architecture of the library's central buildings attracted requests for location filming, which from the 1980s proved another welcome source of income and one that interested a worldwide audience. The Bodleian features in television series such as *Brideshead Revisited*, *Inspector Morse*, *Lewis* and *Endeavour*, and in films such as *Another Country* (1984), based on the early life of the spy and double agent Guy Burgess; *Shadowlands* (1993), about the relationship between the Oxford don and author C.S. Lewis and the American poet Joy Gresham; Alan Bennett's *The Madness of King George* (1994); *Gulliver's Travels* (1996); *To Kill a King* (2003), which recounted the problematic relations between General Fairfax and Oliver Cromwell as they came to terms with the consequences of the execution of King Charles I; and *The New World* (2005), the story of the English exploration of Virginia. Most popular of all were the films of J.K. Rowling's Harry Potter books, which featured Duke Humfrey's Library as the library of Hogwarts School and the Divinity School as its sanatorium.

By 1992 it had become clear that the level of light coming through the wonderful windows of the Divinity School, even with the precautions routinely exercised, was damaging the books and manuscripts on display. Attention switched to the School of Natural Philosophy, which had since 1968 been used to augment the exhibition space in the Divinity School. In 1993–94 it was transformed into the library's principal exhibition room, meeting modern standards for the display of library materials. A unique contribution came from Bodley's Librarian, David Vaisey, who ran the London Marathon in April 1990, finishing in 4 hours and 15 minutes, and through sponsorship raising over £21,000. The refurbished and redesigned exhibition room was opened in July 1994.

In 1993 another dependent library, the Bodleian Japanese Library, was opened in the newly constructed building of the Nissan Institute of Japanese Studies in the grounds of St Antony's College, with space to store about 98,000 volumes and to seat some thirty-two readers. It houses collections of modern publications, early printed books and manuscripts relating to the history and culture of Japan from the earliest times to the present day. Later that year the Oriental Institute Library and the Eastern Art Library in the Ashmolean Museum, and in 1994 a new library for Chinese studies, became dependent libraries. All four came under the administration of the Bodleian's Department of Oriental Books.

In January 1995 David Vaisey announced his intention to retire at the end of the following year and the university returned to the vexed question, shelved in 1987, of how best to organize its libraries, in the light of the savings to be made if the purchasing policies of the individual libraries, and their efforts to automate their catalogues and to provide facilities for the preservation and conservation of their collections, could be better coordinated. A committee chaired by Sir Keith Thomas, president of Corpus Christi College, reported in June 1995, recommending, as the Nicholas Committee had done nine years earlier, that all the libraries should be brought under the governance of one university committee, and managed by the holder of a newly created post of director of University Library Services and Bodley's Librarian. The proposal was approved and Reg Carr, then University Librarian and Keeper of the Brotherton Collection at Leeds, took up the new post in January 1997. Three years later detailed proposals for the integration of the university's libraries were agreed and the Bodleian became the largest library in what was to be known as Oxford University Library Services (OULS). In 2001 the Vere Harmsworth Library, which holds collections relating to the history, culture and politics of the United States (the bulk transferred from Rhodes House Library), joined the university libraries. It was housed in the adjacent Rothermere American Institute which was opened by former president Bill Clinton on 25 May that year.

Discussion about management and governance did not delay consideration of how to bring the Old Bodleian building up to modern standards, both for the provision of service to readers and for the care of the many thousands of books it housed. An infestation of death watch beetle in the damp roof timbers of Duke Humfrey's Library prompted a major consultation and fund-raising exercise, leading in 1998 to a four-year programme of renovation that was reminiscent of the work Sir Thomas Bodley had undertaken on the fifteenth-century library 400 years earlier, between 1598 and 1602. The copper roof was repaired, the floors were replaced, the heating system made more controllable, the lighting improved, the windows coated with ultraviolet and solar filters, and all the readers' desks wired up for personal computers. The frieze of painted heads in the Upper Reading Room was carefully restored, and the copper roof over Duke Humfrey's Library was raised to provide the ventilation necessary to keep the roof timbers dry and free from death watch beetle. In 2002, four centuries after it had first opened its doors to scholars and students, the library that Sir Thomas Bodley had founded was once again ready to meet the needs of contemporary students and scholars and to serve their successors in future generations. Celebration of the library's quatercentenary included two major exhibitions (*Sir Thomas Bodley and his Library* and *Wonderful Things from Four Hundred Years of Collecting*), 'An Evening with Alan Bennett' in the Sheldonian Theatre and a concert in Merton College Chapel featuring seventeenth-century music with Oxford associations, performed by the Taverner Consort, the Orchestra of the Age of Enlightenment and the choir of New College.

Celebration of the library's four-hundredth anniversary provided an opportunity to launch another fund-raising campaign, this time to assist in the much-needed renovation of the New Bodleian. At first the campaign focused on alterations to the bookstack primarily to reduce the fire risk, but also to improve the shelving and the air circulation system to provide more stable temperatures and relative humidity for the storage of the collections. The university pledged £10 million towards the project, but only a couple more million pounds had been raised by mid-2004. It became clear that potential benefactors thought that the university itself should cover the cost of such essential improvements to the storage of its library collections. Prompted by the vice-chancellor, John Hood, a re-evaluation of the campaign produced a broader vision for the New Bodleian, combining alterations in the bookstack and compliance with national standards for the storage of archival material (BS 5454) with improvement of the reading rooms, provision of seminar rooms, a lecture theatre and two state-of-the-art

Fig. 104 **The Upper Reading Room in the Old Bodleian.**

exhibition rooms designed to display to the general public the great
interest of the library's collections.

Meanwhile, rapid advances in information technology necessitated
and facilitated major changes in the organization of Oxford's libraries
and in the means by which services were delivered to readers within the
university and throughout the world. Under Reg Carr, who continued
in post as director of University Library Services and Bodley's Librarian
until the end of 2006, the management of all university-funded libraries
(including the English and History Faculty libraries and, for languages
and classics, the Taylorian and Sackler libraries) was integrated. The
Oxford University Library Services, with the Bodleian at the centre,
developed into the largest unitary academic library system in the world.
Automation of all stages of the cataloguing process was followed by the
introduction of an automated stack request system that enabled readers
at their own work stations to order books from the closed storage areas
in advance of a visit to study in a university library.

From the 1990s a series of digitization projects provided online
access to an increasing range of library materials, making many of

its collections available for study outside the Bodleian buildings for the first time. The John Johnson Collection showed the way with a project in collaboration with Toyota, featuring printed ephemera relating to motoring. It was soon followed by further selections of ephemera, illustrating, among other subjects, the book trade, advertising, entertainment and crime in the nineteenth and early twentieth centuries. Early English manuscripts, illuminations in medieval and Renaissance manuscripts, and broadside ballads (popular songs from the sixteenth to the twentieth centuries that had originally been printed and circulated in sheet format) also gradually became available online. From 2006 the Bodleian's participation in the Google digitization project, alongside Harvard University, Stanford University, the University of Michigan and the New York Public Library, provided the texts of over 400,000 out-of-copyright nineteenth-century books. Between 2012 and 2017, in collaboration with the Vatican Library, many Greek and Hebrew manuscripts, with early editions of the Bible and biblical commentaries, were made available to researchers and the general public worldwide. In 2015 the images from all these projects were brought together on one site the Digital Bodleian.

In 2007 Sarah Thomas, formerly Carl A. Kroch Librarian at Cornell University, was appointed director of University Library Services and Bodley's Librarian. Shortly after her arrival in Oxford, she was faced with the collapse of the university's plan to build a book repository at Osney Mead, designed to relieve the pressure of an ever-expanding book stock on the central library buildings. Recognizing, as had been foreseen in the 1980s, that it was no longer feasible for universities to provide enormous closed-access libraries on central sites as constrained as the Bodleian's, she pressed for an out-of-town solution, which was achieved in the construction of a Book Storage Facility (BSF) at South Marston on the outskirts of Swindon, twenty-five miles west of the Bodleian's main buildings (fig. 105). The storage facility has a floor area equivalent to that of 1.6 football pitches, fitted out with a solid shelving system eleven metres high, providing 230 kilometres (153 miles) of shelf space, and a five-level multi-tier structure for the storage of maps. Its completion in 2010 made possible the transfer of the bulk of the millions of lesser-used books from the New Library bookstack and the Camera basement a mammoth undertaking, expertly executed by the library's own book service staff. Beginning in October 2010,

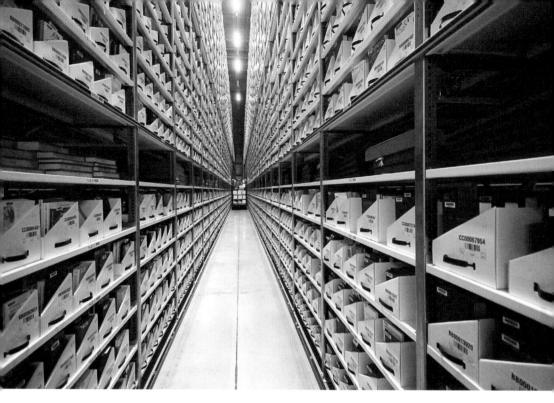

Fig. 105 **The Bodleian's book storage facility at South Marston, near Swindon.**

the volumes were moved at a rate of 35,000 a day and the first readers' requests for items to be transferred from Swindon to the central reading rooms were processed on 8 November, 406 years to the day since readers had first consulted books in Sir Thomas Bodley's library.

The move to the BSF of many little-used books from the Radcliffe Camera's basement made possible the transformation of the two floors of underground bookstore into the Gladstone Link, a stack and reading room with around 270,000 items (the majority of the previous three years' acquisitions in the humanities) immediately available to readers, who could now access them either from the Radcliffe Camera or from the Old Bodleian through a tunnel that had hitherto been used only for the delivery of books. An additional 120 reader places were also provided. Furnished with group study tables behind acoustic screens and easy chairs, as well as more formal desks, the Gladstone Link provides a more relaxed and informal environment for study than the traditional reading rooms elsewhere in the library.

The massive transfer of stock from the central library site paved the way for an ambitious plan to transform the New Bodleian, which

Fig. 106 **The Special Collections Reading Room in the Weston Library,** formerly the Politics, Philosophy and Economics Reading Room.

seventy years earlier had been designed primarily for book storage, into a modern special collections library and research centre. The challenge was to achieve major changes to the interior while retaining the building's historical features. (It had, at the prompting of the Twentieth Century Society, been listed as a Grade II building in 2002.) The core of the 1930s building was gutted, the bookstack redesigned, the three reading rooms greatly improved (fig. 106) and a lecture theatre, seminar and meeting rooms provided. These facilities to support research and teaching inside the building were complemented by alterations to the forbidding Broad Street frontage, which had for so long presented a fortress-like image to the outside world. Under the skilful guidance of the project's architects, WilkinsonEyre, the facade was opened up with shallow steps and sloping ramps inviting the public into the building (fig. 107), and leading through glass doors into the spacious Blackwell Hall (fig. 88), with a cafe, library shop and two small exhibition cases. At the back of the hall are two state-of-the-art exhibition rooms a small 'Treasury' showing a changing selection of some of the best-known items in the library's collections and a larger room used for a succession of major themed displays. Renamed the Weston Library, in recognition of a major donation from the Garfield Weston Foundation, the remodelled New Bodleian opened to readers as the Weston Library in October 2014 (with a formal opening the following May). It is anticipated that with the BSF at Swindon providing for the library's ever-expanding collections, there is no longer the risk that facilities for teaching will be swamped, as they were in the Schools Quadrangle in the eighteenth and nineteenth centuries and in the New Bodleian in the twentieth, by the relentless growth of the library itself. The completion of this development ended the 400-year-old role of Duke Humfrey's Library as the centre for the study of the Bodleian's rare books and manuscripts. Although still open to readers, it is frequented more by visitors who continue to enjoy the magnificent view of the fifteenth-century room as refitted by Sir Thomas Bodley.

During Sarah Thomas's librarianship from 2007 to 2013, collaborative digitization projects with other major research libraries continued to be a significant element in the library's strategy of making the collections more widely available. The integration of libraries within the university was consolidated and the name of Oxford University Library Services changed to the Bodleian Libraries in 2010, in recognition of 'the strength of the Bodleian name worldwide as a library of distinction'. Richard Ovenden, Keeper of Special Collections from 2003 and Deputy Librarian from 2009, played a leading role in the development of digital services within the university, and nationwide from 2009 as chair of the Digital Preservation Coalition. He was the driving force behind the Weston Library, overseeing every aspect of the project. In February 2014 he was appointed Bodley's Librarian, the twenty-fifth since the foundation of the library.

Although discussions about governance and building developments may seem to have dominated the early years of the twenty-first century, the Bodleian continued to acquire important manuscript and printed materials that significantly enhanced its collections and facilitated research. In 2004 the Abinger collection of Godwin and Shelley papers, which had been on deposit in the library for many years, was purchased after an international fund-raising campaign. A major source for British literary and intellectual history during the Romantic period, it includes journals, correspondence and papers of

Fig. 107 **The Broad Street frontage of the Weston Library.**

the philosopher William Godwin, his wife Mary Wollstonecraft, their daughter Mary, and her husband Percy Bysshe Shelley. The Marconi Archive, an important source for studies of wireless telegraphy, sound broadcasting and television, which includes a series of telegrams relating to the disastrous first voyage of the *Titanic*, came in 2004. In 2007 the library received Albi Rosenthal's bequest of his collection of eighty-seven first and early editions of the works of Mozart, all published in the composer's lifetime. The following year the archive

of the Harcourt family of Stanton Harcourt and Nuneham Courtenay was allocated to the Bodleian, having been accepted by the government in lieu of tax. Most of the collection had been on deposit in the library since 1972 and had proved an invaluable resource for political, social, literary and local history. Alongside the papers and correspondence of Sir William Harcourt (1827–1904), Home Secretary and Chancellor of the Exchequer in Gladstone's governments in the 1880s and 1890s, and of his son Lewis (1863–1922), Secretary of State for the Colonies from 1910 to 1915, it included a very large collection of Oxfordshire

Fig. 108 **View from the Weston Library's roof terrace.**

estate and household papers. The year 2008 was also marked by Alan Bennett's gift of his great literary archive, which includes scripts of his plays, short stories, articles, theatre programmes and diaries. The local history collections were enhanced by the ledgers of the shoemakers Ducker & Son of Turl Street in Oxford, and by the archive of the printers Cheney & Sons of Banbury. Papers of the composer Edmund Rubbra, including letters, diaries and annotated scores, were purchased in 2012. He had been a lecturer in Oxford's newly founded Faculty of Music and a fellow of Worcester College.

A history of the Bodleian's first 400 years would be incomplete without some attempt to explain what enabled it to develop from a fifteenth-century library room, beautifully restored at one man's expense, into a national and international research centre, ranking among the foremost university libraries in the world. No single factor can account for its longevity, but there can be no doubt that Sir Thomas Bodley's vision and generosity, combined with his sound business acumen, were crucial in laying the foundations on which it grew. He was a man ahead of his time in establishing a public library in a university setting, one that was, moreover, in the centre of the country. He had seen in the failure of the earlier university library the result of both lax administration and a lack of adequate funding. His library from the outset benefited not only from the endowment he provided but also from a framework of detailed regulations on governance, staffing and use, enshrined in his first draft of the library statutes; these were amended over the centuries by successive generations in the library and university to adapt the Bodleian to the circumstances of their own times, sometimes reflecting and sometimes leading changes in the needs of scholarship. Bodley's adept use of his wide contacts in diplomatic, government and academic circles secured spectacular donations of printed books and manuscripts that, in his own lifetime, formed the basis of a collection of European importance, unparalleled in Britain until the rapid growth of the library in the British Museum after its foundation in 1753. His agreement with the Stationers' Company in 1610 paved the way for the Bodleian's development into a copyright library. The personalities of successive Bodley's Librarians were of enormous importance in the development of the library in their charge. In their cultivation of potential benefactors and their defence of the copyright privilege, and through such purchases as fluctuating funding permitted, they did much to ensure the steady growth of its remarkable collections. Their publication of catalogues made known the contents of the Bodleian, facilitating research, enhancing its reputation and attracting scholars from far and wide. When occasionally they were lax in attending to their duties, momentum was maintained by the governing body of curators, all senior members of the university. This was most noticeable in the last decades of the eighteenth century, when the curators, in response to the criticism of Thomas Beddoes, increased staff, revised regulations, saw to the publication of lists of newly acquired books and took the initiative in making purchases at important auction sales. On many occasions the university provided the funding that the library itself lacked, to enable it to add to the collections as both an ornament to Oxford and an invaluable asset for its students. The importance to scholarship of the Bodleian's collections continued to attract donations, and in the last decades of the twentieth century often provided the basis for successful applications to national grant-giving bodies that enabled the library to continue to purchase on the open market as the prices of manuscripts and rare books escalated.

Bodley's librarians

1599–1620	Thomas James
1620–52	John Rouse
1652–60	Thomas Barlow
1660–65	Thomas Lockey
1665–1701	Thomas Hyde
1701–19	John Hudson
1719–29	Joseph Bowles
1729–47	Robert Fysher
1747–68	Humphrey Owen
1768–1813	John Price
1813–60	Bulkeley Bandinel
1860–81	H.O. Coxe
1882–1912	E.W.B. Nicholson
1912–19	Falconer Madan
1919–31	Arthur Cowley
1931–45	H.H.E. Craster
1945–47	H.R. Creswick
1947–65	J.N.L. Myres
1966–79	Robert Shackleton
1979–81	E.R.S. Fifoot
1982–85	J.W. Jolliffe
1986–96	David Vaisey
1997–2006	R.P. Carr
2007–13	Sarah Thomas
2014–	Richard Ovenden

Notes

Chapter 1

1 See 'Cobham, Thomas (c.1265–1327)', in *Oxford Dictionary of National Biography*.

2 Revd H. Anstey (ed.), *Munimenta Academica; or, Documents Illustrative of Academical Life and Studies at Oxford*, Rolls Series, London, 1868, pt I, pp. 226–8.

3 *Munimenta Academica*, pt I, pp. 261–8.

4 A facsimile of the manuscript (MS. Bodl. 13, part A) was published by the Bodleian Library as *Queen Elizabeth's Book of Oxford* in 2006, edited with an introduction by Louise Durning and an English translation by Sarah Knight and Helen Spurling. Bereblock's drawing was used by David Gentleman as the basis of the logo he designed for the Bodleian in 1982.

5 Anthony à Wood, *The History and Antiquities of the University of Oxford*, ed. John Gutch, vol. 2, pt 2, Oxford, 1796, p. 919.

Chapter 2

1 *The Autobiography of Sir Thomas Bodley*, ed. William Clennell, Oxford, 2006, p. 52.

2 *Autobiography of Bodley*, p. 52.

3 *Trecentale Bodleianum*, Oxford, 1913, p. 24.

4 *Trecentale Bodleianum*, p. 24.

5 *Letters of Sir Thomas Bodley to the University of Oxford*, ed. G.W. Wheeler, Oxford, 1927, p. 6.

6 *Letters of Sir Thomas Bodley to Thomas James*, ed. G.W. Wheeler, Oxford, 1926, p. 1.

7 *Bodley to James*, p. 60.

8 *Calendar of State Papers Domestic, 1598–1601*, London, 1895, p. 35.

9 *The Letters and the Life of Francis Bacon*, ed. James Spedding, 7 vols, London, 1861–74, vol. 3, p. 253.

10 *Bodley to the University*, p. 7.

11 The first statutes of 1610 are headed 'The Statutes of the Public Bodleian Library': see G.R.M. Ward, *Oxford University Statutes*, 2 vols, London, 1845, 1851, vol. 1, p. 240.

12 See Ian Philip, *The Bodleian Library in the Seventeenth and Eighteenth Centuries*, Oxford, 1983, pp. 9–10, 13, 25, and 'Norton, John (1556/7–1612)', in *Oxford Dictionary of National Biography*.

13 *Bodley to James*, p. 168.

14 *Bodley to James*, p. 35.

15 *Bodley to James*, p. 219.

16 *Bodley to James*, pp. 221–2.

17 *Bodley to James*, p. 53.

18 Ward, *Statutes*, vol. 1, p. 247.

19 Ward, *Statutes*, vol. 1, p. 215.

20 *Bodley to James*, pp. 230–31.

21 *Bodley to James*, p. 18, n. 2.

22 Stanley Gillam, *The Divinity School and Duke Humfrey's Library at Oxford*, Oxford, 1988, p. 56.

23 Strickland Gibson (ed.), *Statuta Antiqua Universitatis Oxoniensis*, Oxford, 1931, p. 497.

24 Ward, *Statutes*, vol. 1, pp. 241–9.

25 *Bodley to James*, pp. 147–8.

26 *Bodley to James*, p. 188.

27 G.W. Wheeler, *The Earliest Catalogues of the Bodleian Library*, Oxford, 1928, p. 35.

28 *Trecentale Bodleianum*, p. 49.

29 Ward, *Statutes*, vol. 1, p. 255.

30 *Bodley to James*, p. 76.

31 *Bodley to James*, p. 66.

32 Ward, *Statutes*, vol. 1, p. 264.

33 Ward, *Statutes*, vol. 1, p. 255.

34 *Trecentale Bodleianum*, pp. 51–2; for a full account of the oath and declaration, see William Clennell, 'The Bodleian Declaration: A History', *The Bodleian Library Record*, vol. 20, nos 1–2, 2007, pp. 47–60.

35 *Trecentale Bodleianum*, p. 24.

36 Printed in William Dunn Macray, *Annals of the Bodleian Library Oxford*, 2nd edn, Oxford, 1890, pp. 412–18.

37 Gwen Hampshire (ed.), *The Bodleian Library Account Book 1613–1646*, Oxford Bibliographical Society, NS, vol. 21, 1983, p. 144.

38 Gabriel Naudé, *Advis pour dresser une bibliothèque*, Paris, 1627, p. 154.

39 Philip, *Bodleian Library*, pp. 35–6. Gronovius as a young man travelled extensively in England, France and Italy and was from 1658 to 1671 Professor of Greek at the University of Leiden.

40 Macray, *Annals*, p. 104.

41 Oxford University Archives, WPβ/21/4, p. 11.

42 Oxford, Bodleian Library, Arch. G e. 44, reproduced in Philip, *Bodleian Library*, pl. 11.

43 Macray, *Annals*, p. 100.

44 'Burton, Robert (1577–1640)', in *Oxford Dictionary of National Biography*. The *Anatomy of Melancholy*, first published in 1621, proved very popular and ran to eight editions in the seventeenth century.

45 Philip, *Bodleian Library*, p. 37.

46 Macray, *Annals*, p. 407.

47 Macray, *Annals*, p. 99.

48 Macray, *Annals*, p. 99.

49 Oxford, Bodleian Library, Library Records e. 544.

Chapter 3

1 Oxford, Bodleian Library, MS. Wood donat. 1.

2 Oxford, Bodleian Library, Library Records c. 1073.

3 See William Dunn Macray, *Annals of the Bodleian Library Oxford*, 2nd edn, Oxford, 1890, p. 113, and *Bishop Barlow's State of the Case*, London, 1670, p. ii.

4 *Bishop Barlow's State of the Case*, p. iv.

5 *Bishop Barlow's State of the Case*, p. i.

6 *The Life of Edward, Earl of Clarendon … written by himself*, London, 1759, vol. i, p. 31.

7 Oxford, Bodleian Library, Library Records b. 474–5; *Remarks and Collections of Thomas Hearne*, ed. C.E. Doble, David Watson Rannie and Herbert Edward Salter, Oxford Historical Society, no. 7, 1886, p. 40; Oxford.

8 Monsieur Sorbière, *A Voyage to England*, London, 1709, p. 41.

9 Thomas Sprat, *Observations on Monsieur de Sorbier's Voyage into England*, London, 1665, p. 2.

10 Oxford, Bodleian Library, MS. Smith 47, fol. 140, quoted in Ian Philip, *The Bodleian Library in the Seventeenth and Eighteenth Centuries*, Oxford, 1983, p. 126 n. 64.

11 His deed of gift, witnessed by Thomas Marshall and Obadiah Walker, is Oxford, Bodleian Library, Library Records c. 1138, fols 2–3.

12 For an account of Thomas Tanner and his collections, see above pp. 109–10.

13 Macray, *Annals*, p. 138.

14 *The Life and Times of Anthony Wood, Antiquary, of Oxford, 1632–1695*, ed. Andrew Clark, 5 vols, Oxford Historical Society, no. 26, 1894, pp. 236–7.

15 Oxford, Bodleian Library, MS. Bodl. 907, fol. 11.

16 Oxford, Bodleian Library, MS. Bodl. 907, fol. 4v.

17 S.G. Gillam and R.W. Hunt, 'The Curators of the Library and Humphrey Wanley', *The Bodleian Library Record*, vol. 5, 1954, pp. 85–98, esp. p. 88.

18 Oxford, Bodleian Library, Library Records e. 3, fol. 17, quoted in Philip, *Bodleian Library*, p. 65.

19 Quoted in *A Chorus of Grammars: The Correspondence of George Hickes and his Collaborators on the Thesaurus linguarum septentrionalium*, ed. Richard L. Harris, Toronto, 1992, p. 202.

20 David Lloyd, *Memoires of the Lives ...*, London, 1677, p. 518, quoted in 'Langbaine, Gerard (1608/9–1658), in *Oxford Dictionary of National Biography*.

21 For an account of Samuel Clarke, orientalist and first controller of the university press, see 'Clarke, Samuel (bap. 1624, d. 1669)', in *Oxford Dictionary of National Biography*.

22 In 1859 these portraits were hanging on the staircase, but in the 1870s they were moved into Duke Humfrey's Library, filling the gaps between the windows on the north and south walls when the side galleries were removed; see Sir Edmund Craster, *History of the Bodleian Library, 1845–1945*, Oxford, 1981, p. 9, and Stanley Gillam, *The Divinity School and Duke Humfrey's Library at Oxford*, Oxford, 1988, p. 74.

23 Printed in full in Macray, *Annals*, pp. 170–1.

Chapter 4

1 Ian Philip, *The Bodleian Library in the Seventeenth and Eighteenth Centuries*, Oxford, 1983, p. 73.

2 Oxford, Bodleian Library, MS. Rawl. let. 90, fol. 47, quoted in Philip, *Bodleian Library*, p. 80.

3 Philip, *Bodleian Library*, pp. 70, 85, quoting from *Oxford in 1710, being the Travels of Zacharius Conrad von Uffenbach*, ed. W.H. Quarrell and W.J.C. Quarrell, Oxford, 1926, pp. 2–3, 26.

4 Uffenbach, *Oxford in 1710*, p. 51.

5 Oxford, Bodleian Library, MS. Rawl. B. 399*.

6 William Dunn Macray, *Annals of the Bodleian Library Oxford*, 2nd edn, Oxford, 1890, pp. 192, 199, quoting from Hearne's diaries.

7 This copy of the *Bay Psalm Book* is now the only copy known to have survived outside the United States.

8 See pp. 117-21. Many of his letters to Rawlinson survive in Rawlinson's manuscripts in the Bodleian.

9 Macray, *Annals*, p. 57.

10 For full and illlustrated accounts, see Stanley Gillam, *The Radcliffe Camera*, Oxford, 1992, and Stephen Hebron, *Dr Radcliffe's Library: The Story of the Radcliffe Camera in Oxford*, Oxford, 2014.

11 Thomas Salmon, *The Present State of the Universities and of the Five Adjacent Counties of Cambridge, Huntington, Bedford, Buckingham and Oxford*, London, 1744, p. 37.

12 Philip, *Bodleian Library*, p. 93.

13 Ian Philip, 'Reconstruction in the Bodleian Library and Convocation House in the Eighteenth Century', *The Bodleian Library Record*, vol. 6, 1957–61, pp. 416–27, esp. p. 419.

14 Philip, 'Reconstruction', pp. 416–27, esp. p. 419.

15 Oxford, Bodleian Library, MS. Ballard 2, fol. 48v.

16 Oxford, Bodleian Library, MS. Rawl. D. 1512.

17 Macray, *Annals*, p. 236.

18 *Jackson's Oxford Journal*, 2 April 1768.

19 Thomas Beddoes, *Memorial concerning the State of the Bodleian Library and the Conduct of its Principal Librarian*, Oxford, 1787, Oxford, Bodleian Library, Library Records c. 4.

20 Beddoes, *Memorial*, pp. 6–7.

21 G.R.M. Ward, *Oxford University Statutes*, 2 vols, London, 1845, 1851, vol. 2, p. 15.

22 Ward, *Statutes*, vol. 2, p. 15. With some satisfaction the new library statutes of 1813 referred to the Bodleian collections as 'now greatly increased ... by continual accessions' as a result

of these fees (Ward, *Statutes*, vol. 2, p. 102).

23 A copy of the appeal is in the curators' minute book, 1786–92, Oxford, Bodleian Library, Library Records e. 4, fol. 65.

24 John Nichols and J.B. Nichols, *Illustrations of the Literary History of the Eighteenth Century*, vol. 5, London, 1828, p. 514.

Chapter 5

1 John Nichols and J.B. Nichols, *Illustrations of the Literary History of the Eighteenth Century*, vol. 5, 1828, pp. 514–61, at p. 552.

2 Nichols, *Illustrations*, vol. 5, p. 553.

3 Mary Ward, *A Morning in the Bodleian*, privately printed, 1871, p. 9.

4 'Nicoll, Alexander (1793–1828)', in *Oxford Dictionary of National Biography*.

5 William M. Wade, *Walks in Oxford*, London, 1817, p. 303.

6 Isaac D'Israeli, *Amenities of Literature*, new edn, London, 1867, p. 663, quoted in *The Douce Legacy* (exhibition catalogue), Oxford, 1984, p. 11.

7 The drawings and most of the prints were transferred to the Ashmolean in 1863, the coins and medals in 1920.

8 Frederic Madden's letter to Sir Thomas Phillipps, Oxford, Bodleian Library, MS. Phillipps-Robinson b. 128, fol. 23v, quoted in I.G. Philip, 'The Bodleian Library', in M.G. Brock and M.C. Curthoys (eds), *The History of the University of Oxford*, vol. vi, Nineteenth Century, pt 1, Oxford, 1997, p. 593.

9 William Dunn Macray, *Annals of the Bodleian Library Oxford*, 2nd edn, Oxford, 1890, p. 310 n.

10 Oxford, Bodleian Library, Library Records b. 40, fol. 327.

11 Now displayed on the walls of the south range of the Upper Reading Room.

12 F. Max Müller, *My Autobiography: A Fragment*, Oxford, 1901, p. 249, quoted

in Sir Edmund Craster, *History of the Bodleian Library, 1845–1945*, Oxford, 1952, repr. 1981, p. 26.

13 Extracts from Coxe's diary, Oxford, Bodleian Library, Library Records e. 609, fol. 13.

14 Philip, 'Bodleian Library', p. 595.

15 Müller, *Autobiography*, pp. 250–51.

16 Müller, *Autobiography*, p. 251.

17 Craster, *History of the Bodleian*, p. 30.

18 Macray, *Annals*, p. 371 n.

19 Revd W.D. Macray, 'Mr. Coxe's Work at the Bodleian', *Transactions and Proceedings of the 4th and 5th Annual Meetings of the Library Association, 1884*, pp. 13–16.

20 Macray, 'Mr. Coxe's Work', pp. 13–16.

21 For a full account of the protracted negotiations, see Craster, *History of the Bodleian*, pp. 83–7. Phillipps's collection, which included over 60,000 manuscripts, was dispersed in a succession of sales that began in the mid-1880s and continued for almost a century before the residue was bought by New York book dealers in 1977.

22 Craster, *History of the Bodleian*, p. 9 n. 1.

23 John William Burgon, 'Henry Octavius Coxe – The Large-Hearted Librarian', in *Lives of Twelve Good Men*, London, 1888, vol. 2, pp. 123–48.

24 Burgon, 'Coxe', p. 134.

25 See K.A. Manley, 'E.W.B. Nicholson (1849–1912) and his Importance to Librarianship', D.Phil. thesis, University of Oxford, 1977, Oxford, Bodleian Library, MS. D.Phil. d. 6429, pp. 19–20.

26 See press cuttings in Oxford, Bodleian Library, 2590 d. Oxf. d. 1.10.

27 [E.W.B. Nicholson,] *The Bodleian Library in 1882–7: A Report from the Librarian*, Oxford, 1888.

28 Craster, *History of the Bodleian*, p. 227.

29 Craster, *History of the Bodleian*, p. 227.

30 Craster, *History of the Bodleian*, p. 154.

31 Craster, *History of the Bodleian*, p. 154.

32 Letter of 7 December 1895 in the Phelps papers at Oriel College, Oxford.

33 Oxford, Bodleian Library, MS. Eng. lett. e. 121, fols 99–100.

34 R.H. Hill, 'The Bodleian since 1882 – Some Records and Reminiscences', *Library Association Record*, 4th series, no. 7, 1940, pp. 76–85.

35 Strickland Gibson, 'E.W.B. Nicholson (1849–1912): Some Impressions', *Library Association Record*, 4th series, no. 16, 1949, pp. 137–43.

36 Oxford, Bodleian Library, Library Records d. 142.

Chapter 6

1 *The Bodleian Quarterly Record*, vol. 1, no. 7, 1915, p. 173.

2 *The Bodleian Quarterly Record*, vol. 1, no. 3, 1914, p. 59.

3 *The Bodleian Quarterly Record*, vol. 1, no. 8, 1916, p. 242.

4 Sir Edmund Craster, *History of the Bodleian Library, 1845–1945*, Oxford, 1952, repr. 1981, p. 149.

5 *The Bodleian Quarterly Record*, vol. 8, no. 86, 1935, pp. 73–4.

6 *Library Association Record*, no. 23, 1922, p. 320.

7 *Library Association Record*, no. 23, 1922, p. 325.

8 Craster, *History of the Bodleian*, pp. 347–8.

9 *The Bodleian Quarterly Record*, vol. 6, nos 70–71, 1931, pp. 261–2.

10 See Stanley Gillam, 'The Bodleian Library in the Nineteen Thirties', *The Bodleian Library Record*, vol. 18, no. 1 (2003), pp. 16–30.

11 In the event total expenditure on construction and furnishing was £379,300 (Craster, *History of the Bodleian*, p. 337).

12 Craster, *History of the Bodleian*, p. 342; Robert J. Bruce, 'Deposits in the New Bodleian during the Second World War', *The Bodleian Library Record*, vol. 26, no. 1, 2013, pp. 59–82.

13 Craster, *History of the Bodleian*, p. 342.

14 *Craster, History of the Bodleian*, p. 258.

Chapter 7

1 See Helen Watson, 'Reminiscences of Restoring the Bodleian Frieze in the 1950s', *The Bodleian Library Record*, vol. 28, no. 2, 2015, pp. 197–204.

2 John Walters, *Poems*, London, 1780, p. 48. Walters scrupulously recorded that he had not been able to ascertain firm authority for this account, but he understood that, when the visitors learned of the earl's intention to present the statue to the university, they offered to carry the head back with them to Oxford 'lest it should be injured by a rougher mode of transport'.

3 Quoted in Abigail Williams, 'Ragtime to Riches: The Remarkable Story of Walter Harding's Book and Music Collections', *The Bodleian Library Record*, vol. 25, no. 2, 2012, pp. 243–4.

4 *The Bodleian Library Record*, vol. 12, no. 3, 1986, p. 165.

5 *Oxford University Statutes*, Oxford, 1971, p. 46.

Further reading

Beddoes, Thomas, *Memorial concerning the State of the Bodleian Library and the Conduct of its Principal Librarian*, Oxford, 1787.

Bodley, Sir Thomas, *The Autobiography of Sir Thomas Bodley*, intro. and notes by William Clennell, Oxford, 2006.

Bodley, Sir Thomas, *Letters of Sir Thomas Bodley to Thomas James*, ed. and intro. G.W. Wheeler, Oxford, 1926.

Bodley, Sir Thomas, *Letters of Sir Thomas Bodley to the University of Oxford*, ed. G.W. Wheeler, Oxford, 1927.

Bruce, Robert J., 'Deposits in the New Bodleian Library during the Second World War', *Bodleian Library Record*, vol. 26, no. 1, 2013, pp. 59–82.

Burgon, John William, 'Henry Octavius Coxe – The Large-Hearted Librarian', in *Lives of Twelve Good Men*, London, 1888, vol. 2, pp. 123–48.

Clennell, William, 'The Bodleian Declaration: A History', *Bodleian Library Record*, vol. 20, nos 1–2, 2007, pp. 47–60.

Craster, Sir Edmund, *History of the Bodleian Library, 1845–1945*, Oxford, 1952, repr. 1981.

Garlick, Kenneth (rev.), *Catalogue of Portraits in the Bodleian Library*, by Mrs Reginald Lane Poole, Oxford, 2004.

Gibson, Strickland, 'E.W.B. Nicholson (1849–1912): Some Impressions', *Library Association Record*, 4th ser., no. 16, 1949, pp. 137–43.

Gillam, Stanley, *The Divinity School and Duke Humfrey's Library at Oxford*, Oxford, 1988.

Gillam, S.G., and R.W. Hunt, 'The Curators of the Library and Humfrey Wanley', *Bodleian Library Record*, vol. 5, 1954, pp. 85–98.

Hampshire, Gwen (ed.), *The Bodleian Library Account Book 1613–1646*, Oxford Bibliographical Society, NS, vol. 21, Oxford, 1983.

Hill, R.H., 'The Bodleian since 1882 – Some Records and Reminiscences', *Library Association Record*, 4th ser., no. 7, 1940, pp. 76–85.

Lewis, David Frazer, 'Developing Modernity: Giles Gilbert Scott's Design for the New Bodleian Library', *Bodleian Library Record*, vol. 28, no. 1, April 2015, pp. 47–68.

Macray, William Dunn, *Annals of the Bodleian Library Oxford*, 2nd edn, Oxford, 1890.

Macray, Revd W.D., 'Mr. Coxe's Work at the Bodleian', *Transactions and Proceedings of the 4th and 5th Annual Meetings of the Library Association*, 1884, pp. 13–16.

Manley, K.A., 'E.W.B. Nicholson (1849–1912) and his Importance to Librarianship', DPhil thesis, University of Oxford, 1977.

Müller, F. Max, *My Autobiography: A Fragment*, Oxford, 1901.

Nichols, John, and J.B. Nichols, *Illustrations of the Literary History of the Eighteenth Century*, 8 vols, London, 1817–58.

[Nicholson, E.W.B.,] *The Bodleian Library in 1882–7: A Report from the Librarian*, Oxford, 1888.

Philip, Ian, *The Bodleian Library in the Seventeenth and Eighteenth Centuries*, Oxford, 1983.

Philip, I.G., 'Reconstruction in the Bodleian Library and Convocation House in the Eighteenth Century', *Bodleian Library Record*, vol. 6, 1957–61, pp. 416–27.

Trecentale Bodleianum, Oxford, 1913.

Ward, G.R.M., *Oxford University Statutes*, 2 vols, London, 1845, 1851.

Wheeler, G.W., *The Earliest Catalogues of the Bodleian Library*, Oxford, 1928.

Williams, Abigail, 'Ragtime to Riches: The Remarkable Story of Walter Harding's Book and Music Collections', *Bodleian Library Record*, vol. 25, no. 2, 2012, pp. 238–47.

Wood, Anthony à, *The History and Antiquities of the University of Oxford*, ed. John Gutch, Oxford, 1796.

Wood, Anthony à, *The Life and Times of Anthony Wood, Antiquary, of Oxford, 1632–1695*, ed. Andrew Clark, 5 vols, Oxford Historical Society, nos 19, 21, 26, 30, 40, Oxford, 1891–1900.

Picture credits

Unless otherwise stated, all images are
© Bodleian Library, University of Oxford

52 Oxford, Bodleian Library, MS. Ch. Gloucs. 8
53 Oxford, Bodleian Library, LP 764
54 Oxford, Bodleian Library, Library Records b. 868, no. 1
55 Oxford, Bodleian Library, Library objects 702
56 Oxford, Bodleian Library, MS. Mus. c. 26, fol. 26r
57 Oxford, Bodleian Library, MS. Gough Gen. Top. 16
58 Oxford, Bodleian Library, MS. D'Orville 78, fol. 26r
59 Oxford, Bodleian Library, LP 302
60 Oxford, Bodleian Library, MS. Canon. Bibl. Lat. 60, fol. 48v
61 Oxford, Bodleian Library, MS. Ouseley Add. 3, fols 2v, 3r
62 Oxford, Bodleian Library, G.A. Oxon 40 795, p. 13
63 Oxford, Bodleian Library, MS. Douce 366, fol. 9v
64 Oxford, Bodleian Library, Arch. G b.6, fol. 6r
65 Oxford, Bodleian Library, Library Records b. 868, no. 12
66 Oxford, Bodleian Library, LP 740
67 Oxford, Bodleian Library, LP 307
68 Oxford, Bodleian Library, MS. Ashmole 1511, fol. 75v
69 Oxford, Bodleian Library, Library Records b. 868, no. 27
70 Oxford, Bodleian Library, Library Records d. 137, fol. 18v
71 Oxford, Bodleian Library, Library Records d. 137, unfoliated
72 Oxford, Bodleian Library, Per. 2590 g. Oxford 1.1
73 Oxford, Bodleian Library, Library Records d. 137, fol. 33
74 Oxford, Bodleian Library, MS. Lat. liturg. f. 5, fols 21v–22r
75 Oxford, Bodleian Library, Library Records b. 867, p. 31
76 Oxford, Bodleian Library, LP 807
77 Oxford, Bodleian Library, Byw. Q 1.1
78 Oxford, Bodleian Library, MS. Top. Oxon b. 90, fol. 3r
79 Oxford, Bodleian Library, MS. Don. e. 7
80 Oxford, Bodleian Library, MS. Don. d. 14, fols 22v–23r
81 Oxford, Bodleian Library, Library Records b. 867, p. 191
82 © Francis Frith Collection
83 Oxford, Bodleian Library, LP 822 / © Bridgeman Images
84 Oxford, Bodleian Library, Library Records c. 618, p. 11
85 Oxford, Bodleian Library, Library Records c. 619/7, fol. 11
86 Oxford, Bodleian Library, Library Records b. 868, no. 84
87 Oxford, Bodleian Library, Library Records b. 868, no. 70
88 © Dan Paton
89 Oxford, Bodleian Library, JL 664 (Cons. Res. Objects 63)
90 Oxford, Bodleian Library, LP 854
91 © Greg Smolonski
92 © Ian Jackson
93 Oxford, Bodleian Library, from *Annual Report of the Curators of the Bodleian Library for 1955/6*, pl. 1
94 © Greg Smolonski
95 © Fisher Studios
96 © David Frudd
97 Oxford, Bodleian Library, John Johnson Collection: Games Folder (5)
98 Oxford, Bodleian Library, Harding Mus. Q 563
99 Oxford, Bodleian Library, MS. M. Deneke Mendelssohn d. 71, fol. 13r
100 Oxford, Bodleian Library, MS. Tenbury 346, fol. 66r
101 Oxford, Bodleian Library, Opie EE 28
102 Oxford, Bodleian Library, LP 880, © Paul Brason, 1996
103 Oxford, Bodleian Library, MS. Eng. poet. d. 197, recto
104 © John Cairns
105 © Greg Smolonski
106 © James Brittain
107 © John Cairns
108 © James Brittain

Index

Abbot, George, Archbishop of Canterbury (1562–1633), 47
Abrams, Lieutenant R.A., of the Sherwood Foresters, 179
Acland, Sir Henry Wentworth (1815–1900), 186
Acland, Sarah Angelina (1849–1930), 186, 188
Admiralty, 201; charts, 136
Aesop, *Fables* (1535) 145
Alfred, King (849–901), his translation of St Gregory's *Pastoral Care*, 83
Allen, G.E.H., 224
Allen, Mr and Mrs H.M., 224
Allen, Percy Stafford, President of Corpus Christi College (1869–1933), 192
Allen, Thomas (1542–1632), 25, 34, 56, 62
All Souls College, Oxford, 69, 113, 203, 109, 114, 230
Anne, Queen (1665–1714), 113
Arundel, Thomas, Archbishop of Canterbury (1352–1414), 13
Ashmole, Elias (1617–1692), 85, 86
Ashmolean Museum, Oxford, 85, 90, 118, 126, 158, 167, 168, 189, 196, 198, 199, 237
Asquith, Herbert Henry, 1st Earl of Oxford and Asquith (1852–1928), 223
Aubigné, Théodore Agrippa d' (1552–1630), 66
Aubrey, John (1626–1697), 85, 158
Austen, Jane (1775–1817), 'Volume the First', 186, 187

Bacon, Francis, 1st Baron Verulam and Viscount St Albans (1561–1626), 34
Ball, Ann, *see* Bodley, Ann
Ball, John, Mayor of Totnes, 23
Ballard, George (1706–1755), 121, 123
Balliol College, Oxford, 139, 199
Bandinel, Bulkeley, Bodley's Librarian (1781–1861), 98, 133, 137–53 *passim*
Barocci, Giacomo (1562–1617), 73
Barlow, Thomas, Bodley's Librarian (1607–1691), 71–7, 85, 93
Barratt, Dr Molly, 228
Basire, Jean, 55–6
Bathurst, Ralph, President of Trinity College (1620–1704), 71, 90
Bay Psalm Book (1640), 110, 111
Beaufort, Duke of, *see* Somerset
Beaumont, Francis (1584–1616), 62
Beddoes, Thomas (1760–1808), 124–7
Beesley, G.W., Bedel of Arts, 205
Benedict, St, Rule of (MS. Hatton 48), 83
Benfield & Loxley, builders, of Oxford, 197
Bennett, Alan, 236, 238, 246
Bereblock, John, 10, 15

Berkshire, 54, 107, 157, 223, 234
Bernard, Edward (1638–1696), 81, 83, 87, 94–5, 107, 109
Beroaldus, Matthaeus (d.1576), 20
Beza, Theodore (1519–1605), 20
Bibliographical Society of London, 184
Bill, John, bookseller, 37
Blackstone, Sir William (1723–1780), 105
Blomfield, Sir Reginald Theodore (1856–1942), 185
Blood Transfusion Service, 201
Blount, Charles, 8th Baron Mountjoy, Earl of Devonshire (1563–1606), 34
Boccaccio, Giovanni (1313–1375), 37, 182
Bodleian Japanese Library, 237
Bodleian Law Library, 187, 217
Bodleian Library:
    Benefactors' Register, 28, 43, 56, 95
    Benefactors' Tablet, 185, 221
    catalogues:
        of printed books: (1605), 37–8; (1620), 55, supplement (1635), 62, 65, 77; (1674), 79, 81, 94, 99, 107, 109; (1738) catalogue, 109, 139, 148; of individual collections, 147; (1843) and supplement (1851), 148, 157; 'moveable slip' catalogue (1879), 157, 164, 186; revision (1907–16), 166, 169, 170, 178, 147; pre-1920 transcribed catalogue, 230, 231; post-1920 catalogue, 230, 231; automation of catalogue, 230–31; of Hebrew collections, 169, 184; of western manuscripts, 148, 277–8, 183, 193, 201
    collections:
        general: Chinese books, 37–8, 93; coin collections, 86, 107, 120, 123–4, 144; contemporary scientists' papers, 223; 'curiosities', 97–8, 107–8; Greek manuscripts, 62, 73, 136, 141, 147; Hebrew collections, 37, 76, 87, 105, 141, 169, 184; Mexican manuscripts, 76; modern political papers, 223; music collections, 131, 222, 223; oriental manuscripts, 33, 34, 64, 76, 87, 98, 136, 139, 141–2, 158
        'named': Canonici collection, 141, 147; Conservative Party Archive, 223; Dodsworth manuscripts, 85; Douce collection, 143–5, 147; Gough collection, 128, 131, 133–4, 147; Hatton manuscripts, 83; John Johnson collection of printed ephemera, 218, 240; Junius manuscripts, 83; Laud collection,

258

Chandler, Henry William (1828–1889), 166

Charlemagne, Holy Roman Emperor (742–814), 144

Charles I, King (1600–1649), 65–6, 110, 113, 183, 236; bust of, 64, 65; request to borrow a book, 66, 75; portrait, 77

Charles II, King (1630–1685), 79, 90, 108

Charles V, Holy Roman Emperor (1500–1558), 76

Charles, H.R.H. the Prince of Wales, 233

Charlett, Arthur, Master of University College (1655–1722), 95, 102, 103, 123

Chedworth, Lord, see Howe

Chelles Abbey, France, 144

Cheney & Sons, printers, of Banbury, 246

Cherry, Francis (1665? –1713), 107

Chevalier, Antoine Rodolphe (1523–1572), 20

Chinese Studies Library, 237

Christ Church, Oxford, 19, 65, 66, 68, 69, 77, 79, 85, 94, 103, 109, 114, 139, 143, 151, 199, 209, 213

Civil War tracts, 183

Clare, John (1793–1864), 185

Clarendon, Earl of, see Hyde

Clarendon Press, 167

Clarke, Edward Daniel (1769–1822), 136

Clarke, Samuel (1625–1669), 97

Clarkson, Christopher (1938–2017), 208

Cleaver, William, Bishop of St Asaph (1742–1815), 124

Cobham, Thomas, Bishop of Worcester (d.1327), 11, 13

Coleridge, Samuel Taylor (1772–1834), 185

Collins, George Wolseley, *Hebrew Grammar* (1898), 184

Columba, St, 119

Congregation House, 12

Conservative Party Archive, 223

Contemporary Scientific Archives Centre, 223

Convocation House, 65, 67, 90

Cope, Sir Walter (d.1614), 33

Copyright Act (1709), 40, 136; (1814), 139

Corpus Christi College, Oxford, 192, 199

Cotton, Henry (1789–1879), 139

Coulson, Charles Alfred (1910–1974), 223

Courtenay, Richard, Bishop of Norwich (d.1415), 13

Cowley, Sir Arthur Ernest, Bodley's Librarian (1861–1931), 179

Coxe, Henry Octavius, Bodley's Librarian (1811–1881), 120, 147, 151–2, 154–61, 167, 182

Craster, Sir (Herbert Henry) Edmund, Bodley's Librarian (1879–1959), 154, 169, 179, 192–203

Creswick, Harry Richard, Bodley's Librarian (1902–1988), 205, 209

Crevenna, Pierre-Antoine (d.1792), 128

Crewe, Nathaniel, 3rd Baron Crewe (1633–1721), 103, 127

Cromwell, Oliver, Lord Protector (1599–1658), 73, 75, 110

Crosthwaite, Thomas, of Queen's College, 95

Crynes, Nathaniel (d.1745), 110

Dainton, Frederick Sydney, Baron Dainton (1914–1997), 229

Dante Alighieri (1265–1321), 37

Davies, John, storekeeper at Deptford dockyard, 98

de la Mare, Walter John (1873–1956), 186

Deneke, Margaret Clara Adèle (1882–1969), 223

Desborough, John (1608–1680), 97

Devereux, Robert, 2nd Earl of Essex (1565–1601), 21, 34

Digby, Sir Kenelm (1603–1665), 62

Disraeli, Benjamin, 1st Earl of Beaconsfield (1804–1881), 223

D'Israeli, Isaac (1766–1848), 143–4

Divinity School, Oxford, 15–17, 22, 25, 50–51, 65, 93, 161, 174, 213, 234, 236

Dixon, Miss, 179

Dodsworth, Roger (1585–1654), 85

Donne, John (c.1572–1631), 'Epistle to Lady Carew', 234–5

D'Orville, Jacques Philippe (1696–1751), 136

Douce, Francis (1757–1834), 144–7

Drake, Sir Francis (1540? –1596), 96

Dugdale, Sir William (1605–1686), 66, 85, 158

Dunn, Lieutenant H.J., of the Royal West Kent Regiment, 179

Dunstan, St, manuscripts belonging to, 34

Eastern Art Library, 237

Edinburgh, Advocates' Library, 153

Edinburgh University Library, 231

Edmondes, Sir Clement (1564? –1622), 97

Edward I, King (1239–1307), 144

Edward VI, King (1537–1553), 18

Eleanor of Castile, Queen of Edward I (d.1290), 144

Eliot, Thomas Stearns (1888–1965), 186

Elizabeth I, Queen (1533–1603), 15, 20–21

Essex, Earl of, see Devereux

Eton College, 200

Evelyn, John (1620–1706), 103

Exclusion Crisis of 1681, 90

Exeter College, Oxford, 188, 199, 231

Exeter, dean and chapter of, 34

Fairfax, Thomas, 3rd Baron Fairfax (1612–1671), 85

Faro, Portugal, 34

Fawkes, Guy (1570–1606), 98

Fell, John, Dean of Christ Church and Bishop of Oxford (1625–1686), 69, 85

Fermor, Sir Richard, 38

Fifoot, (Erik) Richard (Sidney), Bodley's Librarian (1925–1992), 230

Fitzwilliam, Sir William, Lord Deputy of Ireland (1526–1599), 123

Fletcher, John (1579–1625), 62

Folger, Henry Clay (1857–1930), 171

Ford, Henry, Principal of Magdalen Hall (d.1813), 131

Forman, Simon (1552–1611), 58
Fortescue, Sir John (1531? –1607), 33
Fosbroke, Thomas Dudley (1770–1842), 131
Furney, Richard (1694–1753), 121
Fysher, Robert, Bodley's Librarian (1698–1749), 109–14

Garfield Weston Foundation, 243
Geneva, 20
Gent, William, of Gloucester Hall, 25
Geological Society, 200
George II, King (1683–1760), 105
George IV, King (1762–1830), as Prince Regent, 233
George VI, King (1895–1952), 205
Gesenius, Wilhelm (1786–1842), *Hebrew Grammar*, 184
Gibbs, James (1682–1754), 113
Gibson, Edmund, Bishop of London (1669–1748), 84
Gibson, Strickland, Keeper of Printed Books, 171, 175, 179, 195
Gillam, Stanley, 195
Gladstone, William Ewart (1809–1898), 168
Glemham, Sir Thomas (1595–1649), 68
Gloucester Hall, Oxford, 25
Godwin, Mary (née Wollstonecraft), (1759–1797), 244
Godwin, William (1756–1836), 244
Golden Hind, chair made from its timbers, 96
Gough, Richard (1735–1809), 128, 131–6
Grahame, Kenneth (1859–1932), 202
Greaves, John (1602–1652), 68
Gregory, St, translation of his *Pastoral Care*, 83
Gronovius, Johann Friedrich (1611–1671), 56–7
Guest, Edith, 120

Hackman, Alfred, 157
Halley, Edmund (1656–1742), 105, 106
Hamlyn, Paul Bertram, Baron Hamlyn (1926–2001), 233
Hampden, John (1595–1643), 110
Handel, George Frideric (1685–1759), 223
Harcourt, Lewis (1863–1922), 245
Harcourt, Sir William (1827–1904), 245
Harding, Walter (1883–1973), 221
Hart Hall, Oxford, 75, 109
Hatton, Christopher, 1st Baron Hatton (c.1605–1670), 83
Havergal, Henry East ((1820–1875), 151
Hawksmoor, Nicholas (1661–1736), 103
Hawley, John, Principal of Gloucester Hall, 25
Hearne, Thomas (1678–1735), 103, 107, 108, 118, 121, 181
Heath, Sir Edward Richard George (1916–2005), 223
Heather, William (1563? –1627), 169
Henrietta Maria, Queen (1609–1669), 66
Henry IV, King (1367–1413), 13
Henry V, King (1387–1422), 13
Henry VIII, King (1491–1547), 18
Henry Frederick, Prince of Wales (1594–1612), 38

Henshall, Samuel (1764/5–1807), 131
Herbert, William, 3rd Earl of Pembroke (1580–1630), 62, 211
Heywood, Robert, of Brasenose College, 98
Hickes, George, non-juror (1642–1715), 97
Hill, Reginald Harrison, Secretary of the Library, 175
Hinton, Henry, ironmonger, of Oxford (1749–1816), 234
Holst, Gustav Theodore (1874–1934), 186
Holsten, Lucas, of Hamburg, 56
Holywell Contractors, of Oxford, 215
Hood, Sir John Anthony, Vice-Chancellor of the University, 238
Hooke Library, 217
Howe, John Thynne, 2nd Baron Chedworth (1714–1762), 121
Hudson, John, Bodley's Librarian (1662–1719), 101–8 *passim*
Humfrey, Duke of Gloucester (1391–1447), 13–15, 185
Hunt, James, chemist, of Oxford (1795–1857), 234
Hunt, Richard William (1908–1979), 221
Hunt, Thomas, orientalist (1696–1774), 105
Huntington, Robert, Provost of Trinity College Dublin (1637–1701), 87
Hurst, Herbert, 182–3
Hyde, Donald F. (1909–1966), 213
Hyde, Edward, 1st Earl of Clarendon (1609–1674), 123
Hyde, Thomas, Bodley's Librarian (1636–1703), 79, 81, 83, 90, 94–8, 118

Isham, Sir Justinian, 2nd Bart. (1610–1675), 73
Indian Institute Library, 188, 216–17

Jackson, Sir Thomas Graham (1835–1924), 160
James I, King (1566–1625), 37, 54
James II, King (1633–1701), 91
James, Richard (1592–1638), 109
James, Thomas, Bodley's Librarian (1572/3–1629), 28–9, 37, 38, 40, 43–4, 54–5, 56, 57, 58, 69, 73, 107, 210
Jenson, Nicolas, printer, of Venice (1420–1480), 145
Jesus College, Oxford, 114
Johnson, John de Monins (1882–1956), 218, 220
Jolliffe, John William, Bodley's Librarian (1929–1985), 230
Jonson, Ben (1573–1637), 62
Jordan, William, apothecary, 98
Junius, Francis (1589–1677), 83, 109

Keats, John (1795–1821), 185
Keiller, Alexander (1889–1955), 221
Kempe, Thomas, Bishop of London (d.1489), 15
Kennett, White, Bishop of Peterborough (1660–1728), 84
Kennicott, Benjamin (1718–1783), 105
King, Peter, 1st Baron King (1669–1734), 223

Knollys, William, Earl of Banbury (c.1545–1632), 34

Lambeth Palace Library, 81
Langbaine, Gerard, Provost of Queen's College (1609–1658), 68, 71, 97, 109
Langford, Emmanuel, vice-principal of Hart Hall, 109
Laud, William, Archbishop of Canterbury (1573–1645), 62–4, 85, 123
Lawes, Jeremy, plumber, 57
Lawes, William (1602–1645), 170
Law Library, 187, 217
Leeds University Library, 230, 237
Leiden University, 118
Lenton, Janet, 210
Leofric, Bishop of Exeter (d.1072), 34
Le Sueur, Hubert, sculptor, 64, 211
Lincoln College, Oxford, 83, 110
Linnaean Society, 200
Lobel, Edgar, sub-librarian (1888–1982), 193, 195
Locke, John (1632–1704), 101, 223
Lockey, Thomas, Bodley's Librarian (1602–1679), 77–9
Loggan, David, engraver, 87
London, Distaff Lane, 54, 66, 90
London Institution, 162
London School of Economics, 200
London University Library, 200
Louis XIV, King of France, 90

Macartney, George, 1st Earl Macartney (1737–1806), 181
Macmillan, (Maurice) Harold, 1st Earl of Stockton (1894–1986), 223
Macray, William Dunn (1826–1916), 85, 120, 148, 154
Madan, Falconer, Bodley's Librarian (1851–1935), 166, 169, 171, 172, 173, 177–84
Madden, Sir Frederic (1801–1873), 143, 147
Magdalen College, Oxford, 19, 121, 171
Magna Carta, 122, 123
Malone, Edmond (1741–1812), 142–3
Malone, Richard, Lord Sunderlin (1738–1816), 142–3
Malta, Imtarfa hospital, 179
Manchester, Earl of, see Montagu
Manning, Percy (1870–1917), 182, 183
Manutius, Aldus, of Venice (1449–1515), 141
Margaret, Saint (d.1093), 172
Marshall, Thomas, Rector of Lincoln College (1621–1685), 83–4, 87
Martin, Sir (John) Leslie (1908–2000), 217
Mary, Queen (1867–1953), 198, 199
Max Müller, Friedrich (1823–1900), 151, 154
Meerman, Gerard (1722–1771), 141
Mellon, Paul (1907–1999), 223
Mendelssohn, Felix (1809–1847), 222
Mendoza, Antonio de, Viceroy of Mexico (1495–1552), 76
Merton College, Oxford, 20, 21, 25, 34, 66, 199, 238

Miers, Sir Henry Alexander (1858–1942), 191
Milton, John (1608–1674), 58
Mineralogical Society, 200
Montagu, Edward, 2nd Earl of Manchester (1602–1671), 79
Montaigne, Michel Eyquem de (1533–1592), 37
More, Sir George (1553–1632), 33
More, John, 15
Morrison, Walter (1836–1921), 185
Mortimer, Edmund, 5th Earl of March (1391–1425), 13
Mountjoy, Lord, see Blount
Museum of the History of Science, Oxford, 86, 189
Myres, John Nowell Linton, Bodley's Librarian (1902–1989), 207–16 passim

Nalson, John (d.1686), 110
Napier, Sir Richard (1607–1676), 57
Nash, Joseph, (1809–1878), 130
Natural History Museum, London, 199–200
Naudé, Gabriel (1600–1653), 55
Netherlands, 21
Neubauer, Adolf, sub-librarian (1831–1907), 169, 184
Newark Priory, 33
New College, Oxford, 28, 44, 66, 131, 137, 151, 183, 199, 238
Newton, Sir Isaac (1642–1727), 103
Nicholas, (John Keiran) Barry (Moylan), Principal of Brasenose College (1919–2002), 229
Nichols, John (1745–1826), 128, 133
Nicholson, Edward Williams Byron, Bodley's Librarian (1849–1912), 162–75, 178
Nicoll, Alexander (1793–1828), 139
Nicolson, William, Bishop of Derry (1655–1727), 84
Nollekens, Joseph (1737–1823), 143
Norris, Francis, Earl of Berkshire (1579–1622), 47
Northumberland, Earl of, see Percy
Norton, John (1556/7–1612), 37
Norwich Cathedral, 144
Nottingham University Library, 230
Nuneham Courtenay, Oxon, book repository, 225, 245

Opie, Iona (1923–2017), and Peter (1918–1982), 223–4
Oppenheimer, David, chief rabbi of Prague, 141
Ordnance Survey, 136
Oriel College, Oxford, 11, 44, 58, 109
Oriental Institute Library, 237
Ormonde, Duke of, see Butler
Osler, Sir William, Regius Professor of Medicine (1849–1919), 171
Ouseley, Sir William (1767–1842), 142
Ovenden, Richard, Bodley's Librarian, 243
Owen, Humphrey, Bodley's Librarian (1702–1768), 114–24 passim
Owen, Thankful, President of St John's College (1620–1681), 69